Morley's Universal Library.

A careful selection of masterpieces of literature, British and Foreign.

Crown 8vo, red cloth neat, cut edges. Each 1/-.

A KEMPIS (Thomas). **Of the Imitation of Christ.** 318 pp.

AESCHYLUS. **Plays,** transl. by POTTER. 288 pp.

ARISTOPHANES: metrical transl. by J. H. FRERE. 282 pp.

ARISTOTLE, On Government, transl. by W. ELLIS. 282 pp.

BACON. **Essays.** 308 pp.

BOCCACCIO. **Decameron.** 312 pp.

BURKE (E.). **Two Speeches and Two Letters.** 284 pp.

Burlesque Plays and Poems. 320 pp. Ed. by H. MORLEY.

BUTLER (Bp. J.). **Analogy of Religion.** 320 pp.

BUTLER (S.). **Hudibras.** 288 pp.

CAVENDISH (G.). **Life of Wolsey.** 284 pp.

CERVANTES. **Don Quixote,** Vol. I.

—— Don Quixote, Vol. II.

CHAMBERS (R.). **Vestiges of the Natural History of Creation.** 286 pp.

Chronicle of the Cid, transl. by R. SOUTHEY. 320 pp.

COBBETT (W.). **Advice to Young Men.** 286 pp.

COLERIDGE (S. T.). **Table Talk.** 298 pp.

CROKER (J. W.). **Popular Songs of Ireland.** 320 pp.

CUNNINGHAM (Allan). **Traditional Tales.** 288 pp.

DANTE. **The Divine Comedy** translated by H. W. LONGFELLOW.

—— The Banquet, transl. 286 pp.

DEFOE. **Journal of the Plague Year.** 316 pp.

DE QUINCEY. **Confessions of an Opium-Eater,** etc. 276 pp.

DRAYTON. The Barons' Wars, etc. 288 pp.

EDGEWORTH (Maria). Stories of Ireland. 288 pp.

ELLWOOD (Thos.). **History of.** By Himself. 288 pp.

EMERSON. **Essays, Representative Men, Society and Solitude.** 288 pp.

EURIPIDES. **Alcestis, Electra,** etc. 286 pp.

—— Bacchanals, Ion, etc. 320 pp.

—— Hecuba, Hercules, Distracted, etc. 288 pp.

Fables and Proverbs from the Sanskrit. 278 pp.

Famous Pamphlets. 316 pp. Ed. by H. MORLEY.

FITZGERALD (EDWARD). Six Dramas of Calderon. 256 pp.

——— Miscellanies. (in preparation).

FROUDE (J. A.). The Nemesis of Faith. 160 pp.

GOETHE. Faust. Part I.: with MARLOWE's Dr. Faustus. 316 pp.

——— Faust, Part II. 288 pp.

GOLDSMITH. Vicar of Wakefield, Plays, and Poems. 256 pp.

HARRINGTON. Commonwealth of Oceana. 282 pp.

HERRICK. Hesperides. 320 pp.

HOBBES (T.). Leviathan. 320 pp.

HOMER. Iliad, transl. by CHAPMAN. 220 pp.

HOOKER. Ecclesiastical Polity. 288 pp.

Ideal Commonwealths. 284 pp.

[*JOHNSON (Dr.).* Rasselas. *See* VOLTAIRE. *infra.*]

JONSON (Ben). Plays and Poems. 320 pp.

LAMB (C.). Essays of Elia. 288 pp.

LEWIS (M. G.). Tales of Terror and Wonder. 284 pp.

LOCKE (J.). On Civil Government, 320 pp.

MACHIAVELLI (N.). The Prince. 320 pp.

[*MARLOWE.* Dr. Faustus. *See* Goethe, *supra.*]

Mediaeval Tales. 288 pp. Ed. by Prof. H. MORLEY.

Miscellany (A.). 272 pp. Ed. by Prof. H. MORLEY.

MOLIÈRE (J. B. de). Plays from. By DRYDEN, WYCHERLEY, FIELDING, etc.

PEELE (G.). Plays and Poems. 288 pp.

PRAED (W.M.). Essays. 280 pp.

RABELAIS (F.). Gargantua. Books I.—II. 320 pp.

——— The Same. Books III.—V. 320 pp.

SCHILLER (F. v.. Poems and Ballads, transl. by LYTTON. 384 pp.

SCOTT (Sir W.). Demonology and Witchcraft. 320 pp.

SHERIDAN (R. B.), Plays. 320 pp.

SOPHOCLES. Plays: transl. by T. FRANCKLIN. 320 pp.

SOUTHEY (R.). Life of Nelson. 282 pp.

STERNE (L.). Tristram Shandy. 186 pp.

VIRGIL. Works. Translated by DRYDEN. 320 pp.

VOLTAIRE. Candide: and JOHNSON's Rasselas. 288 pp.

WALKER (T.). The Original. 316 pp.

WALTON (I.). Lives of Donne, Wotton, Hooker, and Herbert. 284 pp.

Morley's Universal Library

MISCELLANIES OF
EDWARD FITZGERALD

MISCELLANIES
OF
EDWARD FITZGERALD

LONDON
GEORGE ROUTLEDGE AND SONS, Limited
NEW YORK: E. P. DUTTON AND CO.
1904

Contents

	PAGE
OMAR KHAYYÁM	1
EUPHRANOR	21
POLONIUS	85
SALÁMÁN AND ABSÁL	172
MEMOIR OF BERNARD BARTON	212
DEATH OF BERNARD BARTON	240
DEATH OF THE REV. GEORGE CRABBE	245

OMAR KHAYYÁM

THE ASTRONOMER-POET OF PERSIA

OMAR KHAYYÁM was born at Naishápúr in Khorassán in the latter half of our eleventh, and died within the first quarter of our twelfth century. The slender story of his life is curiously twined about that of two others, very considerable figures in their time and country; one of them, Hasan al Sabbáh, whose very name has lengthened down to us us a terrible synonym for murder: and the other (who tells the story of all three), Nizám al Mulk, Vizyr to Alp the Lion and Malik Shah, son and grandson of Toghrul Beg the Tartar, who had wrested Persia from the feeble successor of Mahmúd the Great, and founded that Seljukian Dynasty which finally roused Europe into the Crusades. This Nizám al Mulk, in his *Wasyat* or *Testament*—which he wrote and left as a memorial for future statesmen—relates the following, as quoted in the *Calcutta Review*, No. 59, from Mirkhond's *History of the Assassins*—

" One of the greatest of the wise men of Khorassán was the Imám Mowaffak of Naishápur, a man highly honoured and reverenced,—may God rejoice his soul; his illustrious years exceeded eighty-five, and it was the universal belief that every boy who read the Koran or studied the traditions in his presence, would assuredly attain to honour and happiness. For this cause did my father send me from Tús to Naishápur with Abd-u-samad, the doctor of law, that I might employ myself in study and learning under the guidance of that illustrious teacher. Towards me he ever turned an eye of favour and kindness, and as his pupil I felt for him extreme affection and devotion, so that I passed four years in his service. When I first came there,

I found two other pupils of mine own age newly arrived, Hakim Omar Khayyám and the ill-fated Ben Sabbáh. Both were endowed with sharpness of wit and the highest natural powers; and we three formed a close friendship together. When the Imám rose from his lectures, they used to join me, and we repeated to each other the lessons we had heard. Now Omar was a native of Naishápur, while Hasan Ben Sabbáh's father was one Ali, a man of austere life and practice, but heretical in his creed and doctrine. One day Hasan said to me and to Khayyám, 'It is the universal belief that the pupils of the Imám Mowaffak will attain to fortune. Now, if we *all* do not attain thereto without doubt one of us will; what then shall be our mutual pledge and bond?' We answered, 'Be it what you please.' 'Well,' he said, 'let us make a vow, that to whomsoever this fortune falls, he shall share it equally with the rest, and reserve no pre-eminence for himself.' 'Be it so,' we both replied; and on those terms we mutually pledged our words. Years rolled on, and I went from Khorassán to Transoxiana, and wandered to Ghazni and Cabul; and when I returned, I was invested with office and rose to be administrator of affairs during the Sultanate of Sultan Alp Arslán."

"He goes on to state that years passed by, and both his old school friends found him out, and came and claimed a share in his good fortune, according to the schoolday vow. The Vizier was generous and kept his word. Hasán demanded a place in the government, which the Sultan granted at the Vizier's request; but discontented with the gradual rise, he plunged into the maze of intrigue of an oriental court, and, failing in a base attempt to supplant his benefactor, he was disgraced and fell. After many mishaps and wanderings, Hasan became the head of the Persian sect of the *Ismailians*—a party of fanatics who had long murmured in obscurity, but rose to an evil eminence under the guidance of his strong and evil will. In A.D. 1090, he seized the castle of Alamút, in the province of Rúdbar, which lies in the mountainous tract south of the Caspian Sea; and it was from its mountain home he obtained that evil celebrity among the Crusaders as the

OLD MAN OF THE MOUNTAINS, and spread terror through the Mohammedan world; and it is yet disputed whether the word *Assassin*, which they have left in the language of modern Europe as their dark memorial, is derived from the *hasaish*, or opiate of hemp-leaves (the Indian *bhang*), with which they maddened themselves to the sullen pitch of oriental desperation, or from the name of the founder of the dynasty, whom we have seen in his quiet collegiate days at Naishápur. One of the countless victims of the Assassin's dagger was Nizám-ul-Mulk himself, the old schoolboy friend.

" Omar Khayyám also came to the Vizier to claim his share, but not to ask for title or office. ' The greatest boon you can confer on me,' he said, ' is to let me live in a corner under the shadow of your fortune, to spread wide the advantages of science, and pray for your long life and prosperity.' The Vizier tells us that, when he found Omar was really sincere in his refusal, he pressed him no further, but granted him a yearly pension of 1,200 *mithkáls* of gold from the treasury of Naishápur.

" At Naishápur thus lived and died Omar Khayyám, ' busied,' adds the Vizier, ' in winning knowledge of every kind, and especially in Astronomy, wherein he attained to a very high pre-eminence. Under the Sultanate of Malik Shah he came to Merv, and obtained great praise for his proficiency in science, and the Sultan showered favours upon him."

" When Malik Shah determined to reform the calendar, Omar was one of the eight learned men employed to do it; the result was the *Jaláli* era (so called from *Jalal-ul-Din*, one of the king's names)—' a computation of time,' says Gibbon, ' which surpasses the Julian, and approaches the accuracy of the Gregorian style.' He is also the author of some astronomical tables, entitled ' Kíji-Malik-sháhí,' and the French have lately republished and translated an Arabic treatise of his son on Algebra.

" These severe studies, and his verses, which, though happily fewer than any Persian poet's, and, though perhaps fugitively composed, the result of no fugitive emotion or thought, are probably the work and event of his life, leaving little else to record. Perhaps he liked a little farming too, so often as he speaks of the ' edge of the tilth ' on which he loved to rest with his diwán of verse, his loaf—and his wine.

"His Takhallus or poetical name (Khayyám) signifies a Tentmaker, and he is said to have at one time exercised that trade, perhaps before Nizám-ul-Mulk's generosity raised him to independence. Many Persian poets similarly derive their names from their occupations; thus we have Attár, ' a druggist,' Assár, ' an oil-presser,' etc." (Though all these, like our Smiths, Archers, Millers, Fletchers, etc., may simply retain the surname of an hereditary calling.) "Omar himself alludes to his name in the following whimsical lines—

"' Khayyám, who stitched the tents of science,
Has fallen in grief's furnace and been suddenly burned ;
The shears of Fate have cut the tent ropes of his life,
And the broker of Hope has sold him for nothing ! '

" We have only one more anecdote to give of his life, and that relates to the close, related in the anonymous preface which is sometimes prefixed to his poems ; it has been printed in the Persian in the appendix to Hyde's *Veterum Persarum Religio*, p. 499 ; and D'Herbelot alludes to it in his *Bibliothèque*, under ' Khiam '—[1]

" It is written in the chronicles of the ancients that this King of the Wise, Omar Khayyám, died at Naishápur in the year of the Hegira 517 (A.D. 1123) ; in science he was unrivalled,—the very paragon of his age. Khwájah Nizámi of Samarcand, who was one of his pupils, relates the following story : ' I often used to hold conversations with my teacher, Omar Khayyám, in a garden ; and one day he said to me, ' My tomb shall be in a spot where the north wind may scatter roses over it.' I wondered at the words he spoke, but I knew that his were no idle words. Years after, when I chanced to revisit Naishápur, I went to his final resting-place, and lo ! it was just outside a

---

[1] " Philosophe Musulman qui a vécu en Odeur de Sainteté dans la Fin du premier et le Commencement du second Siécle," no part of which, except the ' Philosophe,' can apply to Khayyám.

garden, and trees laden with fruit stretched their boughs over the garden wall, and dropped their flowers upon his tomb, so as the stone was hidden under them.'"

Thus far—without fear of trespass—from the *Calcutta Review*.

Though the Sultan "showered favours upon him," Omar's epicurean audacity of thought and speech caused him to be regarded askance in his own time and country. He is said to have been especially hated and dreaded by the Súfis, whose practice he ridiculed, and whose faith amounts to little more than his own when stript of the mysticism and formal compliment to Islamism which Omar would not hide under. Their poets, including Háfiz, who are (with the exception of Firdúsi) the most considerable in Persia, borrowed largely, indeed, of Omar's material, but turning it to a mystical use more convenient to themselves and the people they addressed; a people quite as quick of doubt as of belief; quite as keen of bodily sense as of intellectual; and delighting in a cloudy element compounded of all, in which they could float luxuriously between heaven and earth, and this world and the next, on the wings of a poetical expression, that could be recited indifferently whether at the mosque or the tavern. Omar was too honest of heart as well as of head for this. Having failed (however mistakenly) of finding any Providence but Destiny, and any world but this, he set about making the most of it; preferring rather to soothe the soul through the senses into acquiescence with things as they were, than to perplex it with vain mortifications after what they *might be*. It has been seen that his worldly desires, however, were not exorbitant; and he very likely takes a humorous pleasure in exaggerating them above that intellect in whose exercise he must have found great pleasure, though not in a theological direction. However this may be, his worldly pleasures are what they profess to be without any pretence at divine allegory; his wine is the veritable juice of the grape: his tavern, where it was to be had: his Sáki, the flesh and blood that poured it out for him: all which, and where the roses were in bloom, was all he professed to want of this world or to expect of Paradise.

The mathematical faculty, too, which regulated his fancy, and condensed his verse to a quality and quantity unknown in Persian, perhaps in Oriental, poetry, helped by its very virtue perhaps to render him less popular with his countrymen. If the Greeks were children in gossip, what does Persian literature imply but a *second childishness* of garrulity? And certainly if no *ungeometric* Greek was to enter Plato's School of Philosophy, no so unchastised a Persian should enter on the race of Persian verse, with its "fatal facility" of running on long after thought is winded! But Omar was not only the single mathematician of his country's poets; he was also of that older time and stouter temper, before the native soul of Persia was quite broke by a foreign creed as well as foreign conquest. Like his great predecessor Firdúsi, who was as little of a *mystic*, who scorned to use even a *word* of the very language in which the new faith came clothed, and who was suspected, not of Omar's irreligion indeed, but of secretly clinging to the ancient Fire-Religion of Zerdusht, of which so many of the kings he sang were worshippers.

For whatever reason, however, Omar, as before said, has never been popular in his own country, and therefore has been but charily transmitted abroad. The MSS. of his poems, mutilated beyond the average casualties of Oriental transcription, are so rare in the East as scarce to have reached westward at all, in spite of all that arms and science have brought us. There is none at the India House, none at the Bibliothèque Impériale of Paris. We know but of one in England: No. 140 of the Ouseley MSS. at the Bodleian, written at Shiraz, A.D. 1460. This contains but 158 Rubáiyát. One in the Asiatic Society's Library of Calcutta (of which we have a copy) contains (and yet incomplete) 516, though swelled to that by all kinds of repetition and corruption. So Von Hammer speaks of *his* copy as containing about 200, while Dr. Sprenger catalogues the Lucknow MS. at double that number. The scribes, too, of the Oxford and Calcutta MSS. seem to do their work under a sort of protest; each beginning with a tetrastich (whether genuine or not) taken out of its alphabetical order; the Oxford with one of apology; the Calcutta with one of execration too stupid for Omar's, even had Omar been stupid enough to execrate himself.[1]

The reviewer, who translates the foregoing particulars of Omar's life, and some of his verse into prose, concludes by comparing him with Lucretius, both as to natural temper and genius, and as acted upon by the circumstances in which he lived. Both, indeed, men of subtle intellect and high imagination, instructed in learning beyond their day, and of hearts passionate for truth and justice; who justly revolted from their country's false religion, and false, or foolish, devotion to it; but who yet fell short of replacing what they had subverted by any such better *hope* as others, upon whom no better *faith* had dawned, had yet made a law to themselves. Lucretius, indeed, with such material as Epicurus furnished, consoled himself with the construction of a machine that needed no constructor, and acting by a law that implied no lawgiver; and so composing himself into a Stoical rather than Epicurean severity of attitude, sat down to contemplate the mechanical drama of the universe of which he was part actor; himself and all about him (as in his own sublime description of the Roman Theatre) coloured with the lurid reflex of the curtain that was suspended between them and the other sun. Omar, more desperate, or more careless, of any such laborious system as resulted in nothing more than hopeless necessity, flung his own genius and learning with a bitter jest into the general ruin which their insufficient glimpses only served to reveal; and, yielding his senses to the actual rose and vine, only *diverted* his thoughts by balancing ideal possibilities of fate, freewill, existence and annihilation; with an oscillation that so generally inclined to the negative and lower side, as to make such stanzas as the following exceptions to his general philosophy—

---

[1] "Since this paper was written" (adds the *Reviewer* in a note), "we have met with a copy of a very rare edition, printed in Calcutta in 1836. This contains 438 Tetrastichs, with an appendix containing 54 others not found in some MSS."

Oh, if my soul can fling his Dust aside,
And naked on the Air of heaven ride,
  Is't not a Shame, is't not a Shame for Him
So long in this Clay Suburb to abide ?

Or is *that* but a Tent, where rests anon
A Sultán to his Kingdom passing on,
  And which the swarthy Chamberlain shall strike
Then when the Sultán rises to be gone ?

    With regard to the present translation. The original Rubáiyát (as, missing an Arabic guttural, these *tetrastichs* are more musically called) are independent stanzas, consisting each of four lines of equal, though varied, prosody, sometimes *all* rhyming, but oftener (as here attempted) the third line suspending the cadence by which the last atones with the former two. Sometimes, as in the Greek Alcaic, where the third line seems to lift and suspend the wave that falls over in the last. As usual with such kind of Oriental verse, the Rubáiyát follow one another according to alphabetical rhyme—a strange farrago of grave and gay. Those here selected are strung into something of an Eclogue, with perhaps a less than equal proportion of the " Drink and make merry," which (genuine or not) recurs over-frequently in the original. For, Lucretian as Omar's genuis might be, he crossed that darker mood with much of Oliver de Basselin humour. Any way, the result is sad enough : saddest, perhaps, when most ostentatiously merry ; any way, fitter to move sorrow than anger toward the old tentmaker, who, after vainly endeavouring to unshackle his steps from destiny, and to catch some authentic glimpses of To-morrow, fell back upon To-day (which has outlasted so many to-morrows) ! as the only ground he got to stand upon, however momentarily slipping from under his feet.

THE QUATRAINS OF OMAR KHAYYÁM

I

Awake! for Morning in the Bowl of Night
Has flung the Stone that puts the Stars to Flight:
  And Lo! the Hunter of the East has caught
The Sultán's Turret in a Noose of Light.

II

Dreaming when Dawn's Left Hand was in the Sky
I heard a Voice within the Tavern cry,
  "Awake, my Little ones, and fill the Cup
"Before Life's Liquor in its Cup be dry."

III

And, as the Cock crew, those who stood before
The Tavern shouted—" Open then the Door!
  " You know how little while we have to stay,
" And, once departed, may return no more."

IV

Now the New Year reviving old Desires,
The thoughtful Soul to Solitude retires,
  Where the White Hand of Moses on the Bough
Puts out, and Jesus from the Ground suspires.

V

Irám indeed is gone with all its Rose,
And Jamshýd's Sev'n-ring'd Cup where no one knows:
  But still the Vine her ancient Ruby yields,
And still a Garden by the Water blows.

VI

And David's Lips are lock't; but in divine
High-piping Péhlevi, with " Wine! Wine! Wine!
  " *Red* Wine! "—the Nightingale cries to the Rose
That yellow Cheek of her's to incarnadine.

VII

Come, fill the Cup, and in the Fire of Spring
The Winter Garment of Repentance fling:
  The Bird of Time has but a little way
To fly—and Lo! the Bird is on the Wing.

VIII

And look—a thousand Blossoms with the Day
Woke—and a thousand scatter'd into Clay:

And this first Summer Month that brings the Rose
Shall take Jamshyd and Kaikobád away.

IX

But come with old Khayyám and leave the Lot
Of Kaikobád and Kaikhosrú forgot:
　　Let Rustum lay about him as he will,
Or Hátim Tai cry Supper—heed them not.

X

With me along some Strip of Herbage strown
That just divides the desert from the sown,
　　Where name of Slave and Sultán scarce is known,
And pity Sultán Máhmúd on his Throne.

XI

Here with a Loaf of Bread beneath the Bough,
A Flask of Wine, a Book of Verse—and Thou
　　Beside me singing in the Wilderness—
And Wilderness is Paradise enow.

XII

"How sweet is mortal Sovranty"—think some:
Others—"How blest the Paradise to come!"
　　Ah, take the Cash in hand and waive the Rest;
Oh, the brave Music of a *distant* Drum!

XIII

Look to the Rose that blows about us—"Lo,
"Laughing," she says, "into the World I blow;
　　"At once the silken Tassel of my Purse
"Tear, and its Treasure on the Garden throw."

XIV

The Worldly Hope men set their Hearts upon
Turns Ashes—or it prospers; and anon,
　　Like Snow upon the Desert's dusty Face
Lighting a little Hour or two—is gone.

XV

And those who husbanded the Golden Grain,
And those who flung it to the Winds like Rain,
   Alike to no such aureate Earth are turn'd
As, buried once, Men want dug up again.

XVI

Think, in this batter'd Caravanserai
Whose Doorways are alternate Night and Day,
   How Sultán after Sultán with his Pomp
Abode his Hour or two, and went his way.

XVII

They say the Lion and the Lizard keep
The Courts where Jamshýd gloried and drank deep:
   And Bahrám, that great Hunter—the Wild Ass
Stamps o'er his Head, and he lies fast asleep.

XVIII

I sometimes think that never blows so red
The Rose as where some buried Caesar bled;
   That every Hyacinth the Garden wears
Dropt in its Lap from some once lovely Head.

XIX

And this delightful Herb whose tender Green
Fledges the River's Lip on which we lean—
   Ah, lean upon it lightly! for who knows
From what once lovely Lip it springs unseen!

XX

Ah, my Belovèd, fill the cup that clears
To-day of past Regrets and future Fears—
   To-morrow?—Why, To-morrow I may be
Myself with Yesterday's Sev'n Thousand Years.

XXI

Lo! some we loved, the loveliest and the best
That Time and Fate of all their Vintage prest,

Have drunk their Cup a Round or two before,
And one by one crept silently to Rest.

XXII

And we, that now make merry in the Room
They left, and Summer dresses in new Bloom,
  Ourselves must we beneath the Couch of Earth
Descend, ourselves to make a Couch—for whom?

XXIII

Ah, make the most of what we yet may spend,
Before we too into the Dust descend;
  Dust into Dust, and under Dust, to lie,
Sans Wine, sans Song, sans Singer, and—sans End!

XXIV

Alike for those who for To-day prepare,
And those that after a To-morrow stare,
  A Muezzin from the Tower of Darkness cries
"Fools! your Reward is neither Here nor There!"

XXV

Why, all the Saints and Sages who discuss'd
Of the Two Worlds so learnedly, are thrust
  Like foolish Prophets forth; their Words to Scorn
Are scatter'd, and their Mouths are stopt with Dust.

XXVI

Oh, come with old Khayyám, and leave the Wise
To talk; one thing is certain, that Life flies;
  One thing is certain, and the Rest is Lies;
The Flower that once has blown for ever dies.

XXVII

Myself when young did eagerly frequent
Doctor and Saint, and heard great Argument
  About it and about; but evermore
Came out by the same Door as in I went.

XXVIII

With them the Seed of Wisdom did I sow,
And with my own hand labour'd it to grow;
   And this was all the Harvest that I reap'd—
"I came like Water, and like Wind I go."

XXIX

Into this Universe, and *why* not knowing,
Nor *whence*, like Water willy-nilly flowing;
   And out of it, as Wind along the Waste,
I know not *whither*, willy-nilly blowing.

XXX

What, without asking, hither hurried *whence?*
And, without asking, *whither* hurried hence!
   Another and another Cup to drown
The Memory of this Impertinence!

XXXI

Up from Earth's Centre through the Seventh Gate
I rose, and on the Throne of Saturn sate,
   And many Knots unravel'd by the Road;
But not the Knot of Human Death and Fate.

XXXII

There was a Door to which I found no Key:
There was a Veil past which I could not see;
   Some little Talk awhile of Me and Thee
There seemed—and then no more of Thee and Me.

XXXIII

Then to the rolling Heav'n itself I cried,
Asking, "What Lamp had Destiny to guide
   "Her little children stumbling in the Dark?"
And—"A blind Understanding!" Heav'n replied.

XXXIV

Then to this earthen Bowl did I adjourn
My Lip the secret Well of Life to learn:

And Lip to Lip it murmur'd—" While you live
" Drink!—for once dead you never shall return."

XXXV

I think the Vessel, that with fugitive
Articulation answer'd, once did live,
   And merry-make; and the cold Lip I kiss'd
How many Kisses might it take—and give!

XXXVI

For in the Market-place, one Dusk of Day,
I watch'd the Potter thumping his wet Clay:
   And with its all obliterated Tongue
It murmur'd—" Gently, Brother, gently, pray!"

XXXVII

Ah, fill the Cup:—what boots it to repeat
How Time is slipping underneath our Feet:
   Unborn To-morrow and dead Yesterday,
Why fret about them if To-day be sweet!

XXXVIII

One Moment in Annihilation's Waste,
One Moment, of the Well of Life to taste—
   The Stars are setting and the Caravan
Starts for the Dawn of Nothing—Oh, make haste!

XXXIX

How long, how long, in definite Pursuit
Of This and That endeavour and dispute?
   Better be merry with the fruitful Grape
Than sadder after none, or bitter, Fruit.

XL

You know, my Friends, how long since in my House
For a new Marriage I did make Carouse:
   Divorced old barren Reason from my Bed,
And took the Daughter of the Vine to Spouse.

XLI

For " Is " and " Is-not " though *with* Rule and Line,
And " Up-and-down " *without*, I could define,
  I yet in all I only cared to know,
Was never deep in anything but—Wine.

XLII

And lately, by the Tavern Door agape,
Came stealing through the Dusk an Angel Shape
  Bearing a Vessel on his Shoulder; and
He bid me taste of it; and 'twas—the Grape!

XLIII

The Grape that can with Logic absolute
The Two-and-Seventy jarring Sects confute:
  The subtle Alchemists that in a Trice
Life's leaden Metal into Gold transmute.

XLIV

The mighty Mahmúd, the Victorious Lord,
That all the misbelieving and black Horde
  Of Fears and Sorrows that infest the Soul
Scatters and slays with his enchanted Sword.

XLV

But leave the Wise to wrangle, and with me
The Quarrel of the Universe let be:
  And, in some corner of the Hubbub coucht,
Make Game of that which makes as much of Thee.

XLVI

For in and out, above, about, below,
'Tis nothing but a Magic Shadow-show,
  Play'd in a Box whose Candle is the Sun,
Round which we Phantom Figures come and go.

XLVII

And if the Wine you drink, the Lip you press,
End in the Nothing all Things end in—Yes—

Then fancy while Thou art, Thou art but what
Thou shalt be—Nothing—Thou shalt not be less.

XLVIII

While the Rose blows along the River Brink,
With old Khayyám the Ruby Vintage drink :
   And when the Angel with his darker Draught
Draws up to Thee—take that, and do not shrink.

XLIX

'Tis all a Chequer-board of Nights and Days
Where Destiny with Men for Pieces plays ;
   Hither and thither moves, and mates, and slays,
And one by one back in the Closet lays.

L

The Ball no Question makes of Ayes and Noes,
But Right or Left as strikes the Player goes ;
   And He that toss'd Thee down into the Field,
He knows about it all—He knows—HE knows !

LI

The Moving Finger writes ; and having writ,
Moves on : nor all thy Piety nor Wit
   Shall lure it back to cancel half a Line,
Nor all thy Tears wash out a word of it.

LII

And that inverted Bowl we call The Sky,
Whereunder crawling coop't we live and die,
   Lift not thy hands to *It* for help—for It
Rolls impotently on as Thou or I.

LIII

With Earth's first Clay They did the last Man's knead,
And then of the Last Harvest sow'd the Seed :
   Yea, the first Morning of Creation wrote
What the Last Dawn of Reckoning shall read.

LIV

I tell Thee this—When, starting from the Goal,
Over the shoulders of the flaming Foal
  Of Heav'n Parwin and Mushtara they flung,
In my predestin'd Plot of Dust and Soul.

LV

The Vine had struck a Fibre; which about
If clings my Being—let the Súfi flout;
  Of my Base Metal may be filed a Key,
That shall unlock the Door he howls without.

LVI

And this I know: whether the one True Light,
Kindle to Love, or Wrath consume me quite,
  One Glimpse of It within the Tavern caught
Better than in the Temple lost outright.

LVII

Oh, Thou, who did'st with Pitfall and with Gin
Beset the Road I was to wander in,
  Thou wilt not with Predestination round
Enmesh me, and impute my Fall to Sin?

LVIII

Oh, Thou, who Man of baser Earth did'st make,
And who with Eden did'st devise the Snake;
  For all the Sin wherewith the Face of Man
Is blacken'd, Man's Forgiveness give—and take!

* * * * *

KÚZA—NÁMA

LIX

Listen again. One Evening at the Close
Of Ramazán, ere the better Moon arose,
  In that old Potter's Shop I stood alone
With the clay Population round in Rows.

LX

And, strange to tell, among the Earthen Lot
Some could articulate, while others not:
   And suddenly one more impatient cried—
"Who *is* the Potter, pray, and who the Pot?"

LXI

Then said another—"Surely not in vain
"My substance from the common Earth was ta'en,
   "That He who subtly wrought me into Shape
"Should stamp me back to common Earth again."

LXII

Another said—"Why, ne'er a peevish Boy,
"Would break the Bowl from which he drank in Joy;
   "Shall He that *made* the Vessel in pure Love
"And Fansy, in an after Rage destroy?"

LXIII

None answer'n this; but after Silence spake
A Vessel of a more ungainly Make:
   "They sneer at me for leaning all awry;
"What! did the Hand then of the Potter shake?"

LXIV

Said one—"Folks of a surly Tapster tell,
"And daub his Visage with the Smoke of Hell;
   "They talk of some strict Testing of us—Pish!
"He's a Good Fellow, and 'twill all be well."

LXV

Then said another with a long-drawn Sigh,
"My Clay with long oblivion is gone dry:
   "But, fill me with the old familiar Juice,
"Methinks I might recover by and by."

LXVI

So while the Vessels one by one were speaking,
One spied the little Crescent all were seeking,
   And then they jogg'd each other, "Brother, Brother!
'Hark to the Porter's Shoulder-knot a-creaking!"

    *   *   *   *   *

LXVII

Ah, with the Grape my fading Life provide,
And wash my Body whence the Life has died,
   And in a Winding-sheet of Vine-leaf wrapt,
So bury me by some sweet Garden-side,

LXVIII

That ev'n my buried Ashes such a Snare
Of Perfume shall fling up into the Air,
   As not a True Believer passing by
But shall be overtaken unaware.

LXIX

Indeed the Idols I have loved so long
Have done my Credit in Men's Eye much wrong!
   Have drown'd my Honour in a shallow Cup,
And sold my Reputation for a Song.

LXX

Indeed, indeed, Repentance oft before
I swore—but was I sober when I swore?
   And then and then came Spring, and Rose-in-hand
My thread-bare Penitence apieces tore.

LXXI

And much as Wine has play'd the Infidel,
And robb'd me of my Robe of Honour—well,
   I often wonder what the Vintners buy
One half so precious as the Goods they sell.

LXXII

Alas, that Spring should vanish with the Rose!
That Youth's sweet-scented Manuscript should close!
  The Nightingale that in the Branches sang,
Ah, whence, and whither flown again, who knows?

LXXIII

Ah, Love! could thou and I with Fate conspire
To grasp this sorry Scheme of Things entire,
  Would not we shatter it to bits—and then
Re-mould it nearer to the Heart's Desire?

LXXIV

Ah, Moon of my Delight who know'st no wane,
The Moon of Heav'n is rising once again:
  How oft hereafter rising shall she look
Through this same Garden after me—in vain!

LXXV

And when Thyself with shining Foot shall pass
Among the Guests star-scatter'd on the Grass,
  And in thy joyous Errand reach the Spot
Where I made one—turn down an empty Glass!

TAMÁM SHUD

EUPHRANOR

A DIALOGUE ON YOUTH

DURING the time of my pretending to practise Medicine at Cambridge, I was aroused, one fine forenoon of May, by the sound of some one running up my staircase, three or four steps at a time; then, directly, a smart rapping at the door; and, before I could say "Come in," Euphranor had opened it, and, coming up to me, seized my arm with his usual eagerness, and told me I must go out with him—"it was such a day—sun shining—breeze blowing—hedges and trees all in leaf. He had been to Chesterton (he said), and had rowed back with a man who had now left him in the lurch; and I must take his place." I told him what a poor hand at the oar I was, and, such walnut-shells as these Cambridge boats were, I was sure a strong fellow like him must rejoice in getting a whole eight-oar to himself once in a way. He laughed, and said, "The pace, the pace" was the thing. However, that was all nothing, but—in short, I must go out with him, whether to row, or for a walk in the fields, or a game of billiards at Chesterton, whatever I liked, only go I must. After a little more banter about my possible patients, I got up, closed a very heavy treatise on Magnesia I was reading, put on coat and hat, and in three minutes we had run downstairs, out into the open air; where both of us calling out together what a glorious day it was, we struck out briskly for the old wooden bridge, where Euphranor said he had left his boat.

"By-the-bye," said I, as we went along, "it would be a charity to knock up poor Lexilogus, and carry him with us."

Not much of a charity, Euphranor thought—Lexilogus

would so much rather be left with his books. But I declared that was the very reason he ought to be drawn abroad; and Euphranor, who was quite good-humoured, and wished Lexilogus all well (for we were all three Yorkshiremen, whose families lived no great distance asunder), easily consented. So, without more ado, we turned into Trinity great gate, and round by the right up a staircase to the attic in which Lexilogus kept.

The door was *sported*, but I knew he must be at home; so, using the privilege of an old friend, I shouted to him through the letter-slit. Presently we heard the sound of books falling and some one advancing, and Lexilogus' thin, pale, and spectacled face appeared at the half-opened door. He was always glad to see me, I believe, howsoever I disturbed him; and he smiled as he laid his hand in mine, rather than returned its pressure.

The tea-things were still on the table, and I asked him (though I knew well enough) if he were so fashionable as only just to have breakfasted?

"Oh—long ago—directly after morning chapel."

I then told him he must put his books away, and come out on the river with Euphranor and myself.

"He could not possibly," he said; "not so early, at least."

"Why, you walk every day regularly, I hope, do you not?" I asked him.

"Almost every day; but not now—the yearly examination was coming on."

"Come, come, my good fellow," said Euphranor, "that is the very reason you are to go, the doctor says; he will have it so. So make haste."

I then told him (what I then suddenly remembered) that, besides other reasons for going with us, his old aunt, a Cambridge tradesman's widow whom I attended, and whom poor Lexilogus helped to support out of his own little funds, wanted to see him directly on business. He should go with us to Chesterton, where she lodged; visit her while Euphranor and I played a game of billiards at the inn; and that afterwards we would all three take a good walk in the fields.

He supposed we should be back by Hall time, of course; about which I would make no conditions; and he then resigned himself to his destiny. While he was busy changing and brushing his clothes, Euphranor, who had walked somewhat impatiently about the room, looking now at the books, and now out of the window at some white pigeons wheeling about in the clear blue sky, went up to the mantelpiece and called out, "What a fine new pair of screens Lexilogus had got! the present, doubtless, of some fair lady."

Lexilogus said his sister had sent them to him on his birthday; and coming up to me brush in hand, asked if I recognized the views painted on them?

"Quite well, quite well," I said, and told him to finish his toilet—"the old church, the yew tree, your father's house—one cannot mistake them."

"And were they not beautifully done?" he wanted to know; and I answered without hesitation, they were; for I knew the girl who had painted them, and (whatever they might be in point of art) an affection above all art had guided her hand.

At last, after a little hesitation as to whether he should wear cap and gown (which I decided he should *not*, for this time only), Lexilogus was ready; and calling out on the staircase to his bed-maker not to meddle with his books, we ran downstairs, crossed the great court, through the Screens, thronged with Gyps and bed-makers, and redolent of ten thousand dinners; where we stopped a moment to read the names of the preachers appointed at St. Mary's; then through the cloisters of Neville's Court, and out upon the open space before the library. The sun shone broad on the new-shaven expanse of grass, while holiday-looking folks sauntered along the riverside, and under the trees of the walks, now flourishing in freshest green—the chestnuts especially in full leaf, and bending down their white cones over the sluggish current, which seemed indeed more fitted for the merchandise of coal, than to wash the walls and flow through the groves of Academe.

We now considered we had not come quite right for

the wooden bridge; but this was easily amended at a small expense of college propriety. Going along to the Breweries, Euphranor called out to a man who had his boat in charge with many others close by. We descended the grassy slope, stepped into the boat, and settled the order of our voyage. Euphranor and I were to row, and Lexilogus (as I at first proposed) was to steer. But seeing he was averse from meddling with the matter, I agreed to take all the blame of my awkward rowing on myself.

" And just take care of this for me," said Euphranor, handing him a book which fell out of his pocket as he took his coat off.

" Oh, books, books!" I exclaimed, " I thought we were to steer clear of them at all events. Now we shall have Lexilogus reading all the way. What is it, Latin, Greek, Algebra, German, or what ? "

It was none of these, however, Euphranor said, but only Digby's *Godefridus;* and then asking me whether I was ready, and I calling out " Ay, ay, Sir," our oars splashed in the water. Threading the main arch of Trinity Bridge, we shot past the library, I exerting myself so strenuously (as bad rowers sometimes do) that I almost drove the nose of the boat against an office of this college as much visited by the students as avoided by visitors. This danger past, however, we got on better; Euphranor often looking behind him to anticipate our way, and counteracting with his strong oar any misdirection from mine. Amid all this, he had leisure to ask me if I knew Digby's books ?

" Some of them," I told him, " the *Broad Stone of Honour* for one; indeed I had got the first edition of it, the Protestant one, now very rare."

" But not so good as the enlarged Catholic edition," said Euphranor, " of which this *Godefridus* is part; at least, so Hare says."

" Perhaps not," I replied; " but then, on the other hand, not so Catholic; which you and Lexilogus will agree with me is a great advantage."

This I said slyly, Euphranor being rather taken with the Oxford doctrine just then coming into vogue.

"You cannot forgive him his Popery," said he.

"Nay, nay," said I, "I can forgive a true man anything. Digby is a noble writer; and his quotations too—nobody except old Burton beats him in that."

"Oh, but so much finer than Burton," exclaimed Euphranor, "as much as Aeschylus, Dante, Plato, the Fathers, and the old Romancers, are finer than Albertus Magnus, Paracelsus, Cardan, and suchlike."

I admitted this, though Burton quoted from Plato, Cicero, and Seneca too. After a little pause, Euphranor asked me "if I did not remember Digby himself at College; if I did not know him?"

"Not *know* him," I answered, "but I remember him very well."

"What sort of man?"

"Tall, big-boned, high-featured, and of a sad complexion," I said, "like some old Digby stepped down from the canvas."

"And, Hare says, really himself the knight he drew."

"At least," answered I, "he rowed very vigorously on this river, where I am now labouring so awkwardly."

Thus talking of Digby and his books, and constantly interrupted by the little accidents of our voyage, we had threaded our way through the barges congregated at Magdalen Bridge; through the locks, and so to Cross's boathouse; where we surrendered our boat, and footed it over the fields to Chesterton, at whose church we came just as its quiet chimes were preluding twelve o'clock. Close by was the humble house whither Lexilogus was bound. I looked in for a moment at the old lady, and left Lexilogus with her, desiring him privately to stay but a short time, and then to join us at the *Three Tuns Inn*; the *Three Tuns*, which I preferred to any younger rival, because of the many pleasant hours I had spent there in my own college days.

When we got there, we found that all the tables were occupied; but that one, as usual, would be at our service before long. Meanwhile, ordering some light ale after us, we went into the bowling-green, with its lilac bushes now in full bloom and full odour; and there we found Lycion sitting alone upon a bench, with a cigar in his mouth, and rolling the bowls about lazily with his foot.

"What! Lycion! and all alone!" I exclaimed.

He nodded to us both, and said he was waiting till some men had finished a pool of billiards upstairs—"A great bore—for it was only just begun; and one of the fellows is a man I particularly detest, so I am obliged to wait here till he is off."

"Come and share our ale then," said I. "Are you ever foolish enough to go rowing on the river, as we have been doing?"

"Not often," he said; "he did not see the use of perspiring to no purpose."

"Just so," replied I. "But here comes our liquor; sweet is pleasure after pain, at all events."

We then sat down in one of those little arbours cut into the lilac bushes round the bowling-green, and while Euphranor and I were quaffing each a glass of home-brewed, Lycion took up the volume of Digby, which Euphranor had laid on the table.

"Ah, Lycion," said Euphranor, putting down his glass, "there is one who would teach you to like a longer row on the river than we have had."

"Chivalry," said Lycion, glancing carelessly over the book; "I thought people had done talking about that sort of thing."

Euphranor asked him "what sort of thing?"

"Why, dragons, tournaments, old armour, and so on."

"You judge of the book on rather a hasty acquaintance," said Euphranor.

Lycion said he had heard of it before, and heard it laughed at.

"Possibly," replied Euphranor, who began to look a little angry. "Nevertheless, I can assure you this book is *not* about tournaments, dragons, and ' that sort of thing'; that is, not about them only."

"Don't you remember," Lycion said, addressing me,

"what an absurd thing the Eglinton Tournament was? What a complete failure! There was the Queen of Beauty on her throne, and the heralds, and the knights in full armour on their horses—they had been practising for months, I believe—but unluckily, at the very moment of onset, the rain began, and the knights threw down their lances and put up umbrellas."

I laughed at this account, and said, I remembered something like it had occurred, though not to the extent of the umbrellas, which I thought was a playhouse burlesque on the affair. And I asked Euphranor what he had to say in defence of the tournament.

"Nothing at all," he replied. "It was a silly thing, and fit to be laughed at for the very reason that it *was* only an affair of old armour, with little of the essence of chivalry about it—As Digby himself emphatically tells us," he went on, rapidly turning over the leaves—"Here it is" —and he read—"'The error that leads men to doubt of this first proposition'—that is, you know, that chivalry is not a thing past, but, like all things of beauty, eternal— 'the error that leads men to doubt of this first proposition consists in their supposing that tournaments, steel panoply, and coat arms, and aristocratic institutions, are essential to chivalry; whereas these are, in fact, only accidental attendants upon it, subject to the influence of time, which changes all such things.'"

"I am told the old knights were really great blackguards," said Lycion, turning his cigar in his mouth, and glancing at his antagonist, "with all their pretences of fighting for religion, distressed damsels, and so on."

"Come, Lycion," said I, "you must not abuse them, you, whose pedigree links you through Agincourt and Crecy, almost up to the times of King Arthur."

"Oh yes, King Arthur and his round table, and the seven champions; and pray do not forget Don Quixote. He is one of your heroes, is he not, Euphranor?"

Euphranor declared that Don Quixote was a man of truly chivalric soul—only——

"Only that he was mad," interrupted Lycion, "and mistook windmills for giants. And I doubt if King

Arthur's giants, ogres, and dragons were half so substantial as windmills."

"Perhaps Digby would tell us," said I, who saw Euphranor's wrath rising, "that there can be no want of dragons and ogres while oppression and misery are to be found in the world."

"To be sure," said Euphranor, "these old romances are the symbols of the truth, if not the truth itself: nay, they do record the truth itself, inasmuch as they record the warfare which all heroic men must wage for ever with the evil of the world, under whatsoever shape it may appear."

"Does not Carlyle somewhere tell us," said I, "that chivalry must now seek and fulfil its mission in the campaigns, not of war, but of peace? which need no less energy, endurance, and self-devotion. He talks of a 'chivalry of labour,' I think; that the proper conquests for heroes now to make are the victories of the loom and the steam engine; and that in future not '*arms* and the man,' but '*tools* and the man,' must be the Epic of the world."

"Oh, well," said Lycion, "if your King Arthurs and Sir Lancelots are to soften down into peaceable spinners, stokers, and tailors, I shall never object to them. Let them go on conquering and to conquer in that vocation, by all means; and let short bills, especially among the tailors, be the tokens of their prowess."

"Yes, my dear fellow," said I, "but then you must not sit idle, smoking your cigar, in the midst of it all; but, as your ancestors led on mailed troops at Agincourt, so must you put yourself at the head of these spinners and tailors, and be what Carlyle calls 'a captain of industry'; a master-tailor, leading on a host of journeymen to fresh fields and conquests new."

"Besides," said Euphranor, who did not like dropping chivalry so low from its ancient imaginary splendour, "surely chivalry will ever find enough to do with the law, the religion, the welfare, and glory of a country, the defence of the poor, the education of the people. As Tennyson says so nobly, King Arthur, who was carried away to the island valley of Avilion, to be tended and nursed by queens, will, and does, return to us in the shape of a modern gentleman of stateliest port. And whatever Carlyle or any one else may say, war is not yet out of the world; there are people still ready to strike in a bad cause, and it would be hard if there were none to resist in a good."

"Well," said Lycion, who often, seeming not to attend to what was making against him, caught quickly at any favourable turn—"we have a paid army to do all that for us."

"A paid army!" repeated Euphranor with great disgust. "And do you pretend to say, Lycion, that you, for one, would sit there smoking your eternal cigar, if England were to be invaded, for instance?"

Lycion, however, only turned that eternal cigar in his mouth, and glanced rather superciliously at his antagonist. And I, who had been all this while reading in the *Godefridus* at the open page where Euphranor left off, said, "Here we are, as usual, disputing about we know not what; we have not yet agreed upon the meaning of the terms we are using. Here, Euphranor, will you read this passage to us, as to what Digby understands by the word *chivalry*, and then we shall see our way clearer, perhaps.'

I gave him the book, and he read—

"Chivalry is only a name for that general spirit or state of mind which disposes men to generous and heroic actions, and keeps them conversant with all that is beautiful and sublime in the intellectual and moral world. It will be found that, in the absence of conservative principles, this spirit more generally prevails in youth than in the later periods of men's life; and, as the heroic is always the earliest age in the history of nations, so youth, the first period of life, may be considered as the heroic or chivalrous age of each separate man; and there are few so unhappy as to have grown up without having experienced its influence, and having derived the advantage of being able to enrich their imagination, and to soothe their hours of sorrow, with its romantic recollections. The Anglo-Saxons distinguished the period between childhood and manhood by the term 'cnithade,' knighthood: a term which still continued to indicate the connexion between youth and chivalry, when knights were styled "children," as in the historic song beginning,

> Childe Rowlande to the dark tower came,—

an excellent expression, no doubt;—for every boy and youth is, in his mind and sentiment, a knight, and essentially a son of chivalry. Nature is fine in him. Nothing but the circumstances of a singular and most degrading system of education can ever totally destroy the action of this general law; therefore, so long as there has been, or shall be, young men to grow up to maturity; and until all youthful life shall be dead, and its source withered up for ever; so long must there have been, and must there continue to be, the spirit of noble chivalry. To understand therefore this first, and, as it were, natural chivalry, we have only to observe the features of the youthful age, of which examples surround us. For, as Demopho says of young men —

> Ecce autem similia omnia: omnes congruunt:
> Unum cognoris, omnes noris.

Mark the courage of him who is green and fresh in the old world. Amyntas beheld and dreaded the insolence of the Persians; but not so Alexander, the son of Amyntas, ἅτε νέος, τε ἐών, καὶ κακῶν ἀπαθής (says Herodotus) οὐδαμῶς ἔτι κατέχειν οἷός τε ἦν. When Jason had related to his companions the conditions imposed by the king, the first impression was that of horror and despondency; till Peleus rose up boldly, and said—

> "Ὤρη μητιάασθαι ὅ χ' ἔρξομεν· οὐ μὲν ἔολπα
> Βουλῆς εἶναι ὄνειαρ, ὅσον τ' ἐπὶ κάρτεϊ χειρῶν.

'If Jason be unwilling to attempt it, I and the rest will undertake the enterprise; for what more can we suffer than death?' And then instantly rose up Telamon and Idas, and the sons of Tyndarus, and Oenides, although

> ——οὐδὲ περ ὅσσον ἐπανθιόωντας ἰούλους
> Ἀντέλλων.

But Argus, the Nestor of the party, restrained their impetuous valour.'"

"Scarce the down upon their lips, you see" (said I), "Freshmen;—so that you, Euphranor, who are now Bachelor of Arts, and whose upper lip at least begins to show the stubble of repeated harvests, are, alas, fast slipping away from that golden prime of knighthood, while Lycion here, whose shavings might almost be counted——"

"Pshaw!" interrupted Lycion, "I have no ambition to be one of his heroes."

"But you can't help it, it appears," said I, "and you must not, like a bad bird, foul your own nest. And see here again," I continued, having taken the book from Euphranor's hands, "after telling us that Chivalry is only Youth, he goes on to define what Youth is."

"It is a remark of Lord Bacon, that ' for the moral part, youth will have the pre-eminence, as age hath for the politic '; and this has always been the opinion which is allied to that other belief, that the Heroic (the Homeric age) was the most virtuous age of Greece. When Demosthenes was desirous of expressing any great and generous sentiment, he uses the term νεανικὸν φρόνημα, and it is the saying of Plautus when surprise is evinced at the benevolence of an old man, ' Benignitas hujus ut adolescentuli est.' There is no difference, says the philosopher, between youthful age and youthful character; and what this is cannot be better evinced than in the very words of Aristotle. ' The young are ardent in desire, and what they do is from affection; they are tractable and delicate, they earnestly desire and are easily appeased; their wishes are intense, without comprehending much, as the thirst and hunger of the weary; they are passionate and hasty, and liable to be surprised by anger; for being ambitious of honour, they cannot endure to be despised, but are indignant when they suffer injustice: they love honour, but still more victory; for youth desires superiority, and victory is superiority, and both of these they love more than riches; for as to these, of all things, they care for them the least. They are not of corrupt manners, but are innocent, from not having beheld much wickedness; and they are credulous, from having been seldom deceived; and sanguine in hope, for, like persons who are drunk with wine, they are inflamed by nature, and from their having had but little experience of fortune. And they live by hope, for hope is of the future, but memory is of the past, and to youth the future is everything, the past but little; they hope all things, and remember nothing: and it is easy to deceive them, for the reasons which have been given, for they are willing to hope, and are full of courage, being passionate and hasty, of which tempers it is the nature of one not to fear, and of the other to inspire confidence; and thus are easily put to shame, for they have no resources to set aside the precepts which they have learned: and they have lofty souls, for they have never been disgraced or brought low; and they are unacquainted with necessity; they prefer honour to advantage, virtue to expediency; for they live by affection rather than by reason, and reason is concerned with expediency, but affection with honour: and they are warm friends and hearty companions, more than other men, because they delight in fellowship, and judge of nothing by utility, and therefore not their friends; and they chiefly err in doing all things overmuch, for they keep no medium. They love much, and they dislike much, and so in everything, and this arises from their idea that they know everything. And their faults consist more in insolence than in actual wrong; and they are full of mercy, because they regard all men as good, and more virtuous than they are; for they measure others by their own innocence; so that they suppose every man suffers wrongfully.' So that Lycion, you see," said I, looking up from the book, "is a knight of nature's own dubbing—yes, and here we have a list of the very qualities which constitute him one of the order. And all the time he is pretending to be careless, indolent, and worldly, he is really bursting with suppressed energy, generosity, and devotion."

"If one can't help it then," said Lycion rather sulkily, "what is the use of writing books about it?"

"Oh yes, my dear fellow," said I, "it is like giving you an inventory of your goods, which else you are apt to lose in your march to manhood—which you young people are always straining after. Only to repent of it when you have got there; for I see that Digby goes on—'what is termed *entering the world*, assuming its principles and maxims, is nothing else but departing into those regions to which the souls of the Homeric heroes went sorrowing—

ὃν πότμον γοόωσα, λιποῦσ' ἁδροτῆτα καὶ ἥβην.'"

"And do you remember," said Euphranor, "what Lamb's friend said of the Eton boys in their cricket ground?—'What a pity these fine lads should so soon turn into frivolous members of parliament!'"

"Why must they be frivolous?" said Lycion.

Euphranor did not answer this directly, but went on in a musing way. "No doubt what is called *entering the world* is a degradation from chivalrous youth; but I suppose Digby would admit the best Youth is only a preparation for a better Manhood."

I said, "Perhaps so." "And yet," said he, "in the passage you have read, you see he compares the youth of man with the heroic age of a nation."

"Which, however, may not be its *best* age," answered I, "though a very necessary and a very beautiful one. Lycion and I may not agree that Argonautic expeditions, Trojan or holy wars, mark the best epochs of a nation, whatever you heroic gentlemen think."

"Well, but if what Digby says be true, that it is this spirit which keeps men and nations most conversant with what is beautiful and sublime in the moral and intellectual world—And here is Bacon declaring that Youth excels in the Moral, and Age in the Politic only—poor ignoble Politic!"

I asked, smiling, "if by *Age* Bacon might mean *old age*—as much a descent from perfect Manhood on one side as Youth was an ascent to it on the other. Or if '*Politic*' was used in that better sense by which Jeremy Bentham securely proves the expediency of virtue?"

Euphranor, however, rejected all such base notions of virtue, and would have nothing whatever to do with Jeremy Bentham. "And what mighty virtues Aristotle attributes to Youth!" said he.

"And mighty faults too, for that matter," I returned. —"Does he not say it is rash, ambitious, overbearing—insolent even?—faults which manhood with its experience may correct, perhaps?"

"Well, then," said Euphranor, "Lycion may say, the

sooner these Eton boys get into the world and learn that experience the better."

"Yes," said I, "if their stomachs were strong enough to digest it. And even then they might lose more than they gained—for you see how much of this youthful virtue Aristotle draws from *in*experience of the world; as he says it is innocent from not having beheld much wickedness, hopeful from not having been disappointed, trustful from not having been deceived, lofty of soul and despising riches from never having been brought low; and so forth. Your friend Plato, if I remember, will not allow even those who are destined to be judges in his Republic to make acquaintance with crime till near middle life, for fear they should harden into a distrust of human nature—will he?"

Euphranor nodded; and I said that on the same principle he and Lamb's friend might think there was danger of the Eton boys hardening into an ignoble policy, by too early acquaintance with St. Stephen's, before they were established in the good Affection, good fellowship, and generous energy, of which Aristotle's catalogue was so much made up.

"Especially," said Euphranor, "as Plato will not have a man meddle with the laws till he is past thirty."

"Well," said Lycion, "whatever your ancients—or moderns—may say, the law of England settles it otherwise."

"You mean," said I, "in fixing on twenty-one as the age of discretion?"

He nodded; and I said—"Discretion enough to pocket rents, make your will, and so on."

"Yes, and sit in parliament," said he.

I was obliged to admit this. "There is no denying it—only perhaps the law contemplates that you are there not to advise, but only courageously to second, and carry out into vote, what some Nestor Russel or Ulysses Peel proposes—as the knights of Greece and England obeyed the highest wisdom of law or Church in their days."

"Nay, nay," interposed Euphranor, "and to advise too, in order that the generous counsel, the νεανικὸν φρόνημα, of Youth, may vivify and ennoble the cold Politic of Age."

"Ah," said I, "but if by a full apprenticeship of Youth Age could be so fully stocked with its generous spirit and fine affections, that all experience of the world and politic of Age should serve only to direct, not to freeze the genial current of the soul—that boy's heart within the man's never ceasing to throb and tremble even to *old* age, so that

> Ev'n while the vital heat retreats below,
> Ev'n while the hoary head is lost in snow,
> The *life* is in the leaf, and still between
> The fits of falling snow appears the streaky green—

then you know your senators would need no young men to vivify their counsel, having all their virtue in themselves; or could admit the Young without danger of contaminating them by ignoble policy."

"According to you, the virtue of youth consists in its good Affections," said Euphranor.

"Nay," I replied, "I am only following Aristotle's text, whose catalogue is made up of these Affections, you see; 'living by Affection rather than by Reason' he twice says, I think."

"Ah," said Euphranor, "and Bacon somewhere observes, I remember, that Youth doth profit in the Affections, and Age in the Reason, which may help one to the meaning of that other passage of his that puzzled me before, about the Moral and Politic."

"He too," said I, "would perhaps agree with Lamb's friend and Digby, that it would be well to give those affections good time to develop in; that at all events it would be dangerous to forsake them until the Reason was far advanced, which this same Aristotle says, I think, does not reach its maturity till about forty years of age, though I say it who should not, having just passed that noble era."

"Pythagoras, you know," said Euphranor, "had said much the same long before. Setting man's life at fourscore years, he devotes the first twenty to Childhood—the second to Youth—the third to Manhood—and the last to Old Age. A division of life which you and I shall not quarrel with at any rate, doctor."

"No, indeed," cried I, "nor to any one else, I should suppose. Think, my dear Lycion, what a privilege it is for you to have yet more than twenty years before you to enjoy in the Elysian cricket-field of Youth, spared from the contamination of representing your father's borough in Parliament. And Euphranor, too, whom we thought was leaving his prime of youth just as he got his beard, is, in fact, only just entering upon it; and (what is most wonderful of all) I, who have been these fifteen years past bringing people into the world, and regulating their bowels, am myself only just ceased to be a boy!"

Lycion now called up to his friends in the billiard-room, one of whom appeared at the window, cue in hand, and shook his head, saying, however, in a confidential way, that "all would be right in a few minutes," and so retired. On which Lycion had nothing to do for it but light another cigar, and lying down on his back with his hat over his eyes, compose himself to inattention.

Euphranor, who had been musing during this little episode, now said, "To be sure these unreasonable Affections are no very high qualities. Plato would call them the virtues of dogs and horses."

"Let me see," said I, taking up the book again, and running my eye over the passage—"yes, 'ardent of desire,' 'tractable' some of them at least—'without comprehending much'—'ambitious'—'despisers of riches'—except the famous dog and the shadow, but that is a fable—'warm friends and hearty companions'—really a great deal quite applicable to the better breeds of dogs and horses. And why not? The horse, you know, has given his very name to Chivalry, because of his association in the heroic enterprises of men. And as for dogs, Byron says he never had but one friend—'and——'"

"And there *he lies*," cried Euphranor. "Lord Byron!—But there are other affections——"

"Wife and children?" said I, as he paused. "Birds you know, have both—and your knights are supposed as yet to know nothing of either."

"I hope you like it, Euphranor," said Lycion from under his hat.

"Pshaw, doctor!" Euphranor called out rather impatiently—"Religious Affections, for instance, which all children feel, and dogs and horses never come to feel."

"My dear Euphranor," said I, more seriously, "is not *all* Affection, *quoad* Affection, unreasonable? If you speak of the *object* of Affection, that is another thing. Men only (as we suppose) comprehend the idea of God; and, by the way, does not Bacon say that man looks up to God, as a dog to his master?"

"But meaning that man looks up with Reasonable Affection, as a dog to man with unreasonable."

"Well," said I, "*man*, come to forty years of age—(humph!)—may comprehend the Divine idea; but do not the young accept it blindly, on authority, and so bend their Affections to it?"

"But to be able to accept it at all," urged Euphranor, "whether *comprehending* it or not, *is* Reason; and so of Truth, and Justice, and other abstract ideas, which are intuitive by children; remembered, Plato says, from some previous existence, and included by Bacon, I have no doubt, in what he calls the *Moral* of Youth."

"And Wordsworth too," added I, "does not he affirm this Intuition is the more active the younger we are, as being nearer to God, who is our home?"

Euphranor assented, and I said, "But, Euphranor, if this Intuition be *reason*, we overrule Bacon and Aristotle, and say that it is not *Age* that excels in it, but Childhood."

"Unless," said he, "considering the *intuitive* Reason to be drawn out by the *dialectic*, as music from an instrument into the full harmony of *complete reason*, as we see done in Plato's *Dialogues with the Young*."

"Hear these metaphysicians, Lycion!" said I: "the Reason drawn out by Reason into Reason!"

Lycion only answered with one long-drawn sigh of smoke that went the way of most metaphysics.

"Or," said Euphranor, laughing, "suppose I drop the *name* of Reason from my first term, substitute what I believe is an equivalent for the second, put all into a Coleridgean formula (though not with Coleridge's use of terms) —'The Intuition + the Understanding = the whole Reason.'"

We both laughed at this grand proposition, which Euphranor gave out in a mock-heroic way. And then I said, "This poor *reason* has run the gauntlet of definition harder than any word in the language, I believe. Some make it an Instinct, some a process of that Instinct, confounding Reas*on* with Reaso*ning*, perhaps. Milton says it is nothing but *choice*. And, by the way (what has escaped us before, Euphranor), Aristotle, or his translator, seems to identify it with Bacon's *policy*. 'Concerned with expediency,' he defines it. Jeremy Bentham, after all!"

"Aristotle had rather a leaning that way," Euphranor said—" so unlike his glorious master."

"Well," I said, " I, for one, do not pretend to decide among such great authorities, all calling names. I stick to the common phraseology of the country, and when I want to name the supreme faculty of human judgment, whensoever and howsoever begun and completed, give the idol its old name of REASON, and so leave it on its shrine. As for that Intuitive moral-material of it which you say is in us from birth, I should think your friend Plato would agree it should have full room to develop in—that the instrument, as you call it, should be well seasoned and strung before played on by that sceptical agent you told us of, the dialectic Understanding."

"Only to be touched by so delicate a finger as his own Socrates," answered Euphranor, smiling.

"And even he was accused of doing it unskilfully, was he not?—of turning the harmonious instincts of youth into discord, and making sophists of the Etonians of Athens?"

"A great calumny," Euphranor declared.

"Well," said I, "at any rate he might think it dangerous for Youth to tune and question its own Intuitions by its own immature Understanding, which, whether the completion of Reason or not, is, I verily believe, the last growth of the brain, and really scarce mature till middle life. Still less would he let this precious Intuition be tampered with by the finger of worldly, and parliamentary, policy."

Euphranor laughed and nodded, and said that "Lamb's friend was really gathering a cloud of witnesses about him."

"And as to those *affections*," said I, " of which Aristotle's inventory is made up, and which are defined at large in it, Plato may say what he likes, but he would have been especially sorry if his sons, servants, or dogs could have been argued out of them, even by his own *Dialogues*."

"And why?" Euphranor asked.

"Because," I answered, "he probably wanted them to follow and *do* what he thought good for them, whether they understood it dialectically or not, as you will agree with me we want our children to do, and as those children of old, the knights, did."

"And as Plato would have *done* himself," said Euphranor.

"Perhaps, having a good stock of these *affections* at the back of his dialectic. Else, you know my old quotation about 'the native hue of resolution,' etc.," said I, smiling. "And by some of the more irreverent writers on humanity, Reason is said to be the weakest governing part about us; a sign-post, somebody says, which points the way, but by no means urges us along it. Whereas these blind Affections actually push us along the road, being allied in growth and energy to our *animal* affections, which are said to be the strongest governing part about us."

"To which, however, you are not going to draw down Chivalry, I hope," said Euphranor.

"I can't do without some of them for our knights, however," said I. "You and Plato must consider together, if indeed some part of the dog's, horse's, and knight's *a*dialectic affections we spoke of does not in fact result from good *bodily* condition in dogs, horses, and knights; as, for instance, what we are always talking of as *animal spirits*, *animal courage*, and so on—a kind of moral in which Youth proverbially surpasses Age, partly in virtue of its better animal condition."

He looked reproachfully.

"Why, you know," said I, laughing, "your starved horse won't run, and your starved soldier—*will*."

"Chivalry an essence of beefsteaks!" ejaculated he.

"I hope you like it, Euphranor," said Lycion from under his hat.

But I went on laughing.—" No, no, not beefsteaks alone, else your alderman would be a Bayard—he must be well exercised as well as well fed; sent out hunting, for instance, or to cricket with those Eton lads, in order to convert the beefsteak and turtle into pure blood, muscle, sinew, and *pluck.*"

Too much brute strength, however, Euphranor would have it (on Plato's authority again, I believe, for Plato was his great oracle), brutalized the mind. To which I could only answer, I was not (as far as I knew) for too much of anything. However, he would admit that Telamon, and Idas, and Oenides, and those other youthful knights we had read of, wanted a good share of bodily strength to work that very heavy ship, the *Argo*; as did also King Arthur's knights for their fights with giants and dragons; and even those of our own time, " the modern gentlemen," if they were to lead hosts of blacksmiths, for instance, or any other more vigorous trade than a tailor's, to conquest. And I asked him whether, apart from any influence such exercises, or the animal condition they helped to bring about, had upon the soul, Digby did not consider strength of body, and the accomplishments of riding, swimming, fighting with many weapons, and perhaps cricketing, as very necessary accomplishments for his young gentlemen of England?

Euphranor said, " No doubt;" and then, recurring to what I had before spoken of, remembered some observation of Sir Walter Scott (another hero of his), that strong men are usually good-humoured, Scott himself, as Euphranor remarked, being so good an instance of it. And I added Bacon's testimony as to anger being chiefly observable in weakness, old age, childhood, and sickness. " So that, on the whole," said I, tapping on the top of Lycion's hat, " what with the keeping out of knavery till one knows how to join in it properly; and avoiding bad air in more senses than one; and cultivating Good Affections, and Good Health, and perhaps (Euphranor says) Good Humour, and perhaps also some other Good things we cannot now think of, Lamb's friend might have been right after all in lamenting the departure of the Eton lads from the fields of their Youth for a premature Manhood in St. Stephen's; though as to deciding which is fairest, a good Youth or a good Manhood, Euphranor, that may be like deciding which is handsomest, the blossom or the flower."

Whether Lycion would have deigned to reply I know not; but at this very moment his friend put his head out of the billiard-room window, and called out to him that the coast was clear; on which Lycion, getting up, and carelessly nodding to us, went into the house.

"The other day," said Euphranor, when he was gone, "Skythrops was in my rooms, and opened Digby's book at the very passage we have been reading: he read it—with what relish you may imagine."

"What did he say of it?"

"Oh you can fancy—that Youth, so far from 'drawing clouds of glory from God who is its home,' draws clouds of sulphur from—*his* home. He ran over Aristotle's inventory, as you call it; the old talk, he said, of Honour, Glory, and so on—Pagan virtues—very well for a Pagan to record and a Papist to quote; but he wondered I could keep such a book in my rooms. And he especially commented on the ὕβρις, which, as you observed, waits on the very virtues Aristotle records."

"Well," said I, "dead wood doubtless makes best posts, and that is what Skythrops wants. The living tree will sprout out in a manner incomprehensible to such naturalists. *He* would nip the flower of Youth as if it were flower of brimstone:—then Lycion would stifle it in St. Stephen's:—and how many force it to blow before its time, and so ruin it!"

"In the present rage for *intellect*," said Euphranor.

"Yes," I replied, "intellect, not for its own sake only, but for advancement in the peaceful professions, now so thronged since war has been quiet. Jack and Tom, you know, must not only shine at the literary tea-table, they must get fellowships, livings, silk gowns at the Bar—they cannot be crammed too fast; and to this end the order of Nature is reversed, to get early at faculties which come last in the order of growth; the Understanding set to work almost before it is born, the Affections neglected or misdirected, the whole Body, without whose soundness the Soul it encloses cannot, *I* say, be sound, neglected in its hour of growth, or torn to pieces by premature energies within. But Nature has her revenge. We think the world is growing wiser; it may in the end; but, as some one said, we are now rearing a generation of fools."

After a little pause, during which we both applied to our glasses, Euphranor said—"Doctor, you may be right in the main, but I do not like your subjecting the Soul to the carcass as you do."

I laughed, and said, "We doctors were of old infamous for such doctrines—we spoke up for our craft, and would not let Plato and the soul-doctors carry off all the fees. We only wanted to divide the spoil, just as man was divided into body and spirit, and were quite ready to grant that mind acted on carcass as much as carcass on mind. You remember," said I, "Sterne's metaphor of Jerkin and Jerkin's lining,—'rumple one and you rumple the other.'"

"O base metaphor!" cried Euphranor, "just like Sterne, whom I wonder you do not hate as I do,—Soul and Body all of one texture!"

"No, no," said I, laughing; "Jerkin, you know, is generally lined with other material than himself, often finer—silk, for instance."

"Often with coarser too," replied Euphranor, "with diaper, or serge, as I believe Sterne's own jerkin was, for his body was a very delicate one, and his soul one of the grossest upon earth. No, no, if you must have a metaphor, have one at least where soul and body are more essentially distinguished."

"What say you then," said I, "to the old and favourite one of the Body being a house, and the Soul its tenant—'the body's guest'—will that do for you?"

He nodded; and I said that if one were inclined to argue, one might say that the tenant, whether prince or peasant, must be affected according as his lodging is wholesome or not; would catch all manner of rheumatisms and colds and fevers, if it were dilapidated, dirty, and damp. But more especially so if he were not only a tenant, but a prisoner, unable to get out, as was the case with the soul in this life; unless indeed, as some thought, she got abroad through the keyhole at night, when the body was fast locked in sleep; making rather an odd use of her liberty in dreams——"

But here Euphranor called out that the lodger I spoke of, whether peasant or prince, *was* in some sort of the very same matter as his lodgings;—a body built of clay in a clay-built house,—as bad a metaphor, after all, as Jerkin and lining. "Besides," he went on eagerly, "it is well known that persons enfeebled to the last degree by long illnesses, extreme old age, and on the very verge of death, shine brighter than ever in piety, wisdom, and love." And he went on to repeat—

> "The soul's dark cottage, batter'd and decay'd,
> Lets in more light through chinks that time has made;
> Stronger by weakness, wiser men become
> As they draw near to their eternal home."

"Halloo!" I called out, "got back to the clay cottage again!"

"Only to prove," said he, "how it may fall in pieces while its inmate thrives upon its decay and ruin. And what instances we have of the greatest minds dwelling in the craziest and puniest bodies."

"Great *parts* of minds," I answered, "as great Wit in Pope, for instance."

"*Mens curva in corpore curvo*," quoted Euphranor. "No, Wit itself is said to be a kind of dishonesty of thought, so let it e'en be a disease—of the body, if you like. But look at Pascal now——"

"Well," said I, "great mathematical and reasoning faculty. But these do not make up a MAN. A *bon mot*, a poem, a problem, are no more specimens of the whole MAN, than that celebrated brick was of the whole house. What is your author in his Affections and Temper, as well as his Understanding? What as relative, friend, neighbour, and so forth? the 'whole, sound, roundabout' man, as Locke says."

"But Pascal was a notoriously religious and good man," argued Euphranor.

"Notoriously ascetic," said I, "that is to say, of a diseased religion. He would not let his family be too much about him lest their mutual love should deprive God of His due. I should instance Pascal's religion as looking much like the refraction from a sickly body."

Euphranor was again silent a little, and I said, smiling, " Like some objects that will force themselves on one's eyes in a landscape for ever so far, this clay cottage will not be got out of sight. The poets are fond of it. It now occurs to me in that other relation with its tenant which we were speaking of—not where it affects, but is affected—by its lodger's incessant strugglings and batterings within. You remember Dryden's old lines about that soul,

> "Flat o'er-informed its tenement of clay
> Fretting the puny body to decay."

"Well," said Euphranor, " and the sooner the better; so she flies back to her proper element again."

" A great escape, doubtless," I said. "But yet it has pleased God to station her here on probation, to do some work for herself and others. And being certain of eternity —yes, and (as a good soul) of a happy eternity—she should be well content to be imprisoned for such a mere point of time as our threescore years and ten in this clumsy lantern of a body, the only means by which her rays can be so condensed as to lighten her more benighted mortal fellow-spirits. Else, the razor or the halter would furnish a speedy and satisfactory escape for her at any time."

"Well, perhaps so," said he.

" And then, if the body does not die at once, but lingers in long pain," said I, " this divine Soul, though quite independent of the Body she lodges in, and unaffected by its pains, does (out of a divine pity) sympathize greatly with its distresses, and loses much of her precious time in condolence and contriving the means of alleviation: considering the merits of different doctors and medicines. Even in indigestions, which are said to be the plagues of thinking men, how much of her precious self she wastes daily, mourning over some little bit of cheese that will stick in the stomach of the most universal philanthropist!"

Euphranor laughed, and asked, " what could be done

for her?" and I answered, that I supposed, according to that old prescription (the curse of physicians), that "prevention is better than cure," the best way was to build up for her, in the proper season, a tenement strong enough to resist the elements without and her own batterings within; so that when she is called to her great vocations, she may go about them undisturbed by creaking doors and windows, falling timbers, and failing foundations, and by all the repairs they incessantly call for. "Besides," I added, "if for no particular *use*, surely one should in decency provide a handsome, spacious, and airy mansion for so divine a tenant?"

Euphranor, upon this, recalled to me what he called an old paradox of mine (a corollary, however, from that I had just been maintaining), that Beauty of Body and of Mind went together, in spite of such instances as Socrates, whom I always managed to square into my theory to my own satisfaction; citing many notable instances, and, besides that, the instinct there was in all civilized nations to represent their gods and heroes in the most perfect human shape; that even in our religion, in spite of the silence of Evangelists, and even in defiance of a prophecy that was supposed to apply to Him, all the great painters had represented the Divine Author in a shape of godlike perfection, that we should not tolerate the contrary even were it possible, which I could scarcely believe.

"Come, doctor," said Euphranor suddenly, "you, who find such fault with others' education, shall tell me how *you* would bring up a young knight, till you turned him out of your hands a Man."

"My dear fellow," I answered, "like other fault-finders, I have nothing better to propose. People know well enough how to manage these matters, if they will but use their common sense, and not be run away with by new fashions and mistaken interests. And what is become of Lexilogus?"

Euphranor thought there was nothing to be done but to wait for him; and I said, "Besides, you know, I am only a Body doctor, which, as we said, is only half the battle. And then, is your knight to be brought up to shoot partridges, and be a *gentleman*, or to carry his prowess out, as we were talking of, into some calling? Is he to be

> Soldier, sailor,
> Tinker, tailor,
> Gentleman, apothecary, ploughboy, thief,

as boys count on their buttons."

"Nay," said he, "he must be fitted to lead in any calling of life. And as we have agreed that the spirit of Chivalry is only the spirit of Youth, all men, and all trades, inherit it equally, and cannot, I suppose, afford to do without it—except, perhaps, the last."

"Nay," said I, "the proverb says, 'There is honour among thieves,' you know."

"At all events," said he, "if we decide the knight is now to become captain of tailors, we should also lift up the tailor halfway to meet him. It would require, however, a complete recasting of society, to give all classes the advantages necessary for a complete development of our common nature—the tailor must have a turn at the bat and ball, while his young captain takes the shears for an hour or so. We must be content to pick up our hero in a rank of life where these advantages are at hand—an English country squire's, say."

"Well," said I, "such lads are in general very well cared for at home—well suckled, well fed, well clothed, admitted to the full privileges of the chase, protected by gamelaws, and thriving so well in our larger and nobler schools, like Harrow and Eton, that I sometimes wish, with Lamb's friend, they were left longer there."

"Not forgetting my own dear old Westminster, if you please, doctor."

With which I had no quarrel, except its being in the bad air of London; and Euphranor told me I should send Sir Lancelot where I liked, in due time, but at present I must begin with him "*ab ovo*."

"Well," said I. "if I have any hand in the matter, it must certainly be '*ab ovo*;' for it is part of my profession to herald Sir Lancelot into the world. But really, my dear Euphranor, after that process (which, perhaps, you would not care to hear about), I must repeat, I have nothing new to tell you, except, perhaps, some medical recipes."

"Never mind," said he, "tell me the common sense of the matter—that will be new to me, anyhow. Come, let us suppose Sir Lancelot fairly launched into the world by your art."

"Here he is, then," said I, "a very queer-looking, squeaking lump of flesh as ever you saw, neither fitted for sword or toga. I protest, Euphranor, I think he must be given up to me and to the nurses only, to wash and do for. I think there is no use of any soul-doctor at all as yet—the creature appears to me all jerkin, and no lining."

"Ah, but the lining, as you call it, is there," said he, "the immortal soul."

"A little bit of a soul, then!" said I, "for her manifestations are scarcely so decided as a puppy's."

"No wonder," answered Euphranor; "how should she exert herself, the delicate Psyche, suddenly shut up in the foul grub again?"

"Cannot at all use her senses."

"It would be still more wonderful if she could," said he, "understand directly the use of the totally new set of fleshly tools she is doomed to work with for a time."

"Bravo!" I exclaimed, "you have vindicated her handsomely. I only meant to say that for some time Sir Lancelot is little else but a *body*, so far as *our* treatment of him goes—to be suckled, washed, and *done for*."

"Very well," said Euphranor.

"By degrees he begins, as you hinted, to use his senses—to discriminate sounds with his ears, objects and distances with eyes and hands, and so forth, much like other animals."

"Well, go on."

"Well, then, will you say that those objects impressing themselves on the brain, memory wakes? 'The burned child dreads the fire;' remembers faces, voices, and persons; likes some, dislikes others, *physically* at first, and then from *custom*, and from some glimmer of moral affection, perhaps; but still much as the beasts that perish."

"Oh, but *speech*," said Euphranor.

"Well," I answered, "even speech at first is but an

organic imitation, like a parrot's. But I have no desire to keep Sir Lancelot down among the beasts; he soon lifts his head above them; his words become, to himself, the sign of things, of thoughts; he begins to *reflect*, to reflect on the past, and to guess at the future, from it; a short future indeed, as a short past, scarce extending beyond yesterday's and to-morrow's dinner. By-and-bye, too, he begins to collect the scattered images of memory, and re-cast them in new shapes, which you call *fancy*, I believe. And by-and-bye, too, he is drawn up from the visible love and authority of parents and nurses, to the idea of a Father unseen—the Father of his father, Father of all, Maker of all, who, though we do not see Him, sees us, and all we do, and even all we think; who has bid us obey, love, and honour our parents, tell the truth, keep our hands from picking and stealing, and who will one day reward or punish us according as we have done all this."

"Halloa, doctor," said Euphranor, smiling, "you have brought on your child at a fine rate, far faster than I should have dared; instilling religion when you were pretending to give him a dose."

"Not I," I answered, "nor Mr. or Miss Skythrops either. Mamma and nurse have done it imperceptibly. It is through the mother's eyes, Fellenberg finely said, that heaven first beams upon a child. But, as you say, '*ne sutor ultra*.' I return to my soothing syrups."

But Euphranor declared that, having once begun, I must go on, carrying Sir Lancelot's mind along with his body; especially since I had given out that any mismanagement of the mind would injure the body I was employed to protect. So I agreed to look after our young knight so long as he was in the women's apartments, "which was, according to Xenophon (was it not ?), for the first seven years of life."

Euphranor thought Xenophon reported that as the ancient Persian usage. "But," said I, "I cannot be bound to your Aristotelian and Baconian terms of *affections*, *reason*, and so on, which I perhaps do not understand in the sense they do, after all."

He told me to use what terms I liked. "Well, then," I

went on, " I will give the women one general rule : that for those first seven years Sir Lancelot shall only be put to do what he can do *easily*, without effort either of mind or body, whatever his faculties may be, or may be called. He shall only meddle with what Plato calls the *music of education*—does he ?——"

" Part of it, at least, I dare say," Euphranor answered, smiling. And I went on to say that luckily, for the first years of life, the bodily and mental music went together. Nurse finding nonsense songs the best accompaniment to dandling Sir Lancelot in her arms, or rocking him to sleep in the cradle, and that from the lyrical fragment of " Little Bo-peep," the progress was easy to the more dramatic and intellectual Death of Cock Robin ; and after that, to stories in numerous verse and prose about certain good dogs and cats, and little boys and girls, and even little hymns by sweet Jane Taylor and Watts, about the star, and the daisy, and Him who made them ; all which, beside exercising speech and memory, sometimes under cover of fable, sometimes in pure plain-spoken affection, dispose the mind toward the Good, the Beautiful, and the Holy. " Then you know," said I, " there are pictures,—' that is the horse ' —' that is the cat '—which easily lead to ' A was an Apple ' —the alphabet itself—Newton's true *Principia*, after all, as Vincent Bourne said."

" Well, then, there he is instituted in letters," said Euphranor. " But what have you been doing for his bodily exercises all the while ? "

" Ah, there I am more in my element," I returned, " and mamma and nurse want quite as much looking after in this as in the other matter. They are too apt in the pride of their hearts to make Sir Lancelot walk before he can stand, and when he *can* use his legs, will not give him verge enough to ply them in."

" What is to be done for him ? "

" Oh, after the due dandling and rocking of first infancy, give him a clear stage to roll in : he will find his own legs when they are strong enough to bear him. Then let him romp as much as likes ; and roar too—a great part of children's fun, and of great service to the lungs. And that (beside the fresh air) is so great an advantage in sending children to play out of doors, they don't disturb the serious and nervous elders of the house, who ruin the health and spirits of thousands by, 'Be quiet, child—Don't make such a noise, child,' et caetera."

"Ah, I remember," said Euphranor, "how you used to play at hide-and-seek with us in the shrubbery, rather exciting us to rebellion, when my aunt ran out to warn us in, or reduce us to order."

"Or for fear your dresses should be dirtied," rejoined I "for that is one of the fetters laid upon children's wholesome growth. They must early learn to look *respectable*: as also shouting is vulgar, you know. Then what screaming from the window if a little dew lay on the grass, or a summer cloud overcame the sky."

"I suppose you would have shoes with holes in them on purpose to let in water, as Locke does," said Euphranor, laughing.

"I wouldn't keep a child from exercise in the dirt because he has no whole shoes at home, at all events," answered I.

"He catches cold."

"I dose him instantly and effectually."

"But he dies."

"Then, as a sensible woman said, 'he is provided for.' Your own Plato, I think, says it is best the sickly and delicate should die off early at once."

"Rather a pagan doctrine, if he does," replied Euphranor. "However, we will suppose Sir Lancelot survives—what else?"

"Where did we leave him?" said I,—"Oh, yes—I remember—in the mud—where, by-the-bye (much better than if shut up in a schoolroom or parlour), he makes acquaintance with external nature, sun, moon, stars, trees, flowers, stones, so wholesome in themselves, and the rudiments of so many *ologies* for hereafter."

"Not forgetting animals," said Euphranor.

"By no means," said I, "and especially the horse and the dog, whose virtues we said he would do well to share."

"Horses and dogs in the women's apartments!" said

Euphranor, laughing. "Oh yes," I said, "his acquaintance with the dog begins in the cradle; and the horse, who, as we said, has given his very name to the spirit of Youth, Devotion, and Courage, we began talking about—Sir Lancelot cannot too soon make his acquaintance—to pat him—to feed him—to be set upon his back, either in the stable or during exercise up and down the avenue."

"And it is wonderful," Euphranor observed, "what forbearance the nobler animals show for children; how great dogs suffer themselves to be pulled about for hours by them; and horses will carry boys with a kind of proud docility, who would kick and plunge under a grown-up rider. Perhaps they like children's soft voices and light weights; for which very reason, I have heard, they are more manageable by women."

"Yes," said I, "and have they not also a sense of humour that is amused at being bestrid by urchins? ay, and real generosity too, that will not take advantage of weakness."

After a little pause, Euphranor said, "When you lay it down that children are scarcely to be compelled against the grain for their first seven years, I suppose you make some reservation as to *moral* restraint—the repression of passion, for instance."

"Not only that," answered I, "he must also learn to submit himself to order—to *some* daily indoor restraint—silence—and task-work—all when he would be out of doors romping: only let there be but *a little* of such compulsion day by day."

"And if he be refractory, even against this gentle discipline?"

"Then, if the withdrawal of confidence and love, and appealing to his faculty of shame and remorse, are not enough, a taste of the rod, the compendious symbol of might and right. Only, I am quite sure, as a general rule, it is better to lean to the extreme of indulgence than of severity: you at least get at *truth*, if ugly truth, by letting a child display his character without a fear; and faults that determine outwardly are far more likely to evaporate than when repressed to rankle within. Anyhow, the ugliest truth is better than the handsomest falsehood."

To this Euphranor willingly assented; and after a time said, "Well, we have now got Sir Lancelot pretty fairly through his first septenniad."

"And what sort of chap do you find him?" said I.

"Nay, he is your child," answered Euphranor.

"The very reason," said I, "why I should be glad of a neighbour's candid opinion about him. However, I am not his father, but only his doctor; and, moreover, I will not say what he *is*, but only that I shall be content if he be a jolly little fellow, with rosy cheeks, and a clear eye, with just a little mischief in it at times: passionate, perhaps, and (even with his sisters) apt to try right by might; but generous, easily pacified, easily repentant, and ready to confess his faults: rather rebellious against women's domination, and against all the wraps and gruels they force upon him; but fond of mother and of good old nurse; glad to begin and end each day with a prayer and a little hymn at their knees. Decidedly fonder of play than of books; rather too fond, it is supposed, of the stable, and of Will and Tom there; but submitting, after a little contest, to learn a little day by day from books which lead his mind toward hope, affection, generosity, and piety."

"So much for Sir Lancelot's first septenniad," said Euphranor. "And now for his second."

"That is your affair then," said I, taking the last draught from my tumbler. "I only engaged to see him through the first."

"Then," replied Euphranor, laughing, "I must give him up to Skythrops, who is now coming down the avenue."

"In a white neck-cloth, and with a face of determined asperity! Yes, he has often condoled with me before on Sir Lancelot's backwardness and depravity, and now his hour is come."

"Hark, he knocks at the door," said Euphranor. "Will you give your boy up to him?"

"No; I will oppose my portly person in the doorway; thin as he is, he slips no farther,—he cannot melt me with his vinegar. I stand firm while he proposes his plans;—twelve hours a day indoor work at Grammar, Latin, Greek, Modern Languages, Euclid, Geography, *et caetera*;

and two hours' recreation and exercise, videlicet, a walk with Skythrops himself."

"But you don't keep him standing in the passage all this time, doctor?"

"Well, that would not be polite,—I take him into the library, and as soon as possible propose lunch, of which Skythrops very largely partakes; and carrying him abroad to see an improvement in the lawn, escort him safely along the avenue, out of the gates."

"His scheme does not suit you?" said Euphranor.

"And if it did," I answered, "*he* would not suit me. There is magnetism in all these things. Boys cannot learn of one who has nothing of the boy in him."

"Ah! I remember," said Euphranor, "how good Dr. Arnold insists on that;" and he quoted Arnold's beautiful image of the difference between drinking from a living spring and a stagnant pond. "And, no doubt," he continued, "Skythrops' division of play and work please you as little as he himself does?—his twelve hours' work to two of recreation."

I answered, "It only wanted reversing."

Euphranor looked incredulous; and I told him of a table I had lately seen made by a German physiologist, who, proposing to begin education at seven years old (and not a whit earlier) with but *one* hour's indoor study, keeps adding on an hour every year, so as, by fourteen years old, the boy studies eight hours out of the twenty-four.

"Distinctions of age," Euphranor remarked, "which, ever so good, could not be made in schools."

"They *were* made, however, in one school," I replied —"Fellenberg's—the best school, on the whole, that I have read of."

"Ah, he agreed with you, I think," said Euphranor, "how much may be taught out of doors, and by wholesome experiment, in fresh air and exercise. Certainly, a child may learn to love and obey parents, pastors, and masters, as well indoors as out; nay, better, while owing to them the freedom and happiness he enjoys."

"And God too," said I, "while enjoying his fields, streams, and breezes, quite as much as when listening to

Skythrops concerning the origin of evil in a stived-up room. For Skythrops hates fresh air and open windows, I am sure."

Euphranor laughed. "And then," said I, "does not your Plato tells us that drills, marches, and other rhythmical out-of-door exercises, beside the good they do the body, unconsciously instil a sense of order and harmonious obedience into the soul?"

"And now, too," Euphranor went on, "we may suppose Sir Lancelot's acquaintance with nature, having begun in love, will go on to knowledge, in the way of some of those *ologies* you talked about."

"Not forgetting that most necessary geology, agriculture," said I, "eldest, healthiest, and most necessary of sciences; so loved and practised by the Roman gentlemen in the most heroic days of Rome."

"And which Aristotle says rears up the best peasantry," said Euphranor, "'βέλτιστος δῆμος ὁ γεωργικός,' he says; whom, by the way, I suppose you would certainly have your English gentleman well acquainted with, especially if he be a landowner."

"Ah! to be sure," said I, "we might have remembered before to bring him well acquainted with the poor,—a lesson which children cannot learn too soon, which they will always learn gladly when taught, not by dry discourse, but by living experiment; especially in the sweet fields and clean country cottages."

Here, however, Euphranor broke in, declaring how often he had heard me declaim against Skythropical tutors, who would not leave their victims alone even during their scanty play-hours, but must pursue them with exhortations still, and soil even the fair page of nature with their running commentaries.

To which I answered, there was discretion in this as in other things: that no doubt children ought to have much time given up to the most unreasonable sport—to the most total rest of mind; that the real fault of the Skythropical sect was not so much combining instruction with recreation, but *unfit* instruction, which negatived all recreation,—dry theory, whether of science or morals.

Anyhow, I would rather carry the experiments of the fields into the schoolroom, than the theories of the schoolroom into the fields.

"We are agreed, however, to have *some* books, and *some* indoor study," said Euphranor, smiling; "what shall they be?"

"Oh," said I, "the records of good and great men, following properly on those of great dogs and good horses we spoke of before; not theories of heroic virtue, but living examples of it, as found in our own histories, in translations from others, then in Cornelius Nepos, Livy, Caesar, and so on to old Homer himself. For where is the school boy who does not side with Hector or Achilles, Greek or Trojan? Then there is Virgil, with his seedy Aeneas, but lovely vernal *Georgics*, welcome whether in schoolroom or field; and Ovid's stories of wonder."

"Which Plato says is the father of Philosophy," said Euphranor, "to which I suppose you will lead up Sir Lancelot in good time, though scarcely perhaps in his second septenniad. But, doctor, we have unawares got him into Latin and Greek, a thing only to be done by very hard work in Grammar, in itself about as difficult a theory as may be. I am sure I now wonder at the jargon I had to learn and repeat when I was a boy, and only now in happy hour light upon the *reason* of the rules I repeated mechanically."

"True," said I, "but you were only expected, I hope, to *use* them mechanically; ascertaining the different parts of speech, and then how a verb governs an accusative, and an adjective agrees with a noun; to all which relations you are guided by certain terminations of *us, a, um,* and *do, das, dat,* and so on; till you are able to put the scattered words together, and so ford through a sentence. And the repetition by heart of those rules fixed them in your mind, and was a proper exercise for your memory."

"We must not forget arithmetic also," said Euphranor, "where, by-the-bye, the rules are also used mechanically at the time, to be understood, perhaps, afterwards, just as those of grammar. Well, so much for Sir Lancelot's studies in his second septenniad; and now for his bodily exercises;

I suppose they advance proportionably in labour and energy."

"No doubt," said I, "the horse he was taken to look at, feed, and be held on, he now bestrides—a pony at all events—trots, gallops, gets a peep at the hounds throwing off; in due time a run with them, fleshes his maiden courage at a leap, rises up Antaeus-like from a tumble."

"Ah," said Euphranor, "we poorer fellows are cut out of this."

"Well, there are the ditches and rivers for you to fall into, and be drowned in, whether in leaping, skating, swimming, or boating; nay, in this dear old England of ours, the sea itself ready to embrace and strangle the whole youth of Britain, in her arms."

"Ah," said Euphranor, "there again, if mamma was frightened at her boy dabbling in the dew, without his hat too, what will she say now he is brought home half drowned in a ditch, or his arm broken by a fall from his pony?"

"I must console her as before," said I—

> "'If he fall in, good night!
> Send danger from the east unto the west,
> So Honour cross it from the north to south.'

It is better to die well ever so young than to grow up a valetudinary and poltroon. He can only grow strong in body and soul by such exercises as carry danger along with them; and strong in body and soul our knight must be, must he not?"

"Nay, but," said Euphranor, "*I* have not yet agreed that his soul can only grow strong by being in a strong body; and mamma will not agree that the body can only be made strong by dangerous exercises."

"All strong exercise is more or less dangerous," I replied; "in digging, sowing, running, we may sprain, strain, and rupture, if we do not break limbs. There is no end to finding out dangers if you look for them. Men have died of grape-stones sticking in the throat—are we never to eat grapes again, or are they to be carefully picked of their stones first? And as for Courage, which is the strength of soul I speak of, some men are born with it under a lucky star, and, the phrenologists say, under a good constellation of bumps. But even then it will require *exercise* to keep it in repair. But if men have it not naturally, how is it to be acquired except in the demand for it—that is to say, in danger? and to be laid in in youth, while the mind is growing, and capable of nerving, so as to become a *habit* of the soul, and to act with the force and readiness of instinct?"

"Mamma will say it is to be found in good books, good principles, religion, and so on," said Euphranor.

"And there may be found the long-concocted resolution, that, after all the struggles of natural fear, may nerve a man to be a martyr at last. But while it succeeds in one, it fails in a thousand. For here comes the ancient difference between *resolving* and *doing;* which latter is what we want. Nay, you know, the habit of resolving without acting (as we do necessarily in facing dangers and trials in books and in the closet) is worse for us than never resolving at all, inasmuch as it gradually snaps the natural connexion between thought and deed."

"Ah," said Euphranor, "you stole that from the Newman I lent you, doctor; how true and good it is!"

"Very true and very good," answered I, "and I dare say I stole it from him; though I had long before been familiar with an ancient proverb (as old as the Fathers, for anything I know) as to what Thought did as he lay in bed."

"What in fact some folks of weak nerves are said to do before a battle," said Euphranor, with a burst of laughter.

"Just that. And then if this closet courage could certainly brace us up to any long-foreseen emergency, would it help us at any sudden pinch of accident of which life is full, and for which our knight must assuredly be prepared? I mean, when there is no time to *make up our minds*, but the mind must act at once, ready made."

"What is called *presence of mind*," said Euphranor.

"A very wonderful thing," said I; "as, for instance, what a sudden resolution the mind is put upon in hunting, by which men, if their horses fall with them in all the violence and excitement of full cry, know how *to fall well*

—to launch themselves out of their horse's way, for instance —which I remember even dear old Parson Adams knew how to do in the good old days."

"I have often thought," said Euphranor, "what a wonderful act of the soul it is in cricket, where the batter has to make up his mind what to do with the ball, whether to hit, tip, or block, all in the twinkling of an eye between the ball's being delivered from the bowler's hand and its arrival at his own wicket. How much is to be 'willed, done, and performed,' in that moment of time!"

"Yes," said I, "and the boxer, whose mind is to decide, and his fists to follow his mind so instantaneously, as to put in a blow upon his adversary at the very moment of guarding one off from him."

"But," said Euphranor, "mamma will perhaps protest that the presence of mind will be learned in the harmless emergencies of battledore and shuttlecock."

"But not presence of mind *in danger*," said I, "which we are talking of, and which we must therefore include in the exercises fitted to meet it."

"But then," Euphranor went on, "will experience of one emergency avail us in another? For instance, will the power of falling well with our horse help us to put a blow into our adversary's rib?"

"It will so far help us, that the mind, having learnt to abide unshaken in one trial, will be more likely to abide unshaken in another, and bring all the knowledge and art she has to bear upon it. It is like mathematics, you know. Euclid will not help you to the solution of a logical argument, but Euclid disposes you to a logical disposition of all argument. However, Sir Lancelot, we have agreed, is to be practised in many resources—swimming, sailing, rowing, boxing, fencing, riding—time out of mind the indispensable accomplishments of a gentleman, and from whose equal proportionable development of all the parts of the body a gentleman is known by his carriage, whatever effect they may have on his soul."

Euphranor nodded, but said that, after all, there was less need for such preparation now in these days of peace and safe contrivance. Men were not called on to fight, it seemed; hunting was certainly not a duty *per se*; and all life was made a first-class carriage of well-padded security.

But I asked if he had forgotten his own assertion, that war was not dead, but only sleeping; and Sir Walter's assertion, that the strong were good-humoured; and a yet older assertion, that only the brave could be truly merciful; so that even if courage were not wanted for war, was it not wanted for peace ?—life itself, the smoothest life, being all a battle, made up of perpetual little conflicts, harder to bear, many thought, than a few hard raps of fate; which if a man (naturally deficient in women's passive courage of non-resistance) did not meet with active courage, he was sure to fail under, and make himself and all about him miserable. "Depend upon it," I said, "your carpet knight will fight his battles *on* the carpet—over the tea-table—with wife, children, servants. Besides," I went on, laughing, "accidents will happen in the best regulated families. The house will take fire, the coach will break down, the boat will upset;—is there no gentleman who can swim, to save himself and others; no one who can do more to save the maid or the child snoring in the garret, heedless of the flames, than merely to repeat, 'How *very* awful!' Some one is taken ill at midnight: John is drunk in bed; can no gentleman put a saddle on the horse, much less get a collar over his head or adjust the crupper, without such awkwardness as brings on his abdomen the kick he fears, and spoils him for the journey?"

Euphranor laughed at this picture of impotence, and I said, "'I tell you, my Lord Fool, out of this nettle *danger*, we pluck this flower *safety*.' Why, the most timid valetudinarian is ordered by his doctor a gentle ride: the quietest pony is bought; but only he trots safely who has galloped hard: no one is so sure to come down in the road as your heavy sack of a sitter, with no seat in his saddle nor hand on his bridle; and no one so sure to break his nose when he does come down. Besides," I continued, "what after all is the amount of danger in all the hunting, wrestling, boating, etc., that a boy goes through? Half a dozen boys are drowned, half a dozen shot instead of rabbits by their friends, half a dozen get broken arms or collar-bones by falls from ponies, in the course of the year; and for this little toll paid to death, how large a proportion of the gentry of this country are brought up manfully fitted for peace or war! If I have to do with Sir Lancelot he shall take his chance, either to grow up a man fit to live, or to die honourably in striving towards it. And so I leave him at the end of his second septenniad."

"Close upon the age of those young Argonauts," said Euphranor, "upon whose lips the down yet was not. Really closely upon the threshold of Chivalry."

"Yes," said I, "push him on three or four years, and you may dub him a knight according to ancient practice, I believe."

"Fitted in body and mind to his calling?"

"Well, Euphranor," said I, "I cannot tell: my mind misgives me when I am about to send my pupil into the lists, whether Nature originally endowed him well enough, and whether I have helped to make the best of Nature's bounty. I doubt my ideas of knighthood may fall very far short of Digby's; short of what they ought to be perhaps."

"Well, what sort of a fellow do you turn out, at any rate?" said Euphranor.

"I doubt I shall be content with him," said I, "if (at sixteen, say) he shows me outwardly, as before, a glowing cheek, an open brow, copious locks, a clear eye, and looks me full in face withal; his body a little uncouth and angular perhaps, as compared to his earlier self, because now striking out into manly proportion, not yet filled up; flesh giving way to fibre and muscle; the blood running warm and quick through his veins, and easily discovering itself in his cheeks and forehead at the mention of what is noble or shameful; his voice, 'sweet and tuneable,' as Margaret of Newcastle notices of her brothers,—she does not mean, she says (nor do I), an emasculate treble, but no 'husking or wharling in the throat,'—that is her word, —a clear, open, bell-like voice, telling of a roomy chest, and in some measure, I think, of a candid soul. However that may be," continued I, seeing Euphranor shake his head at me with a smile, "candid of soul I hope he is; for I have always sought his confidence, and never used it against himself; never arraigned him severely for the smaller outbreaks of youthful spirit; never exacted sympathy where it was not in the nature of Youth to sympathize. He is still passionate, perhaps, as in his first septenniad, but easily reconciled; subdued easily by affection and the appeal to old and kindly remembrance, but stubborn against force; generous, forgiving; still liking to ride rather than to read, and perhaps to settle a difference by the fist than by the tongue; but submitting to those who do not task him above Nature's due; apt to sleep under the sermon, but not ceasing to repeat morning and evening the prayers he learned at his mother's knee: ambitious of honour, perhaps, but of honour in action rather than in talk; somewhat awkwardly disposed to dancing, and the accomplishments of the drawing-room, which even now he shirks in order to go earth-stopping with Tom and Jack, who used to set him on Topsail's back in days gone by. In short, I shall be content to find him with all the faults of a vigorous constitution of soul and body, which time and good counsel may direct into a channel of action that will find room for all, and turn all to good. One must begin life with all the strength of life, subject to all danger of its abuse: strength itself, even of evil, is a kind of virtue; whereas weakness is the one radical and incurable evil, growing worse instead of better with every year of life."

"And this is your education," said Euphranor, "for all boys indiscriminately, without regard to any particular genius they may show,"

"But without injury to it, I hope," said I; "for instance, should it lie toward any of those *ologies* which we thought Sir Lancelot's free intercourse with Nature especially opened to him, or even toward looking into Plato and Digby for qualities he already unconsciously possesses. But," I continued, seeing no sign of self-consciousness in Euphranor's own earnest face, "if Sir Lancelot not only *has* a Genius (as I suppose all men have some), but *is* a Genius,—big with Epic, Lyrical, or Parliamentary inspiration,—I do not meddle with him—he will take his own course in spite of me. What I have to turn out is not a Genius, but a YOUNG GENTLEMAN, qualified at least for the common professions, or trades, if you like it. Or if he have means and inclination to live independently on his estate, may, *in spite* of his genius, turn into a very good husband, father, neighbour, and magistrate. No mean vocation, in my opinion, who really believe that healthy, courageous good humour, and activity of soul, do radiate a more happy atmosphere throughout a little circle, and, through that, imperceptibly, to the whole world, than cart-loads of poems, sermons, and essays, by dyspeptic divines, authors, and universal philanthropists, whose fine feelings and bad stomachs generally make them tyrants in their own families, and whose books go to draw others into a like unhappy condition with themselves."

Euphranor mused a little within himself, and then observed that all I had been saying applied to private education only, in a young man's home; or, at most, where only a few pupils were to be attended to. In a great school boys must be lumped together in a rougher way.

"That lumping together had, however, its advantages," I said, "which compensated for the absence of others. Boys got knocked out of family delusions, and got to know themselves, by comparing themselves with others. Only let the schools be large and liberal enough—Eton, Harrow, Westminster, and some others."

"But what becomes of your horses?" said Euphranor; "Eton and Harrow could not supply them to their pupils."

"Fellenberg," I replied, "had a riding-school as part of his much poorer German institution."

"But our great schools," argued Euphranor, "do not make it part of their system to provide for the bodily instruction of their youth; it is supposed lads will find out their own play and exercise, and devote themselves too much to it without further assistance."

"That seems to me a mistake, however," said I, "in these days, when, besides the school duties, now so increased in quantity and quality, and the prospective claims of the peaceful professions, young people have so many sedentary accomplishments courting their own or their parents' fancy. If my theory of Body and Mind (which is everybody's who chooses to think) is right, the one ought to be trained as much as the other. The Greeks, you know, made gymnastics a necessary part of their education. So do the German schools; that at Hofwyl, for instance, from which our greatest and noblest foundations might take many good hints, if they were not too proud to do so. At all events, our smaller schools might greatly profit by imitation. If they could not compass the riding-school, there was at least the swimming-bath, which Fellenberg found one of the best remedies for an indolent habit of body and mind—gardens to work in— not only the hours of exertion, whether bodily or mental, proportioned to the ages of the pupils, but even the hours of sleep—no lesson lasting longer than an hour at a time— and wholesome changes of subject, master, and schoolrooms, to refresh the boy's mind. Fellenberg's first principle seems a truism till people come to act upon it —that a child should never be employed in any exercise, physical, moral, or intellectual, beyond his powers."

"Ah, that is very good," said Euphranor. "And have not these Swiss and German schools military exercise also?"

"Yes," said I, "which, you see, is another advantage that a school may possess over home education. Milton expressly recommends military exercises, drills, and watches; good in peace as well as in war, I say; teaching order, submission, and endurance."

"Arnold," said Euphranor, "was all either for home education or one of our large schools. He hated the little ones."

"Yet," said I, "the largest and best of them have other faults; as, for instance, exacting so huge a proficiency in Latin and Greek verse; a fault imputable, I am told, to these universities, which require a great amount of that rather useless accomplishment. They also do too little in the way of training boys to sympathy with the lower classes—not by moral essays, but by living contact with the poor; where Fellenberg again had the advantage, having a large school of agriculture and trade for the poorer boys joined to that of the rich, so that all classes should in some way mingle beneficially with each other."

"Where, as I was saying before," said Euphranor, "the young tailor might have a turn at a bat, and the young lord at the plough, now and then."

"And all the better, if the young lord were put to earn his bread there for a week or so every now and then," said I, "affording him light as to the condition of the poor, 'unquenchable by logic and statistics,' Carlyle says, 'when he comes, as Duke of Logwood, to legislate for them in Parliament.'"

"To hear you talk, doctor, any one would suppose you would send your son to Germany for his schooling; but I know your old dogmas about an Englishman being brought up in England, imbibing English air and English associations into his very nature from the first."

"Yes," said I, "I am for growing up by the Thames under Windsor Castle, rather than by the Rhine under Heidelberg."

"Not forgetting glorious Westminster Abbey!" cried he with exultation.

"No," said I, "we must not go abroad for Fellenberg, but bring a slip of him hither if we can. And yet even this I say with some hesitation, and not without awe of the old Genius of these noble schools. But as to the smaller ones, my dear Euphranor, you cannot imagine the pusillanimous, sordid, soul-and-body-stunting method of some of these, which, if English good sense did not explode just before it was too late (as English good sense has somehow a knack of doing) would ruin the middle-class Chivalry of England altogether. Nor are the poor masters only to blame—they are often one-sided, pedantic men, ignorant of the constitution of man; the boys' parents are quite as ignorant and mercenary as the master— they must have their full pennyworth. Then, you know, there are your Religious Establishments, where the *intellectual and moral culture* of the boys is incessantly attended to—not a moment spared for mischief; and then such care taken of their healths'! Ten hours a day hard at the hardest stuff, most indigestible by the young;

moral essays; sermons; the little play-time cut up into little intercalary snips of time, not allowing of any generous and invigorating game, even if the few square yards of gravel, or the strict edict against all amusements that threaten the boys' limbs or the master's window-panes ever so remotely, should allow it. No cricket, no football —perhaps a little gymnastic gallows, where boys may climb, and turn over, and swing like monkeys, in perfect safety; no rowing, no sailing, no stolen ride on horseback or on the coach-box; no running and leaping over hedge and ditch, animated by the pursuit of some infuriated gamekeeper; but a walk, two and two, in clean dresses, along the high road, dogged by the sallow usher——"

"Of course no fighting," said Euphranor, "and, I suppose, no flogging neither."

"And yet," said I, "the clenched fist so soon resolved into the open hand, when once the question of might and right was settled—how much better than the perpetual canker of a grudge never suffered to explode!—and the good flogging had its humour—soon passed away, shame and smart, from fore and aft—much better than the heart-pining, body-contracting confinements and impositions which double the already overloaded task-work, and revenge a temporary fault with lasting injury."

"You get quite excited about it, doctor," said Euphranor. "But it is enough to make one angry, if it be as you say."

"Oh, it succeeds well," I continued; "the boy who came to school with but *some* troublesome activity about him is soon tamed down, grows pale, cheerless, spiritless, hopeless, and *very good*—a credit to the school—likely to be a blessing to his parents. It is only one of Nature's 'best earthly mould,' with the spirit of her chivalry strong in his blood, who kicks over the traces, throws the whole 'very eligible establishment' into disorder, and rouses the whole dastard soul of Skythrops into a meagre attitude of expulsion, however unwilling he may be to part with any victim who pays. But 'he must go—nothing can be done with him.' He goes: he is sent to sea—rolls and tosses over the world—comes back a good-humoured, active, lively, sunburnt fellow, with tobacco and cheroots for his old Dad; some silks for mother and sisters; a parrot for old Aunt Deborah; a bamboo, which he says he would give old Skythrops but for fear he should lick the boys with it. So he travels, and returns, and travels again: has at last scraped a little money together; marries a good-humoured girl who has even less world's wealth than himself; nay, I believe he had married her long before he was even as rich as he is;—has a large family of children healthy as himself—the more the merrier, he says; and so whistles through and over the ups and downs of life."

"And the *good* boy," said Euphranor, "what becomes of him?"

"I have no heart to follow him," said I. "Poor fellow! the last I heard of him was, that after a most unimpeachable progress through school and college, getting all the prizes, he was going off to some new German baths, covered with boils and blotches; or, at the Old Bailey, laying his hand on that part of his coat under which the heart is supposed to beat, and calling God to witness the innocence of a murderer who had already confessed his crime to him."

"Do you remember," said Euphranor, "that fine passage in the *Clouds* of Aristophanes—whom in general I do not love, by-the-bye—where the δίκαιος and ἄδικος λόγος each solicit the young man who stands hesitating between them?"

I had forgotten, I said, my little Latin and less Greek; and Euphranor told me I must positively read this play again—it was quite in my way—" it is, you see," he said, "Old Athens, who reared the Μαραθωνομάχοι ἄνδρες, against Young Athens, who forsakes the simple rhythmical exercises of his ancestors for intricate and enervating measures—leaves the Gymnasium for the Law Courts and the Sophists. Young Athens pleads for his system, and then the old one replies, ending with those delicious lines, musical as the whisper of the trees they tell of—

'Ἀλλ' οὖν λιπάρος γε καὶ εὐανθής—'"

"Come, my good fellow," said I, "you must interpret." And Euphranor, with a little sly smile, and looking down, recited—

O listen to me, and so shall you be stout-hearted and fresh as a
    daisy:
Not ready to chatter on every matter, nor bent over books till
    you're hazy:
No splitter of straws, no dab at the laws, making black seem white
    so cunning;
But wandering down outside the town, and over the green meadow
    running,
Ride, wrestle, and play with your fellows so gay, like so many birds
    of a feather
All breathing of youth, good humour, and truth, in the time of the
    jolly spring weather,
In the jolly springtime, when the poplar and lime dishevel their
    tresses together."

"Well, but go on," said I, when he stopped. "I am sure there is something more of it, now you recall the passage to me—about broad shoulders and little——"

"Oh," said he, "only the outward signs of inward strength—I remember no more of it."

I then asked him who translated the passage, suspecting it was himself; to which he replied, it was more a paraphrase than a translation, and I might criticize it as I liked. To which I said I had not much to object—perhaps the trees "dishevelling their tresses" was a little Cockney, which he agreed it was—far inferior to the *psithurizing* together of the original. And then I observed to him how the degradation Aristophanes saw in the Athenian youth went on and on, so that, when Rome aided Greece against Philip of Macedon, Livy says the Athenians could only contribute to the common cause declamations and despatches—"*quibus solum valent*," he says; a sentence I could never forget.

"Ay," said Euphranor, "and to think that when Livy wrote so of Athens, his own Rome was just beginning to go downhill in the same way and for the same causes—

> "'Nescit equo rudis
> Haerere ingenuus puer,
> Venarique timet, ludere doctior
> Graeco seu jubeas trocho,
> Seu malis vetitâ legibus aleâ:'

how unlike those early times, when the heroic father begot

and bred an heroic son : generation following generation through ages of national glory, crowned with laurel and with oak ; reared by a system of education, the same Livy says, handed down, as it were an art, from the very foundation of Rome, and filling her senate with generals, equal, he says, to Alexander."

"But come, my dear fellow," said I, jumping up, " here have I been discoursing away like a little Socrates, while the day is passing over our heads. We have forgotten poor Lexilogus, who (I should not wonder) may have stolen away to Cambridge. Let us go after him directly."

Euphranor, who seemed yet desirous to converse, nevertheless rose up. On looking at my watch I saw we could not take anything like the walk we proposed and be at home by college dinner ; so I said that as it was I who had wasted the day, I would stand the expense of mutton chops and ale at the inn ; after which we could all return at our ease to Cambridge in the evening. As we were leaving the bowling-green, I called up to Lycion, who thereupon appeared at the billiard-room window with his coat off, and a rather gorgeous waistcoat revealed, and asked him if he had nearly finished his game ? In reply, he asked us if we had finished our ogres and giants ? On which I told him, laughing, " pretty nearly ; "—that we were going into the fields for a walk—would he come with us ? or, if he meant to go on playing billiards, would he dine with us on our return ? " He could not walk with us, certainly," he said,—" was engaged to play some games more." And when I spoke of dinner again, seemed rather to hesitate about it ; but at last said, " Very well ; " and, nodding to us, retired with his cue and waistcoat back into the room.

Then Euphranor and I, leaving the necessary orders within, sallied out towards the church, observing, as we went, how much pains Lycion took to spoil the good within him. For, at Harrow, he was (as Euphranor understood) a good-humoured, lively, and rather gallant boy. But dining with ambassadors and at clubs, and going to Almack's, was spoiling him. And Euphranor spoke of the affectation of indifference and apathy now so fashionable—

so contrary to the spirit of youth—especially ungraceful, he thought (and so did I), in women. In all of which we judged, both of us, rather from what we heard, and read, and saw of fine people in their carriages, than from any actual knowledge; for neither of us were much in great company. And he observed, I remember, that even if there were no other ill effects of London dissipation on women, yet the simply being present in so many crowds was a sort of prostitution, especially of the eye; and noticed the hackneyed look which even young and handsome women soon acquired. We were walking thus, when, on coming close to Chesterton Church, we saw Lexilogus passing through a turnstile on his way toward us. In half a minute we had met; and he had explained to us why he was so late: he had been delayed by one of Aunt Martha's fits of asthma, and he did not like to leave the house till the fit was over. She had now fallen into a gentle sleep.

After expressing our sympathy, we turned back again; and I told Lexilogus how, after all, Euphranor and I had played no billiards, but been had arguing all the time about Digby and his books.

Lexilogus smiled, but made no remark, being naturally slow of speech, and perhaps of thought also. But the day was delightful, and we walked along the road briskly, conversing on many topics, till, a little farther on, we got into the fields. These were now in their prime; thick with grass, crowded with daisies and buttercups; and, as we went along, Euphranor quoted Chaucer's lines:—

" Embroidered was he as it were a mede,
All full of fresh flowris, both white and rede."

And instantly added, " What a lovely picture that was of a young knight!"

I agreed, and asked Lexilogus if he knew it; but he had never read Chaucer: so I begged Euphranor to repeat it to us; which he did, with an occasional pause in his memory, and jog from mine.

" ' With him there was his Sonn, a yongé Squire,
A Lover, and a lusty Bachelire,
With lockis curle, as they were leid in press;

Of twenty yere of age he was, I ghesse ;
Of his stature he was of evin length,
Wonderly deliver, and of grete Strength ;
And he had been sometime in Chevauchie
In Flandris, in Artois, and Picardie,
And born him wel, as of so litil space,
In hope to standin in his Lady's grace.
Embroidered was he as it were a mede,
All full of fresh flowris, both white and rede ;
Singing he was or floyting all the day ;
He was as fresh as is the Month of May :
Short was his gown with slevis long and wide,
Well couth he set an hors, and fair yride ;
And songis he couth make, and wel endyte,
Just, and eke daunce, and well portraye and write.
So hote he lovid that by nighter tale
He slept no more than doth the Nightingale.
Curteys he was, lowly, and servisable,
And karft before his Fadir at the table.'"

"Chaucer, however," said Euphranor when he had finished the passage, "allows his young squire more accomplishments than you would trust with him, doctor. See, he dances, draws, and even writes songs—quite a *petit-maître*."

"But also," I added, "is of 'grete strength,' 'fair yrides,' and had already 'born him well in Chevauchie.' Besides," continued I (who had not yet recovered, I suppose, from my former sententiousness), "in those days, you know, there was scarce any reading, which usurps so much of knighthood now. Men left that to the clergy; contented, as we before agreed, to follow their bidding to pilgrimages and holy wars. Some gentler accomplishments were needed then to soften manners, just as we want rougher ones to fortify ours."

"One may see this exemplified," said Euphranor, "among us now. Music, you will say, only helps to *Mollyfy* the rich,—pardon the vile pun,—but all the education people say it is of excellent use among the poor."

"And who was it," said I, "who, when some one grumbled at a barrel-organ in the street, said prettily that one should tolerate, and even respect, the instrument that carried Orpheus down into dark alleys and cellars. It has struck me strangely to hear in one of our Yorkshire scars a delicate air of Mozart all of a sudden."

Euphranor then observed that, in the days of Elizabeth and the Stuarts, the lute and viol were common accomplishments of young gentlemen: so, to be sure, were all martial exercises.

"And more than exercises," added I: "young fellows going to serve as soldiers abroad as part of their education, if there were no war in hand at home. Sir Philip Sidney might well be allowed a little conneteering; and one would not quarrel with a midshipman practising his flute in the cockpit now."

"Even Pepys, tailor as he was," Euphranor said, "takes horse and rides to Huntingdon from London and back without comment."

"And without a sore bottom, I dare say," rejoined I. "People could only travel so in those days, and could hardly help being hardily brought up in all respects. There is a delightful little horseback tour in Derbyshire, made and recorded by a son of Sir Thomas Browne's—he, and one friend, I think; with all their wet jackets, tumbles, benightings, and weariness, so well compensated by the welcome inn at last, with its jovial host. Travelling has lost its proper relish for the young now,—there is no fun, no adventure, no endurance. And look at dear old Chaucer himself," said I, "how the fresh air of the Kent hills, over which he rode four hundred years ago, breathes in his verses still. They have a perfume like fine old hay, that will not lose its sweetness, having been cut and carried so fresh. All his poetry bespeaks a man of sound mind and body."

"As he really was, I think," said Euphranor. "I remember Lydgate speaks highly of his good-humour, candour, and liberality. I cannot now recollect the lines," he added, after pausing a little.[1]

---

[1] The verses Euphranor could not remember are these—
"For Chaucer that my master was, and knew
What did belong to writing verse and prose,
Ne'er stumbled at small faults, nor yet did view
With scornful eyes the works and books of those
That in this time did write, nor yet would taunt
At any man, to fear him or to daunt."

"A famous man of business too," said I, "employed by princes at home and abroad. And ready to fight as to write; having, he says, when some City people had accused him of untruth, ' prepared his body for Mars his doing, if any contraried his saws.' "

"A poet after your own heart, doctor," said Euphranor. "In general, however, the poets are said to be a sickly, irritable, inactive, and solitary race."

"The great ones?" I asked, "No, I think, are the only ones worth naming—Homer, Aeschylus, Shakespeare, for instance?"

"We don't know much of them—of the two first, at all events," said he.

I asked if Homer did not go about camp and court singing his verses? To which Euphranor answered that the stories of his beggarhood were quite exploded, by those omniscient critics the Germans, whom he knew how much I reverenced; and I said, "About as much a beggar, I suppose, as his own divine Demodocus at Alcinous' palace, or as the bards were to Irish and Scotch chieftains. Then as to Aeschylus, pray is his service at Salamis only a *myth*, as you call it?"

Euphranor laughed, and believed we must admit this to be authentic, so clearly as the trumpet that woke the Greeks to battle on that morning still rung in his verse. I then asked about Shakespeare's poaching, which Euphranor said he was sure I should vindicate, however exploded by German and English critics too.

"Well," said I, "whether Shakespeare was a poacher or not (and I firmly believe he *was*, in the days of his knighthood), he, at least, was no dyspeptic solitary, but, like Chaucer, a good man of business, managing a theatre so unlike modern managers, who are not great poets, that he made a sufficient fortune by it; which, when he got, desiring no more, he retired from London and all his glory, to dear old Stratford, the town of his birth—the fields of his knighthood and poaching—and there spent the rest of his life, an active burgess of the town, esteemed by all the neighbouring gentry, Aubrey tells us, for his pleasant conversation."

"He does not, however," said Euphranor, "quite bear

out your old theory. His very sound mind appears to have dwelt in rather a heavy body, judging by the figure on his tomb. And he died young."

"The monument, which is a very clumsy one, however, only indicates that he grew plump at last," said I; "but the only probable pictures of him exhibit great beauty of face, and every appearance of its growing on a well-proportioned and well-developed body. Perhaps he drank a little too much sack latterly at the country dinner tables of the Cloptons and Lucys; for no doubt he took his glass with the rest."

"Ah," said Euphranor, "Ward's *Journal* says he died of a kind of fever, I think, resulting from a carousal with Ben Jonson, who came to see him from London."

"Very likely," said I; "he would, no doubt, pledge Ben stoutly, having no idea that his life was necessary to the world. And, after all, fifty-two (the age he died at) was not so young in those days when people drank sack and ale for breakfast, and were much less careful of their health."

"And had, perhaps, not such good doctors as we have now," added Euphranor, slyly. "Well, who does not wish that *his* clay cottage had been built up so strong, or patched up so well, that he might have dictated from it some more imperial manifestoes to posterity? However, doctor, if you have saved your theory one way with him (and I am not quite sure you have), what will you say to two poets, whom I know you admit to be of the highest, and who, as far as we know, had well-conditioned bodies in active times, when you declare that men must have been hardily brought up, and yet were both, I believe, morose kind of men—Dante and Milton?"

I said, supposing the fact were as he stated, both these men lived in bad times for the temper: civil war; neighbour set against neighbour, and, even after the dispute is settled, victor and vanquished settling down cheek by jowl. No wonder if Dante hated, and damned, those who had banished him—in verse, at least. I had not heard he was morose out of his poetry. As to Milton, when he had worn out his eyes "in Liberty's defence," and when the Restoration made that defence treason, he was obliged to live in seclusion, besides being compelled by poverty. Certainly, if his own word were to be believed, he never bated a jot of heart or hope to the last; and, in my turn, I asked Euphranor from what *myths* he drew his conclusion about the temper of these two men?

Euphranor did not like the acerbity of Milton's prose tracts, and fancied he was an awkward husband.

"Ah, Lexilogus," said I, "you know know Euphranor cannot forgive the Republicans, and their treatment of those martyrs, Charles and Laud. Were, however, Shakespeare ever so fat, and Milton and Dante ever so surly, I should not abandon my theory. For who doubts that men, however nobly constituted in body and mind, may ruin both by misuse? as Burns his by intemperance of all kinds, and Walter Scott by striving too hard to redeem his own and his friend's fortune? The poetic spirit in itself is a fiery one, apt to fret its body to decay, made up of some dangerous elements, which, as you say and as Wordsworth has hinted, may lead to melancholy and madness, unless aired by perpetual contact with reality, action, and wholesome communion with men."

"I suppose," said Euphranor, "if you found a young Apollo, you would knock him about in his education like the rest of us coarser vessels."

"To be sure I would, and rather more, perhaps."

"And so break half the tribe in course of moulding."

"And live the better with the other half," I replied. "Yes, certainly, I would pass the young aspirants through such a fire of action as should do these two good things—only the true poetic stuff should abide the trial, and that should come all the purer and stronger from it. I would immediately set young Edwin on a rough colt, and pit your Cockneys and Lakers at a wrestling match, and see if some external bruises would not draw off some of that inner sensibility which is the main stock of most so-called poets."

"And which *is* a vital part of the poetic nature," said Euphranor. "Some one says the poet has more of the woman than the man in him."

"If that were true," answered I, "it would be a final argument for smothering the whole tribe as early as possible, small and great, if they are not only to be women themselves, but to make us so by their incantations. But I don't believe a syllable of this : I believe the poetic sensibility to be wholly different from that of women, resulting not from tenderness of nerves, but susceptibility of imagination, or some vital difference which I, who am neither poet nor metaphysician, cannot understand. I only believe the sensibility of Homer, Dante, Shakespeare, and Scott must have been totally different from that of Laura Matilda, Shenstone, or those Minor Poets, whom I would very readily resign into the rank of female authors."

Euphranor said I was always too tyrannical about what are called the Minor Poets ; that there was a hand fitted for everything under the sun ; that if Homer sung of the Atreidae and Cadmus, we also wanted smaller men to sing of smaller matters, which common men can sympathize in.

" What ! *Love*, for instance ? " I asked—" which Anacreon could only sing of, he says."

" Well, *Love*, if you please," replied Euphranor, " though not precisely Anacreon's."

" Thomas Little's, then, which nearly all common men sympathize in ? "

He shook his head, and quoted Petrarch ; to whose Sonnets I opposed some of Dante's on the same subject, but far grander ; and then passing to other affections, which Minor Poets take a right to celebrate, asked which of them had equalled the parting of Hector and Andromache ; or that close of evening that drew the pilgrim home, and marked by the bell that seems to mourn the dying day—the pictures and associations of Nature in the *Allegro* and *Penseroso*—such pastoral lyrics as " Under the Greenwood Tree," the very careless notes of the blackbird, it seemed to me—or the whole familiar tenderness of this very Shakespeare and Chaucer of ours ? It was only these great poets, I contended, who did indeed respond to the common sympathies of men, but in a way that ennobled them.

" And then," said I, laughing, " consider how a strong active body, capable of endurance and exposure, enables your Poet to be with Nature in all her humours, and to penetrate all her mysteries—of calm, of storm, land and sea, day and night, mountain or forest. Your Cockney can only get up Hampstead Hill with some labour, with an umbrella, cork soles, and a cold muffin in his pocket, having promised Miss Briggs by the sacred Moon to be at home in Bidborough Street before the dews fall. And even if the daisies and buttercups there, were, at this time of day, sufficient object for poetic meditation, yet cannot he make even *his* best of them, for has he not gone out *prepared* to be poetical? Whereas Poetry is said to be an Instinct—an Inspiration—or, in other words, a Madness (as the Platonic Ion argues), that will not come at call, like a Laureate's Odes, but must leap out of its own accord at the unpremeditated contact with Nature (or, at least, the recollection of such a contact), which alone dashes Reality into his words. Just as in those physical emergencies we were speaking of, which called out the Moral Instinct of Courage. In this way one fancies language itself began: so Adam named all things as each presented itself to him, appealing to the divine organ of speech within him. Let any scholar sit down in his study and try to invent *words* now; whereas one *does* see something of the faculty among more illiterate people—Sportsmen, for instance, and the Brethren of the Ring—where a new sudden occasion calls out a suitable word somehow from the unconscious Poet of the field—the very name 'slang' we give all such vocabulary being itself an instance of such felicitous invention, and doubtless owing its rise to some such occasion."

Euphranor then read to us as we walked a delightful passage from his Godefridus, to the effect that, if the Poet could not invent, neither could his reader understand him, when he told of Ulysses and Diomed listening to the crane clanging in the marsh by night, without having *experienced* something of the kind. And so we went on, partly in jest, partly in earnest, drawing Philosophers of all kinds into the same net in which we had entangled the Poet and his Critic—how the best Histories had been written by those who had been busy actors in them—how the moralist who worked alone and dyspeptic in his closet was most apt to mismeasure Humanity, and be very angry when his system would not fit; and so on a great deal more, till I, suddenly observing how the sun had declined from his meridian, looked at my watch, and asked my companions if they did not begin to feel hungry, as I did. They agreed with me, and we turned homeward; and as Lexilogus had hitherto borne so little part in the conversation, I began to question him about Herodotus and Strabo (whose books I had seen lying open upon his table), and drew from him some information about the courses of the Nile and the Danube, and the Geography of the Old World: till, all of a sudden, our conversation stepped from Hymettus to the hills of Yorkshire—our own old hills—and the old friends and neighbours who dwelt among them. And as we were talking of old places, and old people, and old times, we suddenly heard the galloping of horses behind us (for we were now in the main road), and, looking back just as they were coming up, I saw Phidippus was one of the riders, with two others whom I did not know. I held up my hand, and called out to him as he was passing; and Phidippus, drawing up his horse all snorting and agitated with her arrested course, came back to us and held out his hand.

I asked him what he was about, galloping along the road; I thought scientific men were more tender of their horses' legs and feet. But the roads, he said, were quite soft with late rains, and they were only trying each other's speed for a mile.

By this time his two companions had pulled up some way forward, and were calling to him to come on; but he said, laughing, "they had quite enough of it," and addressed himself to pacify Miss Middleton, as he called her, who still curvetted about, and pulled at her bridle; while his friends shouted out to him louder—" why the devil he didn't come on."

He waved his hand, and shouted to them in return not to wait for him; and with a " confound " and " deuce take " the fellow, they set off helter-skelter toward the town. On which Miss Middleton began to caper afresh, plunging, and blowing out a peony-coloured nostril after her flying fellows, until, what with their dwindling in distance, and some expostulation addressed to her by her master as to a fractious child, she seemed to make up her mind to the indignity, and went pretty quietly beside us.

I then asked him if he did not remember Lexilogus (Euphranor he had already recognized), and Phidippus, who really had not hitherto seen who it was (Lexilogus looking down all the while), called out heartily to him, and, wheeling his mare suddenly behind us, took hold of his hand, and began to inquire about his family in Yorkshire.

"One would suppose," said I, "you two fellows had not met for years."

"It was true," Phidippus said, "they did not meet so often as he really wished; but Lexilogus would not come to his rooms, and he did not like to disturb Lexilogus in his reading."

I then asked him about his own reading, which, though not large, was not neglected, it seemed; and he said he had meant to ask Euphranor or Lexilogus to beat something into his stupid head this summer in Yorkshire.

Lexilogus, I knew, meant to stop at Cambridge all the long vacation; but Euphranor said he should be at home, for anything he then knew, and they could talk the matter over when the time came. We then again fell to talking of our county, and among other things I asked Phidippus if his horse were Yorkshire—a county of old famous for its breed—and how long he had her, and so on.

Yorkshire she was, a present from his mother, "and a great pet," he said, bending down his head, which Miss Middleton answered by a dip of hers, and breaking into a little canter, which, however, was easily suppressed.

"Miss Middleton?" said I—"what, by Bay Middleton out of Coquette, by Tomboy out of High-Life Below Stairs, *et caetera, et caetera.*"

"Right," he answered, laughing, "as far as Bay Middleton is concerned."

"But, Phidippus," said I, "she's as black as coal!"

"And so was her dam, a Yorkshire mare," he answered; which, I said, saved the credit of all parties. And then I began to ask him some questions as to his mode of making up his mind in some of those equestrian emergencies Euphranor and I had talked of: all which Phidippus

thought was only my usual banter—" he was no judge—
I must ask older hands—he never made up his mind at
all," and so on, till he declared he must be off directly to get
marked in Hall. But I told him we were all going to dine
at Chesterton, now close at hand; he must come too; all
Yorkshiremen, except Lycion, whom he knew a little of.
There was to be a boat race, however, in the evening, which
Phidippus said he must leave us to attend, if he did dine
with us; for though not one of the rowers on the occasion
(not being one of the best), yet he must see his boat (the
Trinity) keep the head of the river. As to that, I said, we
would all go to the boat race, which indeed Euphranor had
proposed before; and so the whole thing was settled.

On reaching the inn, I begged Euphranor to order dinner
directly, while I and Lexilogus accompanied Phidippus to
the stable. There, after giving his mare in charge to the
hostler, with due directions as to her toilet and table, he
took off her saddle and bridle himself, and adjusted the
head-stall. Then pausing a moment on the threshold to
ask me if she were not a beauty (for he persisted always in
the delusion that I knew more of horses than I chose to
admit), we left the stable and went into the house.

There, having first washed hands and faces, we went up
into the billiard-room, where we found Euphranor and
Lycion playing—Lycion very lazily, like a man who had
too much of it, but yet nothing better to do. After a short
while the girl came to tell us dinner was ready; and, after
that little hesitation as to precedence which Englishmen
rarely fail in even on the most offhand occasions—Lexilogus, in particular, pausing timidly at the door, and Phidippus pushing him gently and kindly before him—we got
down to the little parlour, very airy and pleasant, with its
window opening on the bowling-green, and a table laid
with a clean white cloth, and upon that a good dish of
smoking beefsteaks, at which I, as host, sat down to
officiate. For some time the clatter of knife and fork, and
the pouring out of ale, went on, mixed with some conversation among the young men about college matters: till
Lycion began to tell us of a gay ball he had lately been at,
and of the families who were there, among whom he men-

tioned three young ladies from a neighbouring county, by far the handsomest women present, he said.

"And very accomplished too, I am told," said Euphranor.

"Oh, as for that," replied Lycion, "they *valse* very well, which is enough for me,—I hate your accomplished women."

"Well, there," said Euphranor, "I suppose the doctor will agree with you—won't you, doctor?"

I said, certainly *valsing* would be no great use to me personally.

"One knows so exactly," said Lycion, "what accomplishments the doctor would choose—a woman

> 'Well versed in the arts
> Of pies, puddings, and tarts,
> And the lucrative skill of the oven.'

as one used to read in some book, I remember."

"And do not forget," said I, "being able to help in compounding a pill or a plaster, which I dare say your great-grandmother knew something about, Lycion, for in those days, you know, great ladies studied simples. Well, so I am fitted,—and Lycion wants a partner who can *valse* through life with him."

> "'And follow so the ever-rolling year
> With profitable labour to their graves,'"

added Euphranor, laughing.

"I don't want to marry her," said Lycion testily.

"Then Euphranor," said I, "looks out for a 'strong-minded' woman, who will read Plato's *Republic* with him, and Wordsworth, and Digby, and become a mother of Heroes. As to Phidippus, there is no doubt—Diana Vernon——"

But Phidippus disclaimed any sympathy with sporting ladies.

"Well, come," said I, passing round a bottle of sherry I had just called for, "every man to his taste, only all of you take care at least to secure the accomplishments of health and good-humour."

"Ah! there it is, out at last!" cried Euphranor, clapping

his hands; "I knew the doctor would choose as Frederic did for his grenadiers."

"Well," said I, "you wouldn't choose an ill-made, ill-conditioned mare to breed from, would you, Phidippus?"

He smiled, and asked me if I remembered Miss Prince, a governess his mother had for his sisters, and who really worked them so hard he was obliged to appeal against her in their behalf.

I did not remember Miss Prince; but I asked what effect his appeal had on his mother.

"Oh, I was a schoolboy then: she patted my head, and said Miss Prince knew best; she had perfect confidence in her. And then, you know, if one of them did not get on with her music, there was no use suggesting she had perhaps no talent for it, and had better not learn it at all; the master's conclusion was that she must practise double time at it."

"Yes, that is the way," I answered. "Well?"

Well, after a time, his mother herself, he said, took notice the girls began to look pale and dispirited. "Why, I assure you, doctor, Miss Prince would scarce let them run about alone, even in play-hours, but followed them with a book, so that if they plucked a daisy, they told me, out came a little Wordsworth from her reticule, to have something appropriate read. Not a moment, she said, was to be unimproved."

"Better for her if that Wordsworth had been tied about her neck, and she cast—Well," I went on, seeing Euphranor look grave, "I presume Miss Prince was not fitted to be the dam of heroes or hunters."

"Poor thing," said Phidippus, "she was an excellent woman. I used to be vexed with myself for getting out of patience with her. She worked hard for her bread, and to do her duty, as she thought."

"And besides, your remonstrances had no effect," said I.

"I don't know," answered he, laughing; "though she accused me of making them romp, which I assure you I did not mean to do, they used to tell me I had more effect upon her than any one else, even my mother. I don't know how that was."

Poor governesses! so much to be pitied, and reverenced, as Phidippus said, but rarely, in these days, to be complied with. Early divorced from their own home and its affections, and crammed themselves in order to cram others, they are very ignorant of the nature of children. I was almost going to be didactic about it all, but thinking I had preached quite enough for that day. I only filled up my glass, passed the bottle round, told them to drink Miss Prince's health, and then, unless they would have more wine, we might go and have a game of bowls, which Euphranor would tell us was the noble custom of our forefathers after dinner.

Phidippus instantly jumped up. He was for no more wine, he said. Lycion said he should have liked another glass, if the sherry had been tolerable. Euphranor and Lexilogus, I knew, were no topers; so we sallied forth upon the bowling-green.

Lycion, as a matter of course, pulled out his cigar-case, and offered it to us, telling Phidippus he could recommend his cigars as some of Pontet's best; but Phidippus did not smoke, he said; which, together with his declining to bet on the boat race, caused Lycion, I thought, to look on him with some indulgence.

And now Jack was rolled upon the green; and I bowled after him first, pretty well; then Euphranor, still better; then Lycion, with great indifference, and indifferent success; then Phidippus, who about equalled me; and, last of all, Lexilogus, whom Phidippus had been instructing in the mystery of the bias with little side-rolls along the turf, and who, he said, only wanted a little practice to play as well as the best of us.

Meanwhile, the shadows lengthened along the bowling-green, and, after several bouts of play, Phidippus said he must be off to see his friends start. I told him we should soon follow; and Euphranor begged him to come to his rooms after the race, for some tea, but Phidippus was engaged to sup with his crew.

"Where you will all be drunk," said I.

"No, there," said he, "you are quite mistaken, doctor."

"Well, well," I said, "away, then, to your race and your supper."

"' Μετὰ σώφρονος ἡλικιώτου,' " added Euphranor, smiling.

"' Μετὰ,' ' with,' or ' after,' " said Phidippus, putting on his gloves.

"Well, go on, sir," said I, "' Σώφρονος? ' "

" A temperate—something or other——"

" 'Ηλικιώτου ? "

" Supper ? "—he hesitated, smiling—" ' after a temperate supper ? ' "

" Go down, sir ; go down this instant ! " I roared out to him as he ran from the bowling-green. And in a few minutes we heard his horse's feet shuffling over the threshold of the stable, and directly afterwards breaking into a canter outside the gate.

Shortly after this, the rest of us agreed it was time to be gone. We walked along the fields past the church, crossed the boathouse ferry, and mingled with the crowd upon the opposite bank. Townsmen and Gownsmen, with the laced Fellow-commoner sprinkled among them here and there— reading men and sporting men—Fellows, and even Masters of Colleges, not indifferent to the prowess of their respective crews—all these, conversing on all topics, from the slang in *Bell's Life* to the last new German Revelation, and moving in ever-changing groups down the banks, where, at the farthest visible bend of the river, was a little knot of ladies gathered up on a green knoll, faced and illuminated by the beams of the setting sun. Beyond which point was heard at length some indistinct shouting, which gradually increased, until "They are off—they are coming!" suspended other conversation among ourselves ; and suddenly the head of the first boat turned the corner, and then another close upon it, and then a third ; the crews pulling with all their might, but in perfect rhythm and order; and the crowd upon the bank turning round to follow along with them, cheering, "Bravo, St. John's!" "Go it, Trinity!" and waving hats and caps — the high crest and blowing forelock of Phidippus' mare, and he himself shouting encouragement to his crew, conspicuous over all—until, the boats reaching us, we also were caught up in the returning tide of spectators, and hurried back toward the boathouse, where we arrived just in time to see the ensign of Trinity lowered from its pride of place, and the eagle of St. John's soaring there instead. Then, waiting awhile to hear how it was the winner had won, and the loser had lost, and watching Phidippus engaged in eager conversation with his defeated brethren, I took Euphranor and Lexilogus, one under each arm (Lycion having strayed into better company elsewhere), and walked home with them across the meadow that lies between the river and the town, whither the dusky troops of gownsmen were evaporating, while twilight gathered over all, and the nightingale began to be heard among the flowering chestnuts of Jesus.

Preface to Polonius

FEW books are duller than books of Aphorisms and Apophthegms. A Jest-book is, proverbially, no joke; a Wit-book, perhaps, worse; but dullest of all, probably, is the Moral-book, which this little volume pretends to be. So with men: the Jester, the Wit, and the Moralist, each wearisome in proportion as each deals exclusively in his one commodity. "Too much of one thing," says Fuller, " is good for nothing."

Bacon's *Apophthegms* seem to me the best collection of many men's sayings; the greatest variety of wisdom, good sense, wit, humour, and even simple *naiveté* (as one must call it for want of a native word), all told in a style whose dignity and antiquity (together with perhaps our secret consciousness of the gravity and even tragic greatness of the narrator) add a particular humour to the lighter stories.

Johnson said Selden's *Table-talk* was worth all the French " Ana " together. Here also we find wit, humour, fancy, and good sense alternating, something as one has heard in some scholarly English gentleman's after-dinner talk—the best English common sense in the best common English. It outlives, I believe, all Selden's books; and is probably much better, collected even imperfectly by another, than if he had put it together himself.

What would become of Johnson if Boswell had not done as much for his talk ? If the Doctor himself, or some of his more serious admirers, had recorded it !

And (leaving alone Epictetus, à Kempis, and other Moral aphorists) most of the collections of this nature I have seen are made up mainly from Johnson and the Essayists of the last century, his predecessors and imitators; when English thought and language had lost so much of their vigour, freshness, freedom, and picturesqueness—so much, in short, of their native character, under the French polish that came in with the second Charles. When one lights upon " He who "—" The man who " —" Of all the virtues that adorn the breast "—etc.,— one is tempted to swear, with Sir Peter Teazle, against all "*sentiment*," and shut the book. How glad should we be to have Addison's *Table-talk* as we have Johnson's! and how much better are Spence's *Anecdotes of Pope's Conversation* than Pope's own letters!

If a scanty reader could, for the use of yet scantier readers than himself, put together a few sentences of the wise, and also of the less wise—(and Tom Tyers said a good thing or two in his day [1])—from Plato, Bacon, Rochefoucauld, Goethe, Carlyle, and others—a little Truth, new or old, each after his kind—nay, of Truism too (into which all truth must ultimately be dogs-eared), and which, perhaps, " the wit of one, and the wisdom of many," has preserved in the shape of some nameless and dateless Proverbs which yet " retain life and vigour," and widen into new relations with the widening world——

Not a book of *Beauties*—other than as all who have the best to tell have also naturally the best way of telling it; nor of the " limbs and outward flourishes " of Truth, however eloquent; but in general, and as far as I understand, of clear, decided, wholesome, and available insight into our nature and duties. " Brevity is the soul of *Wit* " in a far wider sense than as we now use the word. " As the centre of the greatest circle," says Sir Edward Coke, " is but a little prick, so the matter of even the biggest business lies in a little room." So the *Sentences*

---

[1] " Tom Tyers," said Johnson " describes me best, ' a ghost who never speaks till spoken to.' Another sentence in Tom's *Resolutions* still remains in my memory, ' Mem.—to think more of the living and less of the dead; for the dead have a world of their own.'" Tom was the original of Tom Restless in the *Rambler*, a literary gossip about London in those days, author of *Anecdotes of Pope, Addison, Johnson, etc.* Johnson used to say of him, " I never see Tom but he tells me something I did not know before."

of the Seven are said to be epitomes of whole systems of philosophy: which also Carlyle says is the case with many a homely proverb. Anyhow that famous Μηδὲν ἄγαν, the boundary law of Goodness itself, as of all other things (if one could only know how to apply it), brings one up with a wholesome halt every now and then, and nowhere more fitly than in a book of this kind, though, as usual, I am just now violating in the very act of vindicating it.¹

The grand Truisms of life only life itself is said to bring to life. We hear them from grandam and nurse, write them in copy-books, but only understand them as years turn up occasions for practising or experiencing them. Nay, the longest and most eventful life scarce suffices to teach us the most important of all. It is Death, says Sir Walter Raleigh, " that puts into a man all the wisdom of the world without speaking a word." Only when we have to part with a thing do we feel its value—unless

---

¹ These oracular Truisms are some of them as impracticable as more elaborate Truths. Who will do " too much " if he knows it *is* " too much " ? " Know thyself " is far easier said than done ; and might not a passage like the following make one suppose Shakespeare had Bacon in his eye as the original Polonius, if the dates tallied ?

" He that seeketh victory over his nature, let him not set himself too great, nor too small, tasks ; for the first will make him dejected by often failings, and the second will make him a small proceeder, though by often prevailings. And at the first let him practise with helps, as swimmers do with bladders or rushes ; but after a time let him practise with disadvantages, as dancers do with thick shoes. For it breeds great perfection if the practice be harder than the use. Where nature is mighty, and therefore the victory hard, the degrees had need be, first, to stay and arrest nature in time ; like to him that would say over the four and twenty letters when he was angry ; then to go less in quantity, as if one should, in forbearing wine, come from drinking healths to a draught at a meal," etc. [Essay 38.]

If all chance of controlling nature depended on advice like this ! What *is* too great for a man's nature ?—what too little ? what *are* bladders, and what thick shoes ? *when* is one to throw off one and take the other ? He has a more effectual philosopher who thought of repeating the alphabet when he was angry ; though it is not every man who knows when he is that.

indeed *after* we have parted with it—a very serious consideration.

When Sir Walter Scott lay dying, he called for his son-in-law, and while the Tweed murmured through the woods, and a September sun lit up the towers whose growth he had watched so eagerly, said to him, " Be a good man; only that can comfort you when you come to lie here!" *" Be a good man!"* To that threadbare Truism shrunk all that gorgeous tapestry of written and real Romance!

" You knew all this," wrote Johnson to Mrs. Thrale, rallying for a little while from his final attack—" You knew all this, and I thought that I knew it too: but I know it now with a new conviction."

Perhaps, next to realizing all this in our own lives (when just too late), we become most sensible of it in reading the lives and deaths of others, such as Scott's and Johnson's; when we see all the years of life, with all their ambitions, loves, animosities, schemes of action—all the " *curas supervacuas, spes inanes, et inexspectatos exitus hujus fugacissimae vitae*" [1]—summed up in a volume or two; and what seemed so long a history to them, but a Winter's Tale to us.

Death itself was no Truism to Adam and Eve, nor to many of their successors, I suppose; nay, some of their very latest descendants, it is said, have doubted if it be an inevitable necessity of life: others, with more probability, whether a man can fully comprehend its inevitableness till life itself be half over; beginning to believe he must Die about the same time he begins to believe he is a Fool.

" As are the leaves on the trees, even so are man's generations:
   This is the truest verse ever a poet has sung:
Nevertheless few hearing it hear; Hope, flattering alway,
   Lives in the bosom of all—reigns in the blood of the Young."

" And why," says the note-book of one " *nel mezzo del cammin di nostra vita*," " does one day still linger in my memory? I had started one fine October morning on a ramble through the villages that lie beside the Ouse. In high health and cloudless spirits, one regret perhaps

[1] See Petrarch's Inscription in his *Virgil*.

hanging upon the horizon of the heart, I walked through Sharnbrook up the hill, and paused by the church on the summit to look about me. The sun shone, the clouds flew, the yellow trees shook in the wind, the river rippled in breadths of light and dark; rooks and daws wheeled and cawed aloft in the clanging spaces of blue above the spire; the churchyard all still in the sunshine below."

Old Shallow was not very sensible of Death even when moralizing about old Double's—" Certain, 'tis very certain, Death, as the Psalmist saith, is certain to all—all shall die.—How a good yoke of bullocks at Stamford Fair?"

Could we but on our journey hear the Truisms of life called out to us, not by Chapone, Cogan, etc., but by such a voice as called out to Sir Lancelot and Sir Galahad, when they were about to part in the forest—" Thynke for to doo wel; for the one shall never see the other before the dredeful day of dome!"

Our ancestors were fond of such monitory Truisms inscribed upon dials, clocks, and fronts of buildings; as that of "Time and Tide tarry for no man," still to be seen on the Temple sundial; and that still sterner one I have read of, "Go about your business"—not even moralizing upon me. I dare say those who came suddenly and unaware upon the Γνῶθι Σεαυτόν over the Delphian temple were brought to a stand for a while, some thrown back into themselves by it, others (and those probably much the greater number) seeing nothing at all in it.

The parapet balustrade round the roof of Castle Ashby, in Northamptonshire, is carved into the letters, "NISI DOMINUS CUSTODIAT DOMUM, FRUSTRA VIGILAT QUI CUSTODIT EAM." This is not amiss to decipher as you come up the long avenue some summer or autumn day, and to moralize upon afterwards at the little *Rose and Crown* at Yardley, if such good Homebrewed be there as used to be before I knew I was to die.[1]

---

[1] " A party of us were looking one autumn afternoon at a country church. Over the western door was a clock with, 'THE HOUR COMETH' written in gold upon it. Polonius proceeded to explain, rather lengthily, what a good inscription it was. 'But not very apposite,' said Rosencrantz, ' seeing the clock has stopped.' The sun was

We move away the grass from a tombstone, itself half buried, to get at any trite memento of mortality, where it preaches more to us than many new volumes of hot-pressed morals. Not but we can feel the warning whisper too, when Jeremy Taylor tells us that one day the bell shall toll, and it shall be asked, " For whom ? " and answered, " For *us*."

Some of these Truisms come home to us also in the shape of old Proverbs, quickened by wit, fancy, rhyme, alliteration, etc. These have been well defined to be " the Wit of one and the Wisdom of many," and are in some measure therefore historical indexes of the nation that originates or retains them. Our English Proverbs abound with good sense, energy, and courage, as compactly expressed as may be, making them properly enough the ready money of a people more apt to act than talk. " They drive the nail home in discourse," says Ray, " and clench it with the strongest conviction."

A thoughtful Frenchman says that nearly all which expresses any decided opinion has "*quelque chose de métrique, ou de mesure.*" So as even so barefaced a truism as " Of two evils choose the least " (superfluous reason, and no rhyme at all !) is not without its secret poetic charm. How much vain hesitation has it not cut short ?

So that if Cogan and Chapone had not been made poetical by the gods, but only brief——

Sometimes indeed our old friend the Proverb gets too much clipt in his course of circulation : as in the case of that very important business to all Englishmen, a Cold —" STUFF A COLD AND STARVE A FEVER," has been grievously misconstrued, so as to bring on the fever it was meant to prevent.

indeed setting, and the hands of the clock, glittering full in his face, pointed up to noon. Osric however, with a slight lisp, said, the inscription was all the more apt, ' for the hour *would* come to the clock, instead of the clock following the hour.' On which Horatio, taking out his watch (which he informed us was just then more correct than the sun), told us that unless we set off home directly we should be late for dinner. This was one way of considering an inscription."

Certainly Dr. Johnson (who could hit hard too) not only did not always drive the nail home, but made it a nail of wax, which Fuller truly says you can't drive at all. "These sorrowful meditations," the Doctor says of Prince Rasselas, "fastened on his mind; he passed four months in resolving to lose no more time in idle resolves; and was awakened to more vigorous exertion by hearing a maid, who had broken a porcelain cup, remark that 'what cannot be repaired is not to be regretted.'"

But perhaps this was a Maid of Honour. If so, however, it proves that Maids of Honour of Rasselas' court did not talk like those of George the Second's. Witness jolly Mary Bellenden's letters to Lady Suffolk. Swift has a fashionable dialogue almost made up of vulgar adages, which I should have thought the Beaux and Belles left to the Mary Bellendens and Country Squires of his day—

> Grounding their fat faiths on old country proverbs.

Nor do I see any trace of it in the comedies of Congreve, Vanbrugh, etc.[1]

Erasmus says that the Proverb is "*a nonnullis Graecorum*," thus defined, λόγος ὠφέλιμος ἐν τῷ βίῳ, ἐν μετρίᾳ παρακρύψει πολὺ τὸ χρήσιμον ἔχων ἐν ἑαυτῷ. The definition, it might seem at first, rather of a Fable, or Parable, than a Proverb. But, beside that the titles of many fables *do* become proverbs—"Fox and Grapes," "Dog in Manger," etc., the title including the whole signification (like

[1] I find in my *Complete Correspondent*, which seems begotten by Dr. Johnson on Miss Seward, the following advice about Proverbs. "STYLE. Vulgarity in language is a proof either of a mean education, or of associating with low company. Coarse Proverbial expressions furnish such with their choicest flowers of rhetoric. Instead of saying, 'Necessity compelled,' such an one would say, 'Needs must when the devil drives.' Such vulgar aphorisms ought especially to be rejected as border upon profaneness. A good writer would not say, 'It was all through you it happened,' but 'It happened all through your inattention,'" etc.

This elegance of style however does not always mend the matter; as we read in Boswell that Dr. Johnson, having set the company laughing by saying of some lady in the good English so natural to him, "She's good at bottom," tried to make them grave again

those *Sentences of the Seven*)—so many of our best proverbs *are* little whole fables in themselves; as when we say, "The Fat Sow knows not what the Lean one thinks," etc.

We are fantastic, histrionic creatures; having so much of the fool, loving a mixture of the lie, loving to get our fellow-creatures into our scrapes and make them play our parts—the Ass of our dulness, the Fox of our cunning; and so on—in whose several natures those of our Neighbours, as we think, come to a climax. Certainly, swollen Wealth is well enacted by the fat Sow reclining in her sty, as a Dowager in an opera-box, serenely unconscious of all her kindred's leanness without. The phrase "rolling in wealth," too, suggests the same fable.

Indeed, is not every Metaphor (without which we cannot speak five words) in some sort a Fable—one thing spoken of under the likeness of another? And how easy (if need were) it is to dramatize, for instance, Bacon's figure of discovering the depth, not by looking on the surface ever so long, but beginning to *sound* it!

by "What's the laugh for? I say the woman is fundamentally good."

The following is one of *Punch's* jokes; I do not know if true of the author referred to—not true, I should suppose, of the class to which he belongs (except as regards the foolish and vulgar use of French)—but very true of the Hammersmith education, of which my complete Letter-writer—Correspondent, I mean—is an exponent.

DESULTORY REFLECTIONS

BY LORD WILLIAM LENNOX

INIQUITOUS intercourses contaminate proper habits.

One individual may pilfer a quadruped, where another may not cast his eyes over the boundary of a field.

In the absence of the feline race, the mice give themselves up to various pastimes.

Feathered bipeds of advanced age are not to be entrapped with the outer husks of corn.

Casualties will take place in the most excellently conducted family circles.

More confectioners than are absolutely necessary are apt to ruin the *potage*.—LENNOX's *Lacon*.

And are these Fables so fabulous after all? If beasts do not really rise to the level on which we amuse ourselves by putting them, we have an easy way of really sinking to theirs. It is no fable surely that Circe *bodily* transformed the captives of Sensuality into apes, hogs, and goats; as Cunning, Hypocrisy, and Rapacity, graft us with the sharp noses, sidelong eyes, and stealthy gait, of wolves, hyaenas, foxes, and serpents; sometimes, as in old fable too, the misfeatures and foul expressions of two baser animal passions—as lust and cunning for instance, with perhaps cruelty beside—conforming man into a double or triple monster, more hideous than any single beast. On the other hand, our more generous dispositions determine outwardly into the large aspect of the lion, or the horse's speaking eye and inspired nostril. "There are innumerable animals to which man may degrade his image, inward and outward; only a few to which he can properly (and that in the Affections only) level it: but it is an ideal and invisible type to which he must erect it."

"Such kind of parabolical wisdom," says Bacon, "was much more in use in the ancient times, as by the Fables of Aesop, and the brief *Sentences of the Seven*, and the use of hieroglyphics may appear. And the cause was, for that it was then of necessity to express any point of reason which was more sharp or subtle than the vulgar in that manner, because men in those times wanted both variety of examples and subtlety of conceit; and as Hieroglyphics were before letters, so Parables were before arguments."

We cannot doubt that Christianity itself made way by means of such Parables as never were uttered before or after. Imagine (be it with reverence) that Jeremy Bentham had had the promulgation of it!

And as this figurative teaching was best for simple people, " even now," adds Bacon, " such Parables do retain much life and vigour, because Reason cannot be so sensible nor example so fit." Next to the Bible parables, I believe John Bunyan remains the most effective preacher, among the poor, to this day.

Nor is it only simple matters for simple people that

admit such illustration.[1] Again, Bacon says, "It is a rule that whatsoever science is not consonant to presuppositions must pray in aid of Similitudes." "Neither Philosopher not Historiographer," says Sir Philip Sidney, "could at the first have entered into the gates of popular judgments, if they had not taken a great Passport of Poetry," which deals so in Similitudes. "For he" (the poet) "doth not only show the way, but giveth so sweet a prospect into the way as will entice any man to enter into it. Nay, he doth, as if your journey should lie through a fair vineyard, at the very first give you a cluster of grapes, that, full of that taste, you may long to pass further."

Who can doubt that Plato wins us to his Wisdom by that skin and body of Poetry in which Sir Philip declares his philosophy is clothed? Not the sententious oracle of one wise man, but evolved dramatically by many like ourselves. The scene opens in Old Athens, which his genius continues for us for ever new; the morning dawns; a breeze from the Aegaean flutters upon our foreheads; the rising sun tips the friezes of the Parthenon, and gradually slants upon the house in whose yet twilight courts gather a company of white-vested, whispering guests, "expecting till that fountain of wisdom," Protagoras, should arise.

Carlyle notices, as one of Goethe's chief gifts, "his emblematic intellect, his never-failing tendency to transform into *shape*, into *life*, the feeling that may dwell in him. Everything has *form*, has visual existence; the poet's imagination *bodies forth* the forms of things unseen,

---

[1] Fable might be made to exemplify the syllogism, but not to illustrate it. "The Lion swore he would eat all flesh that came in his way. One day he set his paw on the Polecat: the Polecat pleaded that he was small, ill-flavoured, etc.; but the Lion said, 'I have sworn to eat all flesh that came in my way: you are flesh come in my way; therefore I will eat you.'" The syllogism is proved; but the speakers do not illustrate, but obscure it, but because it is a matter of *understanding*, of which no animal but man is the representative. Your Lion, noble beast as he is, is only to be trusted with an Enthymeme. One sees this fault in the Eastern fables. Birds and beasts are made to *reason*, instead of representing the passions and affection they really share with men. This also is the vital fault of Dryden's *Hind and Panther*.

and his pen turns them into shape." The same is, I believe, remarkable, probably *too* remarkable, in Richter; and is especially characteristic of Carlyle himself, who to a figurative genius, like Goethe's, adds a passion which Goethe either had not or chose to suppress, which brands the truth double-deep. And who can doubt that Bacon, could it possibly have been his own, would have clothed Bentham's bare argument with cloth of gold?

He says again, " Reasons plainly delivered, and always after one manner, especially with fine and fastidious minds, enter heavily and dully; whereas, if they be varied, and have more life and vigour put into them by these forms and imaginations, they carry a stronger apprehension, and many times win the mind to a resolution." Which, if it be true in any matter, most of all surely in morals, for the most part so old, so trite, and, in this naughty world, so dull. Are not *all* minds grown " fine and fastidious " in these matters, apt to close against any but the most musical voice?

Which also (to join the snake's head and tail of this rambling overgrown Preface) may account, rightly or wrongly, for my rejection of those essayists aforesaid (who crippled their native genius by a style which has left them " more of the ballast than the sail ") and my adoption of earlier and later writers. Not, as I said before, in copious draughts of their eloquence—and what pages of Bacon and Browne it is far easier to bear than forbear!—but where the writer has gone to the heart of a matter, the centre of the circle, hit the nail on the head and driven it home—Proverb-wise, in fact. For in proportion as any writer tells the truth, and tells it figuratively or poetically, and yet so as to lie in a nutshell, he cuts up sooner or later into proverbs shorter or longer, and gradually gets down into general circulation.

Some extracts are from note-books, where the author's name was forgot; some from the conversation of friends that must alike remain anonymous; and some that glance but lightly at the truth are not without purpose inserted to relieve a book of dogmatic morals. " *Durum et durum non faciunt murum.*"

And now Mountain opens and discovers—

Polonius

A COLLECTION OF WISE SAWS AND MODERN
INSTANCES

Therefore, since brevity is the soul of wit,
And tediousness the limbs and outward flourishes,
I WILL BE BRIEF.

QUICKNESS OF WIT.

I MAKE no more estimation of repeating a great number of names or words upon once hearing, or the pouring forth of a number of verses or rhymes extempore, *or the making of a satirical simile of everything, or the turning of everything to a jest, or the falsifying or contradicting of everything by cavil,* or the like (whereof in the faculties of the mind there is great copia, and such as by device and practice may be brought to an extreme degree of wonder), than I do of the tricks of tumblers, funambules, paladines—the one being the same in the mind that the other is in the body; matters of strangeness without worthiness.—*Bacon.*

"Quickness is among the least of the mind's properties, and belongs to her in almost her lowest state; nay, it doth not abandon her when she is driven from her home, when she is wandering and insane. The mad often retain it; the liar has it; the cheat has it; we find it on the racecourse and at the card-table; education does not give it; and reflection takes away from it."

> "WHEN THE CUP IS FULLEST LOOK THOU BEAR HER
> FAIREST."

POWER to do good is the true and lawful end of aspiring. For good thoughts, though God accept them, yet towards men they are little better than good dreams, except they be put in act; and that cannot be without power and place, as the vantage and commanding ground.—*Bacon.*

We are all here fellow-servants, and we know not how our Grand Master will brook insolences in His family. How darest thou, that art but a piece of earth that Heaven has blown into, presume thyself into the impudent usurpation of a majesty unshaken?

The top feather of the plume began to give himself airs, and toss his head, and look down contemptuously on his fellows. But one of them said, "Peace! we are all of us but feathers; only he that made us a plume was pleased to set thee highest."—*Feltham.*

It is a sure sign of greatness whom honour amends.—*Bacon.*

> "THE HIGHER THE APE GOES THE MORE HE SHOWS
> HIS TAIL."

DE TE FABULA.

AN Ass was wishing in a hard winter for a little warm weather, and a mouthful of fresh grass to knab upon, in exchange for a heartless truss of straw, and a cold lodging. In good time, the warm weather and the fresh grass comes on; but so much toil and business for asses along with it, that this ass grows quickly as weary of the spring as he was of the winter. His next longing is for summer; but what with harvest-work, and other drudgeries of that season, he is worse now than he was in the spring: and so he fancies he never shall be well till autumn comes. But then again, what with carrying apples, grapes, fuel, winter provisions, etc., he finds himself more harassed than ever. In fine, when he has trod the circle of the year in a course of restless labour, his last prayer is for winter again, and that he may but take up his rest where he began his complaint.—*L'Estrange's Fables.*

> And follows so the ever-rolling year
> With profitable labour to his grave.

THE PHILOSOPHER.

THE name of "*Wise*" seems to me, O Phaedrus, a great matter, and to belong to God alone. A man may be more fitly denominated "philosophus," "*would be wise,*" or some such name.—*Plato.*

The philosopher stations himself in the middle, and must draw down to him all that is higher, and up to him all that is lower; and only in this medium does he merit the title of wise.—*Goethe.*

Plato's Philosopher pursues the true light, yet returns back to his former fellows who dwell in the dark, watching shadows.

"EVERY OAK MUST BE AN ACORN."

WHEN the Balloon was first discovered, some one said to Franklin, "What will ever come of it?" Franklin pointed to a baby in its cradle, and said, "And what will ever come of that?"

TROUBLES OF LIFE.

I AM very sorry for your distress; one of which [1] I think is of the number of the τὰ ἐφ' ἡμῖν, any may be put an end to at any time. For what is money given for but to make a man easy? And if others will be iniquitous, there is nothing to be done but to have recourse to the *redime te captum quàm queas minimo :* a very good maxim, which we learn in our Grammar, and forget in our lives. The other trouble [2] is not so easily set aside; but it has the comfort of necessity, and must be borne whether you will or not, which with wise men is the same thing as choice: for a fool in such a case goes about bellowing, and telling everybody

---

[1] Loss of money. [2] Sickness.

he meets (who do but laugh at him) what a sad calamity has happened to him; but a man of sense says nothing and submits. This is very wise, you will say; but it is very true.—*Jeremiah Markland.*

"WHAT CAN'T BE CURED MUST BE ENDURED."

"PENNY WISE, POUND FOOLISH."

The saying of a noble and wise counsellor in England is worthy to be remembered, that, with a pretty tale he told, utterly condemned such lingering proceedings. The tale was this :—A poor widow (said he) in the country, doubting her provision of wood would not last all the winter, and yet desiring to roast a joint and a hen one day to welcome her friends, laid on two sticks on the fire; but when that would scarce heat it, she fetched two more; and so still burning them out by two and two (whereas one faggot laid on at the first would have roasted it), she spent four or five faggots more than she needed: and yet when all was done, her meat was scorched of one side, and raw of the t'other side; her friends ill content of their fare; and she enforced, ere winter, went about to borrow wood of her poor neighbours, because so many of her own faggots were spent.—*Sir J. Harrington.*

VALOUR AND MERCY.

That Mercy can dwell only with Valour is an old sentiment, or proposition, which, in Johnson, again receives confirmation. Few men on record have had a more merciful, tenderly affectionate nature than old Samuel. He was called the Bear, and did indeed too often look and roar like one, being forced to it in his own defence; yet within that shaggy exterior of his there beat a heart warm as a mother's, soft as a little child's. Nay, generally his very roaring was but the anger of affection; the rage of a bear, if you will; but of a bear bereaved of her whelps. Touch his religion; glance at the Church of England, or the divine right; and he was upon you! These things were his symbols of all that was good and precious for men; his very ark of the covenant: whoso laid his hand on them tore asunder his heart of hearts. Not out of hatred to the opponent, but of love to the opposed, did Johnson grow cruel, fierce, contradictory: this is an important distinction, never to be forgotten in our censure of his conversational outrages. But observe also with what humanity, what openness of love, he can attach himself to all things—to a blind old woman, to a Doctor Levett, to a Cat Hodge—" His thoughts in the latter part of his life were frequently employed on his deceased friends; he often muttered these or such-like words, 'Poor man! and then he died!'" How he patiently converts his poor home into a Lazaretto; endures, for long years, the contradiction of the miserable and unreasonable—with him unconnected, save that they had no other to yield them refuge! Generous old man! Worldly possessions he has little, yet of this he gives freely; from his own hard-earned shilling, the halfpence for the poor, that waited his coming out, are not withheld; the poor waited the coming out of one not quite so poor! A Sterne can write sentimentalities on dead asses: Johnson has a rough voice, but he finds the wretched daughter of vice fallen down in the streets, carries her home on his own shoulders, and, like a good Samaritan, gives help to the half-needy, whether worthy or unworthy.—*Carlyle.*

Il n'y a que les personnes qui ont de la fermeté qui puissent avoir une veritable douceur; celles qui paroissent douces n'ont ordinairement que de la foiblesse qui se convertit aisément en aigreur.—*Rochefoucauld.*

"It is the best metal that bows best," says Fuller: and "*the sweet wine that makes the sharpest vinegar,*" says an old proverb.

HONESTY.

DOTH not consist in the doing of one, or one thousand, acts never so well, but in the spinning on the delicate thread of life, though not exceeding fine, yet free from breaks and stains.—*Sidney.*

Of great deeds I make no account; but a great life I reverence.—" *Splendida facinora* " every sinner may perpetrate.—*Richter.*

What is to be undergone only once we may undergo: what must be comes almost of its own accord. The courage we desire and prize is, not the courage to die decently, but to live manfully.—*Carlyle.*

SOWING THE SEED.

Σπείρειν τε καρπὸν Χάριτος ἡδίστης Θεῶν.

Two travellers happened to be passing through a town while a great fire was raging.

One of them sat down at the inn, saying, " It is not my business." But the other ran into the flames, and saved much goods and some people.

When he came back, his companion asked him, " And who bid thee risk thy life in others' business ? "

" He," said the brave man, " who bade me bury seed that it may one day bring forth increase."

" But if thou thyself hadst been buried in the ruins ? "

" Then should I myself have been the seed."—*German.*

"FUN IN THE OLD FIDDLE."

As Wilhelm, contrary to his usual habit, let his eye wander inquisitively over the room, the good old man said to him, " My domestic equipment excites your attention. You see here how long a thing may last; and one should make such observations, now and then, by way of counterbalance to so much in the world that rapidly changes and passes away. This same tea-kettle served my parents, and was a witness of our evening family assemblages; this copper fire-screen still guards me from the fire, which these stout old tongs help me to mend; and so it is with all throughout. I had it in my power to bestow my care and industry on many other things, and I did not occupy myself in the changing these external necessaries, a task which consumes so many people's time and resources. "An affectionate attention to what we possess makes us rich; for thereby we accumulate a treasure of remembrances connected with indifferent things. In us little men such little things are to be reckoned virtue¹—."—*Wilhelm Meister.*

And as of family, so of national, monuments—" Ce sont les crampons qui unissent une génération à une autre. Conservez ce qu'ont vu vos Pères."—*Joubert.*

" WISH AND WISH ON."

Such as the chain of causes we call fate, such is the chain of wishes; one links on to another; and the whole man is bound in the chain of wishing for ever.—*Seneca.*

Who has many wishes has generally but little will. Who has energy of will has few diverging wishes. Whose will is bent on one, must renounce the wishes for many things. Who cannot do this is not stamped with the majesty of human nature. The energy of choice, the unison of the various powers for one, is only will—born under the agonies of self-denial and renounced desires.

Calmness of will is a sign of grandeur. The vulgar, far from hiding their will, blab their wishes. A single spark of occasion discharges the child of passion into a thousand crackers of desire.—*Lavater.*

Always let oneness of purpose rule over a boy. He wanted perhaps to have, or to do, some certain thing: oblige him then to take or to do it.—*Richter.*

" HUNT MANY HARES AND CATCH NONE."

" THE EYE SEES ONLY WHAT IT HAS IN ITSELF THE POWER OF SEEING."—*Goethe.*

To many this will seem a truism, who would think it a paradox should you tell them they saw another tree than the painter did, looking at the same. No wonder, then, if they see something very different from Goethe in this sentence of his.

1. We do not see nature by looking at it. We fancy we

see the whole of any object that is before us, because we know no more than we see. The rest escapes us as a matter of course; and we easily conclude that the idea in our minds and the image in nature are one and the same. But in fact we only see a very small part of nature, and make an imperfect abstraction of the infinite number of particulars which are always to be found in it, as well as we can. Some do this with more or less accuracy than others, according to habit or natural genius. A painter, for instance, who has been working on a face for several days, still finds out something new in it which he did not notice before, and which he endeavours to give in order to make his copy more perfect. A young artist, when he first begins to study from nature, soon makes an end of his sketch, because he sees only a general outline and certain gross distinctions and masses. As he proceeds, a new field opens to him: differences crowd on differences; and as his perceptions grow more refined, he could employ whole days in working upon a single part, without satisfying himself at last.—*Hazlitt*.

2. So says Bacon. "That is the best part of beauty which a picture cannot express; no, nor the first sight of life neither."

"Directly in the face of most intellectual tea-circles, it may be asserted that no good book, or good thing of any sort, shows its best face at first: nay, that the commonest quality in a true work of art, if its excellence have any depth and compass, is that at first sight it occasions a certain disappointment—perhaps even, mingled with its undeniable beauty, a certain feeling of aversion."—*Carlyle*.

"Most men are disappointed at first sight of the sea; as also of mountains, which a novice thinks he could soon run up, till his eyes learn to distinguish those aerial gradations which soon make themselves understood by the feet."

"The shepherd knows every sheep in his flock: and Pascal tells us, that the more genius a man has, the more he will see of it in other men. Indeed, the clear eye will see in every man something of that which common observers are apt to consider the property of a few. If no two sheep—nay, it is said, no two leaves—are alike, how much less any two men!"

QUANTUM SUMUS SCIMUS.

THE SOLECISM OF POWER.

THE difficulties in Princes' business are many and great; but the greatest difficulty is often in their own mind. For it is common with princes, saith Tacitus, to will contradictories; "*sunt plerumque Regum voluntates vehementes et inter se contrariae.*" For it is the solecism of power to think to command the end, and yet not to endure the mean.

Princes many times make themselves desires, and set their hearts on toys; sometimes upon a building, sometimes upon erecting of an order, etc. This seemeth incredible unto those that know not the principle, that the mind of man is more cheered and refreshed by profiting in small things than by standing at a stay in great.—*Bacon.*

FORGIVE AND FORGET.

"WHEN," said Descartes, "a man injures me, I strive to lift up my soul so high that his offence cannot reach me."

It is certain, that a man who studieth revenge, keeps his own wounds green, which would otherwise heal and do well.—*Bacon.*

And finally,

Without knowing particulars, I take upon me to assure all persons who think that they have received indignities or injurious treatment, that they may depend upon it as in a manner certain, that the offence is not so great as they imagine.—*Bishop Butler.*

INCONSTANCY.

LE sentiment de la fausseté des plaisirs présents, et l'ignorance de la vanité des plaisirs absents, causent l'inconstance.—*Rochefoucauld.*

"THE OTHER SIDE OF THE ROAD ALWAYS LOOKS CLEANEST."

THE POOR.

A DECENT provision for the poor is the true test of civilization. Gentlemen of education are pretty much the same in all countries; the condition of the lower orders, the poor especially, is the true mark of national discrimination.—*Johnson*.

"How often one hears an English gentleman (as good as any gentleman, however) mourning over the loss, as he calls it, of a hundred or two a year in farming his estate—so fine a business for an English gentleman! 'It won't do—it won't pay—he must give it up,' etc. Why, what do his fine houses, equipages, gardens, pictures, jewels, dinners, and operas, *pay?* 'Oh, but there he has something to show for his money.' And is a population of honest, healthy, happy English labourers — honest, healthy, and happy, because constantly employed by him, with proper wages, and not so much labour exacted of them as to turn a man into a brute—is not *this* something to show for your money? as good pictures, jewels, equipage, and music, as a man should desire?"

Not, however, to be bought wholly by money wages—

"LOVE IS THE TRUE PRICE OF LOVE."

CASH payment never was, or could be (except for a few years) the union bond of man to man. Cash never yet paid one man fully his deserts to another; nor could it, nor can it, now or henceforth to the end of the world.—*Carlyle*.

On a rock-side in one of Bewick's vignettes we see inscribed what should never be erased from any Englishman's heart—

Princes and lords may flourish or may fade,
A breath may make them, as a breath has made;
But A BOLD PEASANTRY, their country's pride,
When once destroyed can never be supplied.

Advice well remembered by Sir Walter Scott's Duke of

Buccleugh, " one of those retired and high-spirited men, who will never be known until the world asks what became of the huge oak that grew on the brow of the hill, and sheltered such an extent of ground."

THE THREE RACES.

MACHIAVELLI divides men into three classes—
 1. Those who find truth.
 2. Those who follow what is found.
 3. Those who do neither.

And the same distinction is observed in a pack of foxhounds, only that, in their case, the latter class are soundly beaten, and, if incorrigible, *hung*.

FOUND OUT BY ONE'S SIN.

WHEN the sinner shall rise from his grave, there shall meet him an uglier figure than ever he beheld—deformed—hideous—of a filthy smell, and with a horrid voice; so that he shall call aloud, " God save me ! what art thou ? "— The shape shall answer, " Why wonderest thou at me ? I am but THINE OWN WORKS; thou didst ride upon me in the other world, and I will ride upon thee for ever here."— *Jellaladin*.

The procrastinator is not only indolent and weak, but commonly false. Most of the weak are false.—*Lavater*.

"What a quantity, not of time only, but of soul, has been spent in resolving and re-resolving to get up out of bed in the morning."

" *By and by* is easily said "—and re-said.

Do immedialely whatever is to be done. When a regiment is under march, the rear is often thrown into confusion because the front do not move steadily and without interruption. It is the same thing with business : if that which is first in hand is not instantly, steadily, and regularly dispatched, other things accumulate behind, till affairs begin to press all at once, and no human brain can stand the confusion.—*Sir W. Scott*.

THE SOURCE OF THE GREAT RIVER.

It has been the plan of Divine Providence to ground what is good and true in religion and morals on the basis of our good natural feelings. What we are towards our earthly friends in the instincts and wishes of our infancy, such we are to become at length towards God and man in the extended field of our duties as accountable beings. To honour our parents is the first step towards honouring God; to love our brethren according to the flesh, the first step to considering all men our brethren. Hence our Lord says we must become as little children if we would be saved; we must become in His Church as men, what we were once in the small circle of our youthful homes.

The love of private friends is the only preparatory exercise for the love of others. It is obviously impossible to love all men in any strict and true sense. What is meant by loving all men is to feel well disposed towards all men, to be ready to assist them, and to act towards those who come in our way as if we loved them. We cannot love those about whom we know nothing, except indeed we view them in Christ, as the objects of His atonement; that is, rather in faith than in love. And love, besides, is a habit, and cannot be attained without actual practice, which on so large a scale is impossible. We see then how absurd it is when writers (as is the manner of some who slight the Gospel) talk magnificently about loving the whole human race with a comprehensive affection, of being the friends of mankind, and the like-such vaunting professions. What do they come to? That such men have certain benevolent feelings towards the world,—*feelings*, and nothing more—nothing more than unstable feelings, the mere offspring of an indulged imagination, which exist only when their minds are wrought upon, and are sure to fail them in the hour of need. This is not to love men, but to talk about love.

The real love of man must depend on practice, and therefore must begin by exercising itself on our friends around us, otherwise it will have no existence. By trying to love our relations and friends; by submitting to their wishes though contrary to our own ; by bearing with their infirmities ; by overcoming their occasional waywardness with kindness ; by dwelling on their excellences, and trying to copy them—thus it is that we form in our hearts that root of charity which, though small at first, may, like the mustard seed, at last even overshadow the earth. The vain talkers about philanthropy, just spoken of, usually show the emptiness of their profession by being morose and cruel in the private relations of life, which they seem to account as subjects beneath their notice. And we know, from the highest of all authority, that one can only learn to love God, whom one has not seen, by loving our brothers whom we do see.—*Newman.*

To a lady, who endeavoured once to vindicate herself from blame for neglecting social attention to worthy neighbours, by saying, " I would go to them if it would do them any good," Johnson said, " What good do you expect, madam, to be able to do them ? It is showing them respect, and that is doing them good."—*Boswell's Johnson.*

The joys and loves of earth the same in heaven will be ;
Only the little brook has widen'd to a sea.—*Trench.*

THE WEAK ARE FALSE.

" HE SHUTS HIS EYES AND THINKS NONE SEE."
As the verse noteth,

" Percontatorem fugito, nam garrulus idem est,"

an inquisitive man is a prattler ; so, upon the like reason a credulous man is a deceiver ; as we see it in fame, that he that will easily believe rumours, will as easily augment rumours, and add somewhat to them of his own : which Tacitus wisely noteth when he saith, " *Fingunt simul creduntque.*"—*Bacon.*

Quack and dupe are upper-side, and under, of the selfsame substance ; convertible personages. Turn up your dupe into the proper fostering element, and he himself can become a quack; there is in him the due prominent insincerity, open voracity to profit, and closed sense to truth; whereof quacks too, in all their kinds, are made.—*Carlyle.*

FORMS AND CEREMONIES.

CEREMONY keeps up all things; 'tis like a penny glass to a rich spirit, or some excellent water; without it the water would be spilt, the spirit lost.

There were some mathematicians that could with one fetch of their pen make an exact circle, and with the next touch point out the centre. Is it therefore reasonable to banish all use of compasses? Set forms are a pair of compasses.—*Selden.*

BUILDING.

HE that builds a fair house on an ill seat, committeth himself to prison. Neither is it ill air only that maketh an ill seat; but ill ways, ill markets, and, if you will consult with Momus, ill neighbours.—*Bacon.*

BETTER ONE'S HOUSE BE TOO LITTLE ONE DAY THAN TOO BIG ALL THE YEAR AFTER.

Isaiah says, "great men build desolate places for themselves;" which doing, Camden says, was the ruin of good housekeeping in England.—*Fuller.*

IDLENESS.

LA paresse, toute languissante qu'elle est, ne laisse pas d'en être souvent la maîtresse; elle usurpe sur tous les desseins et sur toutes les actions de la vie; elle y détruit et y consume insensiblement les passions et les vertus.—*Rochefoucauld.*

"AN EMPTY SKULL IS THE DEVIL'S WORKSHOP."

As of a man, so of a people. "The unredeemed ugliness is that of a slothful people. Show me a people energeti-

cally busy—heaving, struggling, all shoulders at the wheel;
their heart pulsing, every muscle swelling with man's
energy and will—I will show you a people of whom great
good is already predicable; to whom all manner of good
is certain if their energy endure."—*Carlyle.*
When the master puts a spade into his servant's hand,
He speaks his wish by the action, needing no words to declare it:
Thy hand, O man, like that spade, is God's signal to thee,
And thine own heart's thoughts are the interpretation
thereof. —*Mesnavi.*

PHILOSOPHY OF INDIFFERENCE.

HORACE WALPOLE begged of Madame du Deffand not to
love or trust him or any one else; not to run into enthusiasm of any sort for anything, etc. " Vos leçons, vos
réprimandes," she replies, " ont eu plus d'effets que vous
n'en esperiez; vous m'avez désabusée de bien des chimères;
*vous avez été parfaitement secondé par la décrépitude—je ne
cherche plus l'amitié,*" etc.

KNOWLEDGE AND HALF-KNOWLEDGE.

KNOWLEDGE is nothing but a representation of truth—for
the truth of being and the truth of knowing are one, differing no more than the direct beam and the beam reflected.—
Bacon.

Qui respiciunt ad pauca facile pronuntiant.—*Bacon from
Aristotle.*

" The quick decision of one who sees half the truth."

SELF-CONTEMPLATION.

FINALLY, we have read in these three thick volumes of
letters[1]—till, in the second thick volume, the reading
faculty unhappily broke down, and had to skip largely
thenceforth, only diving here and there at a venture, with
considerable intervals! Such is the melancholy fact. It

[1] Rahel von Ense's *Memoirs.*

must be urged in defence that these volumes are of the toughest reading; calculated, as we said, for Germany, rather than for England or us. To be written with such indisputable marks of ability, nay, of genius, of depth and sincerity, they are the heaviest business we perhaps ever met with. They are *subjective* letters : what the metaphysicians call subjective, not *objective :* the grand material of them is endless depicturing of moods, sensations, miseries, joys, and lyrical conditions of the writer ; no definite picture drawn, or rarely any, of persons, transactions, or events, which the writer stood amidst—a wrong material, as it seems to us. To what end ? To what end ? we always ask. Not by looking at itself, but by looking at things out of itself, and ascertaining and ruling these, shall the mind become known. "One thing above all other," says Goethe, "I have never *thought* about thinking." What a thrift of thinking faculty there—almost equal to a fortune in these days—"*habe nie das Denken gedacht !*" But how much wastefuller still it is to *feel about feeling !* One is wearied of that ; the healthy soul avoids that. Thou shalt look outward, not inward. Gazing inward on one's own self—why, this can drive one mad, like the monks of Athos, if it last too long. Unprofitable writing this subjective sort does seem ; at all events, to the present reviewer no reading is so insupportable. Nay, we ask, might not the world be entirely deluged by it, unless prohibited ? Every mortal is a microcosm ; to himself a *macrocosm*, or universe large as nature ; universal nature would barely hold what he could say about himself. Not a dyspeptic tailor on any shop-board of this city but could furnish all England, the year through, with reading about himself, about his emotions, and internal mysteries of woe and sensibility, if England would read him. It is a course which leads no whither : a course which should be avoided.
—*Carlyle.*

DIVES.

HAD a great swamp bequeathed him. He drained, and planted, and stocked it with fish-ponds and game preserves, and enclosed it carefully, so that he might have his pleasure there alone.

One day he was showing it to an aged friend, who admired it much, but said it wanted one thing hugely.

Dives asked, "What?"

"Know you not," replied his friend, "that when God Almighty planted Eden, it was for the sake of putting man therein?"

"IT TAKES A LONG TIME TO FEEL THE WORLD'S PULSE."

SUCH is the complication of human destinies, that the same cruelties which stained the conquest of the two Americas have been renewed under our eyes, in times which we believed characterized by a prodigious progress of civilization, and a general mildness of manners; and yet one man, scarcely in the middle of his career, might have seen the reign of terror in France, the inhuman expedition to St. Domingo, the political reactions and the civil wars of continental Europe and America, the massacres of Chios and Ipsara, the recent acts of atrocity in America, its abominable slave legislation, etc. In the two epochs regrets have followed public calamities; but in our times, of which I have traced the gloomy remembrance, still more unanimous regrets have been more loudly manifested. Philosophy, without obtaining victory, has started in defence. The modern tendency is to seek freedom by laws, order by the perfecting of institutions. This is like a new and salutary element of the social order; an element which acts slowly, but which will make the return of sanguinary commotions less frequent and more difficult.—*Humboldt, Ex. Cr.*

TASTE.

IF it means any thing but a paltry connoisseurship, must mean a general susceptibility to truth and nobleness; a sense to discern, and a heart to love and reverence, all beauty, order, goodness, wheresoever or in whatsoever forms and accompaniments they are to be seen.—*Carlyle.*

"Taste is the feminine of genius."

THE NEW CHIVALRY.

Two boys were playing at chess. A knight was broken, so they put a pawn to serve in his stead.

"Ha!" cried the knight to the pawn, "whence come you, Sir Snailpace?"

But the boy said to him, "Peace! he does the same service as you!"—*German.*

WEAKNESS AND VIGOUR OF MIND.

LA foiblesse est le seul defaut qu'on ne sauroit corriger.—*Rochefoucauld.*

Difficult as it is to subdue the more violent passions, yet I believe it to be still more difficult to overcome a tendency to sloth, cowardice, and despondency. These evil dispositions cling about a man and weigh him down. They are minute chains binding him on every side to the earth, so that he cannot even turn himself to make an effort to rise. It would seem as if right principles had yet to be planted in the indolent mind; whereas violent and obstinate tempers had already something of the nature of firmness and zeal in them; or rather, what will become so with care, exercise, and God's blessing. Besides, the events of life have a powerful influence in sobering the ardent or self-confident temper; disappointments, pain, anxiety, advancing years, bring with them some natural wisdom, as a matter of course. On the other hand, these same circumstances do but exercise the defects of the timid and irresolute, who are made more indolent, selfish, and faint-hearted by advancing years, and find a sort of satisfaction of their unworthy caution in their experience of the vicissitudes of life.—*Newman.*

"YOU CAN'T HANG SOFT CHEESE ON A HOOK,
NOR DRIVE A NAIL OF WAX."

CONTENT.

THE fountain of content must spring up in the mind; and

he who was so little knowledge of human nature as to seek happiness by changing anything but his own disposition, will waste his life in fruitless efforts, and multiply the griefs which he purposes to remove.—*Johnson.*

CAELUM NON ANIMUM MUTANT QUI TRANS MARE CURRUNT.

Contentment, says Fuller, consisteth not in heaping more fuel, but in taking away some fire.

CONVERSATION.

COBBETT used to say that people never should sit talking till they didn't know what to talk about.

HE WAS SCANT OF NEWS WHA TAULD HIS FATHER WAS HANGED.

THE RULER.

WHATEVER the world may think, he who hath not meditated much on God, the humane mind, and the *summum bonum,* may possibly make a thriving earthworm, but will most indubitably make a sorry patriot and a sorry statesman.—*Berkeley.*

No man ignorant of history can govern. Neither can the experience of one man's life furnish example and precedents for the events of one man's life. For as it happeneth sometimes that the grandchild, or the descendant, resembleth the ancestor more than the son; so many times occurrences of the present times may sort better with ancient examples than with those of the later or immediate times. And lastly, the wit of one man can no more countervail learning than one man's means can hold way with a common purse.

In the discharge of thy place, set before thee the best examples; for imitation is a globe of precepts: and, after a time, set before thee thine own example; and examine thyself strictly whether thou didst best at first.—*Bacon.*

SNOB AND GENTLEMAN.

THE Fraction asked himself, "How will this look at Almack's, and before Lord Mahogany?" The perfect man asked himself, "How will this look in the Universe, and before the Creator of man?"—*Carlyle.*

This "Fraction" appears to be, in other words, "A SNOB," whom Thackeray has defined to be "one who meanly admires mean things."

If a man faithfully follows this advice of Sir Thomas Browne, he can never hope to be a *snob*: "Be thou substantially great in thyself, and greater than thou appearest unto others; and let the world be deceived in thee as it is in the light of heaven."

It has been said that in all Voltaire's seventy or eighty volumes there is not one great thought—one, for instance, like that of Sir Thomas' above.

"PLAIN LIVING AND HIGH THINKING."

OH, friend, I know not which way I must look
   For comfort, being, as I am, opprest
   To think that now our life is only drest
For show—mere handiwork of craftsman, cook,
Or groom! we must run glittering like a brook
   In the open sunshine, or we are unblest;
   The wealthiest man among us is the best:
No grandeur now in nature or in book
   Delights us—rapine, avarice, expense,
This is idolatry, and these we adore;
PLAIN LIVING AND HIGH THINKING ARE NO MORE!
   The homely beauty of the good old cause
Is gone—our peace, our fearful innocence,
   And pure religion breathing household laws.

Si ad naturam vives nunquam eris pauper: si ad opinionem, nunquam dives.—*Epicurus.*

WORDS THE SHADOWS OF DEEDS.

THERE is in Seneca's 114th Epistle a very remarkable passage about the fashion of speech at Rome in his day, which is unconsciously, but quite substantially, thus translated: "No man in this fashionable London of yours," friend Sauerteig would say, "speaks a plain word to me. Every man feels bound to be something more than plain; to be pungent withal, witty, ornamental. His poor fraction of sense has to be perked up into some epigrammatic shape, that it may prick into me; perhaps (this is the commonest) to be topsy-turvied, left standing on its head, that I may remember it the better. Such grinning insincerity is very sad to the soul of man. A fashionable wit, '*ach Himmel!*' if you will ask which, he or a death's head, will be the cheerier company for me, pray send not him."

Insincere speech, truly, is the prime material of insincere action. Action, as it were, hangs *dissolved* in speech—in thought, whereof speech is the shadow; and precipitates itself therefrom.

Ubicunque videris orationem corruptam placere, ib mores quoque a recto descivisse non erit dubium.—*Seneca.*

KNOWLEDGE—OPINION—IGNORANCE.

PERFECT ignorance is quiet—perfect knowledge is quiet—not so the transition from the former to the latter.—*Carlyle.*

Les sciences ont deux extrémités qui se touchent; la première est la pure ignorance naturelle où se trouvent tous les hommes en naissant. L'autre extrémité est celle où arrivent les grandes âmes, qui, ayant parcouru tout ce que les hommes peuvent savoir, trouvent qu'ils ne savent rien, et se rencontrent dans cette même ignorance d'où ils etoient partis. Mais c'est une ignorance savante qui se connaît.

When Newton was dying, he said he felt just like a little child who had picked up a few pebbles on the shore, while the great ocean lay undiscovered before him.

Opinion in good men is but knowledge in the making.—*Milton.*

PEGASUS IN HARNESS.

MEN of great parts are often unfortunate in the management of public business, because they are apt to go out of the common road by the quickness of their imagination. This I once said to my Lord Bolingbroke, and desired he would observe that the clerks in his office used a sort of ivory knife with a blunt edge to divide a sheet of paper, which never failed to cut it even, only requiring a strong hand. Whereas if they should make use of a penknife, the sharpness would make it go often out of the crease, and disfigure the paper.—*Swift.*

A man had a plain strong-bow with which he could shoot far and true. He loved his bow so well that he would needs have it curiously carved by a cunning workman.

It was done; and at the first trial, the bow snapt.—*German.*

TRAVEL.

FOOL, why journeyest thou wearisomely in thy antiquarian fervour to gaze on the stone pyramids of Geeza, or the clay ones of Sacchara? These stand there, as I can tell thee, idle and inert, looking over the desert foolishly enough, for the last 3,000 years. But canst thou not open thy Hebrew Bible, then, or even Luther's version thereof?—*Carlyle.*

Once it was, " Farewell, Monsieur Traveller; look you lisp, and wear strange suits; disable the benefits of your own country—be out of love with your nativity, and almost chide God for making you that countenance you are; or I will scarce think you have swum in a gondola."

We may now add—" You must swear by Allah, smoke *chibouques.* and spell Pasha differently from every predecessor, or we shall scarce believe you have been in a *hareem!* "

" NEVER WENT OUT ASS, AND CAME HOME HORSE."

Still, " A good traveller," says Shakespeare, " is something at the latter end of a dinner."

If the golden age is passed, it was not genuine. Gold cannot rust nor decay; it comes out of all admixtures, and all decompositions, pure and indestructible. If the golden age will not endure, it had better never arise; for it can produce nothing but elegies on its loss.—*A. W. Schlegel.*

It is the weak only who, at each epoch, believe mankind arrive at the culminant point of their progressive march. They forget that by an intimate concatenation of all truths, knowledge, the field to be run over, becomes more vast the more we advance; bordered as it is by an horizon that continually recedes before us.—*Humboldt.*

Multi pertransibunt, et augebitur scientia.

FAUST.

Is a man who has quitted the ways of vulgar men without light to guide him a better way. No longer restricted by the sympathies, the common interests, and common persuasions, by which the mass of mortals, each individually ignorant,—nay, it may be, stolid, and altogether blind as to the proper aim of life,—are yet held together, and like stones in the channel of a torrent, by their very multitude and mutual collisions are made to move with some regularity,—he is still but a slave; the slave of impulses which are stronger, not truer or better, and the more unsafe that they are solitary.—*Carlyle.*

So it is with that soul who had built herself a lordly pleasure-house wherein to dwell alone. For three years she throve in it—

> . . . but on the fourth she fell,
> Like Herod when the shout was in his ears,
>   Struck through with pangs of hell.
>
> A spot of dull stagnation, without light
>   Or power of movement, seem'd my soul,
> Mid downward sloping motions infinite,
>   Making for one sure goal.
>
> A still salt pool, lock'd in with bars of sand,
>   Left on the shore, that hears all night
> The plunging seas draw backward from the land
>   Their moon-led waters white.

> Remaining utterly confused with fears,
> And ever worse with growing time,
> And ever unrelieved by dismal tears,
> And all alone in crime.—*Tennyson.*

"NETHER BARREL BETTER HERRING."

SEE how in the fanning of this wheat, the fullest and greatest grains lie ever the lowest; and the lightest take up the highest place.—*Leighton.*

Voltaire is always found at top—less by strength in swimming than by lightness in floating.—*Carlyle.*

"HOW WE APPLES SWIM!"

WEIGHT AND WORTH.

AN old rusty iron chest in a banker's shop, strongly locked, and wonderfully heavy, is full of gold. This is the general opinion; neither can it be disproved, provided the key be lost, and what is in it be wedged so close that it will not, by any motion, discover the metal by clinking.—*Swift.*

Lady H. Stanhope records that Pitt had more faith in a man who jested easily than in one who spoke and looked grave and weighty; for the first moved by some spring of his own within, but the latter might be only a buckram cover well stuffed with others' wisdom.

Coleridge used to relate how he formed a great notion of the understanding of a solid-looking man, who sat during dinner silent, and seemingly attentive to his discourse. Till suddenly, some baked potatoes being brought to table, Coleridge's disciple burst out, "Them's the jockeys for me!"

TO-DAY AND TO-MORROW.

IT is no very good symptom either of nations or individuals, that they deal much in vaticination. Happy men are full of the present, for its bounty suffices them; and wise men also, for its duties engage them. Our grand business undoubtedly is not so *see* what lies dimly at a distance, but to *do* what lies clearly at hand.

> Knowest thou YESTERDAY, its aims and reason?
> Workest thou well TO-DAY for worthy things?
> Then calmly wait TO-MORROW's hidden season,
> And fear not thou what hap soe'er it brings.
> Courage, brother! Get honest, and times will mend.—
Carlyle.

GUILELESSNESS.

IN spite of all that grovelling minds may say about the necessity of acquaintance with the world and with sin, in order to get on well in life, yet, after all, inexperienced guilelessness carries a man on as safely and more happily. The guileless man has a simple boldness and a princely heart; he overcomes dangers which others shrink from, merely because they are no dangers to him; and thus he often gains even worldly advantages by his straightforwardness, which the most crafty persons cannot gain. It is true such single-hearted men often get into difficulties, but they usually get out of them as easily; and are almost unconscious both of their danger and their escape—*Newman.*

The same writer notices also the general peace and serenity such persons enjoy, who suspect nobody and nothing; who live in no fear of their own plots failing, counterplots crossing, and equivocations detecting each other.

"We may not be able to change our natures from crooked to straight: but in a few minutes or hours we shall be called on to speak or to act—let us determine to do either, for once at least, truly, and honestly, and guilelessly."

ATHEISM.

DIDEROT'S Atheism comes, if not to much, yet to something; we learn this from it' (and from what it stands connected with, and may represent for us) that the mechanical system of thought is, in its essence, atheistic; that whosoever will admit no organ of truth but logic, and nothing to exist but what can be argued of, must even content himself with this sad result, as the only solid one he can arrive at; and so, with the best grace he can, of the aether make a gas, of God a force, of the second world a coffin, of man an aimless nondescript, little better than a kind of vermin. If Diderot, by bringing matters to this parting of the roads, have enabled or helped us to strike into the truer and better road, let him have our thanks for it. As to what remains, be pity our only feeling: was not his creed miserable enough—nay, moreover, did not he bear its miserableness, so to speak, in our stead, so that it need now be no longer borne by any one?—*Carlyle.*

"ANTICHRIST ALSO BEARS OUR CROSS FOR US."

"Ludovicus Vives has a story of a clown that killed his ass because it had drunk up the moon, and he thought the world could ill spare that luminary. So he killed his ass '*ut lunam redderet.*' Poor ass! 'He has drunk not the moon; but only the reflection of the moon in his own poor water-pail.'"

Tinkler Ducket was convicted of atheism at Cambridge, and brought up to receive sentence of expulsion before eight heads of colleges. An atheist was a rare bird in those days. Bentley, then almost eighty years old, came into the room (he was one of the *caput*, I suppose), and, being almost blind, called out, "Where's the atheist?" Ducket was pointed out to him—a little thin man. "What! is that the Atheist?" cries Bentley; "I expected to have seen a man as big as Burrough the beadle!"[1]

OLD AGE.

It is a man's own fault—it is from want of use—if his mind grows torpid in old age—*Johnson.*

---

[1] One of the three Esquire Bedells of that day, celebrated as "Pinguia tergeminorum abdomina Bedellorum."

"A man should keep always *learning* something—always, as Arnold said, keep the stream running—whereas most people let it stagnate about middle life."

Goethe is a great instance of a mind growing, growing, and putting out fresh leaves up to eighty years of life.

GUILE.

"IN looking over my books some years ago, I found the following memorandum—'I am this day thirty years old, and till this day I know not that I have met with one person of that age, except in my father's house, who did not use Guile, more or less.'"—*John Wesley.*

"ENOUGH IS A FEAST."

A MAN came home from the sea-side, and brought some shells for his little son. The boy was full of wonder and delight: he counted and sorted them over and over again. What a wonderful place must the sea-shore be!

So one day his father took him to the sea-shore. The boy picked up shell after shell, each seeming fairer than the last; threw down one in order to carry another; till growing vexed with himself and the shells, he threw all away, and when he got home, also threw away those his father had given him before.—*German.*

WIT.

DISEUR DE BONS MOTS, MAUVAIS CARACTÈRE.—*Pascal.*

PERHAPS he (Schiller) was too honest, too sincere, for the exercise of Wit; too intent on the deeper relation of things to note their more transient collisions. Besides, he dealt in affirmation, and not in negation: in which last, it has been said, the material of Wit chiefly lies.—*Carlyle.*

A CHAPTER FROM LAVATER.

"FACE TO FACE TRUTH COMES OUT APACE"

(If you have but an eye to find it by.)

THE more uniform a man's step, voice, manner of conversation, handwriting—the more quiet and uniform his actions and character.

Vociferation and calmness of character seldom meet in the same person.

(So thought Bacon, who desires a counsellor to adopt "a steadfast countenance, not wavering with action as in moving the head or hand too much, which showeth a fantastical light and fickle operation of the spirit; and consequently, like mind, like gesture," etc.)

Who writes an illegible hand is commonly rapid, often impetuous in his judgements.

Who interrupts often is inconstant and insincere.

The side-glance, displayed when observed, seeks to ensnare.

He who has a daring eye tells downright truths, and downright falsehoods.

Softness of smile indicates softness of character. An old proverb says, "A smiling boy is a bad servant."

The horse-laugh indicates brutality.

LEARNING.

IT is an assured truth which is contained in the verses—

> Scilicet ingenuas didicisse fideliter artes
> Emollit mores, nec sinit esse feros.

It taketh away the wildness, and barbarism, and fierceness of men's minds; but indeed the accent had need be laid upon *fideliter*: for a little superficial learning doth rather work a contrary effect. It taketh away all levity, temerity, and insolency, by copious suggestions of all doubts and difficulties, and acquainting the mind to balance reasons on both sides, and to turn back the first offers and conceits of the mind, and to accept of nothing but what is examined and tried. It taketh away all vain admiration of anything, which is the root of all weakness; for all things are admired because they are new, or because they are great. For novelty, no man that wadeth in learning or contemplation thoroughly, but will find that printed in his heart—*Nil novi super terram.* Neither can any man marvel at the play of puppets that goeth behind the curtain, and adviseth well of the motion. And for magnitude, as Alexander the Great, after he was used to great armies, and the great conquests of the spacious provinces in Asia, when he received letters out of Greece of some fights and services there, which were commonly for a passage, or a fort, or some walled town at most, he said, " It seemed to him that he was advertised of the Battle of the Frogs and Mice, that the old tales went of; " so certainly, if a man meditate upon the universal frame of nature, the Earth, with men upon it (the divineness of souls excepted), will not serve much other than an anthill, where some ants carry corn, and some carry their young, and some go empty, and all to and fro a little heap of dust. It taketh away or mitigateth fear of death, or adverse fortune; which is one of the greatest impediments of virtue, and imperfections of manners. For if a man's mind be deeply seasoned with the consideration of the mortality and corruptible nature of things, he will easily concur with Epictetus, who went forth one day, and saw a woman weeping for her pitcher of earth that was broken; and went forth the next day, and saw a woman weeping for her son that was dead; and therefore said, " Heri vidi fragilem frangi; hodiè vidi mortalem mori." And therefore did Virgil excellently and profoundly couple the knowledge of causes and the conquest of all fears together as *concomitantia:*

> Felix qui potuit rerum cognoscere causas,
> Quique metus omnes, et inexorabile fatum,
> Subjecit pedibus, strepitumque Acherontis avari.

I will conclude with that which hath *rationem totius ;* which is that it disposeth the constitution of the mind not to be fixed or settled in the defects thereof, but still to be capable and susceptible of growth and reformation. For the unlearned man knows not what it is to descend into himself, or to call himself to account ; nor the pleasure of that " *suavissima vita, indies sentire se fieri meliorem.*" The good parts he hath he will learn to show to the full, and use them dexterously, but not much to increase them ; the faults he hath, he will learn how to hide and colour them, but not much to amend them : like an ill mower, that mows on still, and never whets his scythe. Whereas with the learned man it fares otherwise, that he doth ever intermix the correction and amendment of his mind with the use and employment thereof. Nay, further, in general and in sum, certain it is that *Veritas* and *Bonitas* differ but as the seal and print ; for Truth prints Goodness ; and they be the clouds of error, which descend in the storms of passions and perturbations.—*Bacon's Advancement.*

He a scholar ! No, a Witling can't be a scholar. Knowledge is a great calmer of people's minds.—*Wilson.*

MIMICRY.

" TELL me of any animal I cannot imitate," said the Ape.

" And tell me," answered the Fox, " of any animal that will imitate you."—*German.*

WILL AND REASON.

" NONE SO BLIND AS THOSE THAT WON'T SEE."

BAXTER was credulous and incredulous for precisely the same reason. Possessing by habit a mastery over his thoughts such as few men ever acquired, a single effort of the will was sufficient to exclude from his view whatever he judged hostile to his immediate purpose. Every prejudice was at once banished, when any debateable point was to be scrutinized, and with equal facility every reasonable doubt was exiled when his only object was to enforce or to illustrate a doctrine of the truth of which he was assured.—*Edinburgh Review.*

So says Pascal, who was a good instance of his own theory. "La volonté est un des principaux organes de la croyance : non qu'elle forme la croyance ; mais par ce que les choses paroissent vraies ou fausses, selon la face par où on les regarde. La volonté, qui se plaist à l'une plus qu'à l'autre, détourne l'esprit de considérer les qualités de celle qu'elle n'aime pas ; et ainsi l'esprit marchant d'une pièce avec la volonté, s'arrête à regarder la face qu'elle aime ; et jugeant par ce qu'il y voit, règle insensiblement sa croyance suivant l'inclination de la volonté."

"Happy," continues the *Edinburgh Review*, "happy they, who, like Baxter, have so disciplined their affections as to disarm their temporary usurpation of all its more dangerous tendencies."

HE THAT COMPLIES AGAINST HIS WILL,
IS OF HIS OWN OPINION STILL.

POVERTY.

"THE GOAT MUST BROWSE WHERE HE IS TIED."

POVERTY, we may say, surrounds a man with ready-made barriers, which, if they do mournfully gall and hamper, do at least prescribe for him, and force on him, a sort of course and goal ; a safe and beaten, though a circuitous course. A great part of his guidance is secure against fatal error, is withdrawn from his control. The rich, again, has his whole life to guide, without goal or barrier, save of his own choosing ; and tempted, as we have seen, is too likely to guide it ill.—*Carlyle.*

I cannot but say to Poverty, "Welcome ! so thou come not too late in life."—*Richter.*

CONVERSATION AND TALK.

To make a good Converser, good taste, extensive information, and accomplishments, are the chief requisites; to which may be added an easy and elegant delivery, and a well-toned voice. I think the higher order of genius is not favourable to this talent.—*Sir W. Scott.*

It is a common remark, that men talk most who think least; just as frogs cease their quacking when a light is brought to the waterside.—*Richter.*

"THE EMPTY CASK SOUNDS MOST."

NATIVE AIR.

CHILDREN educated abroad return home to a strange country, not able to mark the places where they found the first bird's nest, the burn where they caught the first trout, or any of those dear associations of childhood, that binds us to our native soil by ties as small and numerous as those by which the Liliputians bound Gulliver to the earth.—*Mrs. Grant.*

HOMO SUM; HUMANI NIHIL A ME ALIENUM PUTO.

THE sentence which, when first spoken in the Roman theatre, made it ring with applause. Trite as it is, we can scarce come upon it now without the whole heart rising to welcome it.

No character, we may affirm, was ever rightly understood till it had been first regarded with a certain feeling, not of toleration only, but of sympathy.—*Carlyle.*

Lavater says, "He who begins with severity in judging of another, commonly ends with falsehood." But what did he *begin* with?

"It is only necessary to grow old," said Goethe, "to become more indulgent. I see no fault committed that I have not myself inclined to."

POETRY.

"MILTON is very fine, I dare say," said the mathematician,

"but what does he prove?" What, indeed, does Poetry prove?

"It doth raise and erect the mind," says Bacon, "by submitting the shows of things to the desires of the mind, whereas Reason doth buckle and bow the mind unto the nature of things."

But Sir Philip Sidney says, the poet shows the "nature of things" as much as the reasoner, though he may not "buckle and bow the mind" to it: "He doth not only show the way, but giveth so sweet a prospect into the way as will entice any man to enter into it. Nay, he doth as if your journey should lie through a fair vineyard, at the very first give you a cluster of grapes, that full of that taste you may long to pass further."

"Some have thought the proper object of Poetry was to *please;* others that it was to *instruct*. Perhaps we are well instructed if we are *well* pleased."

"POETRY ENRICHES THE BLOOD OF THE WORLD."

VAINGLORY.

THEY that are glorious must needs be factious; for all bravery stands upon comparisons. They must needs be violent to make good their own vaunts; neither can they be secret, and therefore effectual: but according to the French proverb—

> BEAUCOUP DE BRUIT
> PEU DE FRUIT.—*Bacon.*

Bacon may be talking of the vainglory of an Alcibiades, troublesome to States; but so it is through all societies of men, from parliaments to tea-tables; for "Vanity is of a divisive, not of an uniting, nature."

THE GUILTY MAN.

MAY escape, but he cannot rest sure of doing so.—*Epicurus.*

"RIVEN BREEKS SIT STILL."

LIBERTY. WHAT IS IT?

"HE IS WISE WHO FOLLOWS THE WISE."

LIBERTY? The true liberty of a man, you would say, consisted in his finding out, or being forced to find out, the right path, and to walk thereon. To learn, or to be taught, what work he actually was able for: and then by permission, persuasion, or even compulsion, to set about doing of the same! That is his true blessedness, honour, liberty, and maximum of well-being: if liberty be not that, I, for one, have small care about liberty. You do not allow a palpable madman to leap over precipices; you violate his liberty, you that are wise; and keep him in strait-waistcoats away from the precipices! Every stupid, every cowardly and foolish man is but a less palpable madman: his true liberty were that a wise man, that any man, and every wiser man, could, by brass collars, or in whatever sharper or milder way, lay hold of him when he was going wrong, and order and compel him to go a little righter. Oh, if thou really art my Senior, Seigneur, my elder, presbyter, or priest—if thou art in very deed my *wiser*—may a beneficent instinct lead and impel thee to conquer me, to command me! If thou do know better than I what is good and right, I conjure thee in the name of God, force me to do it; were it by never such brass collars, whips, and handcuffs, leave me not to walk over precipices! That I have been called by all the newspapers a "freeman" will avail me little if my pilgrimage have ended in death and wreck. Oh that the newspapers had called me coward, slave, fool, or what it pleased their sweet voices to name me, and I had attained not death, but life!—Liberty requires new definitions.—*Carlyle's Past and Present.*

Plato taught the haughty Athenians they could only be free by liberating themselves from their own passions; and so Milton sings at the end of *Comus.* A later poet, however, says—

"Thou can'st not choose but serve; man's lot is servitude:
But thou hast thus much choice—a bad lord, or a good."

"There is a service that is perfect freedom."

SOCRATIS PATERNOSTER.

When Socrates and Phaedrus have discoursed away the noonday heat under that plane tree by the Ilissus, they rise to depart toward the city. But Socrates (pointing perhaps to some images of Pan and other sylvan deities) says it is not decent to leave their haunts without praying to them. And he prays—

O auspicious Pan, and ye other deities of this place—grant to me to become beautiful *inwardly*, and that all my outward goods may prosper my inner soul. Grant that I may esteem wisdom the only riches, and that I may have so much gold as temperance can handsomely carry.

Have we yet aught else to pray for, Phaedrus? For myself I seem to have prayed enough.

Phaedrus. Pray as much for me also; for friends have all in common.

Socrates. Even so be it. Let us depart.

GIVING AND ASKING.

I like him who can ask boldly without impudence; he has faith in humanity; he has faith in himself. No one who is not accustomed to give grandly can ask boldly.

He who goes round about in his demands, commonly wants more than he wishes to appear to want.

He who acepts crawlingly will give superciliously.

The manner of giving shows the character of the giver more than the gift itself. There is a princely manner of giving and of accepting.—*Lavater.*

THE WISE MOTHER SAYS NOT, "WILL YOU?" BUT GIVES.

> Silver from the living
> Is gold in the giving:
> Gold from the dying
> Is but silver a-flying:
> Gold and silver from the dead
> Turn too often into lead.—*Fuller.*

LIFE.

WE deliberate, says Seneca, about the parcels of Life, but not about Life itself; and so arrive all unawares at its different epochs, and have the trouble of beginning all again. And so, finally, it is that we do not walk as men confidently toward death, but let death come suddenly upon us.

VENT AU VISAGE
FAIT UN HOMME SAGE.

When Hercules was taken up to the consistory of the gods, he went up to Juno first of all, and saluted her.

"How," said Jupiter, "do you first seek your worst enemy to do her courtesy?"

"Yea," said Hercules, "her malice it was made me do such deeds as have lifted me to heaven."—*German.*

PRECEDENCY.

1.

A QUESTION of precedence arose among the beasts. "Let Man be the judge," said the Horse, "he is not a party concerned." "But has he sense enough," said the Mole, "to distinguish and appreciate our more hidden excellences?"

"Ay—can you vouch for that?" said the Ass. But the Horse said to them, "He who distrusts his own cause is most suspicious of his judge."

2.

Man was sent for. "By what scale, O Man, wilt thou measure us?" said the Lion.

"By the measure of your usefulness to me," said Man.

"Nay then," replied the Lion, "at that rate the Ass is worthier than I. You must leave us to decide it among ourselves."

3.

"There," cried Mole and Ass, "you see, Horse, the Lion thinks with us!"

4.

But the Lion said, "What, after all, is all the dispute about? What is it to me whether I am considered first or last? Enough—I know myself." And he strode away into the forest.—*German.*

IMAGINARY EVILS.

I AM more afraid of my friends making themselves uncomfortable who have only imaginary evils to indulge, than I am for the peace of those who, battling magnanimously with real inconvenience and danger, find a remedy in the very force of the exertions to which their lot compels them.—*W. Scott.*

A gentlemen of large fortune, while we were seriously conversing, ordered a servant to throw some coals on the fire. A puff of smoke came out. He threw himself back in his chair, and cried out, "O Mr. Wesley, these are the crosses I meet with every day!"

Surely these crosses would not have fretted him so much if he had had only fifty pounds a year instead of five thousand.—*John Wesley.*

"On n'est point malheureux," wrote Horace Walpole to Madame du Deffand, " quand on a loisir de s'ennuyer."

ACTION AND INSPIRATION:

"NEVER SIGH, BUT SEND."

Nihil lacrimâ citius arescit.—*Cicero.*

THE danger of a polite and elegant education is, that it separates feeling and acting; it teaches us to think, speak, and be affected aright, without forcing us to *do* what is right.

I will take an illustration of this from the effect produced on the mind by reading what is commonly called a Romance or Novel. Such works contain many good sentiments; characters too are introduced, virtuous, noble, patient under sufferings, and triumphing at last over misfortune. The great truths of religion are upheld, we will suppose, and enforced; and our affections excited and interested in what is good and true. But it is all a fiction; it does not exist out of a book, which contains the beginning and end of it. *We have nothing to do;* we read, are affected, softened, or roused; and that is all; we cool again: nothing comes of it.

Now observe the effect of all this. God has made us feel in order that we may go on to act in consequence of feeling. If, then, we allow our feelings to be excited without acting upon them, we do mischief to the moral system within us; just as we might spoil a watch, or other piece of mechanism, by playing with the wheels of it; we weaken the springs, and they cease to act truly.

Accordingly, when we have got into the habit of amusing ourselves with these works of fiction, we come at length to feel the excitement without the slightest thought or tendency to act upon it. And since it is very difficult to begin any duty *without* some emotion or other (that is, on mere principles of dry reasoning), a grave question arises, how, after destroying the connexion between feeling and acting, how shall we get ourselves to act when circumstances make it our duty to do so? For instance, we will say we have read again and again of the heroism of facing danger, and we have glowed with the thought of its nobleness. We have felt how great it is to bear pain, and to submit to indignities, rather than wound our conscience; and all this again and again, when we had no opportunity of carrying our good feelings into practice. Now suppose, at length, we actually come to trial, and, let us say, our feelings become roused, as often before, at the thought of boldly resisting temptations to cowardice; shall we therefore do our duty, quitting ourselves like men? rather, we are likely to talk loudly, and then run from the danger.—Why? rather let us ask, why not? what is to keep us from yielding? Because we *feel* aright?

Nay, we have again and again felt aright, and thought aright, without accustoming ourselves to act aright; and though there was an original connexion in our minds between feeling and acting, there is none now; the wires within us, as they may be called, are loosened and powerless.—*Newman.*

HELL IS PAVED WITH GOOD INTENTIONS.

" 'Ah, thank 'ee, neighbour,' said a perspiring sheep-driver the other day, to one who hooted away his flock from going down a wrong road,—' Thank 'ee—a little help is worth a deal o' pity!' "

WAR.

War begets Poverty—Poverty, Peace—
Peace begets Riches—Fate will not cease—
Riches beget Pride—Pride is War's ground—
War begets Poverty—and so the world goes round.
—*Old Saw.*

How all Europe is but like a set of parishes of the same country; participant of the selfsame influences ever since the Crusades, and earlier: and these glorious wars of ours are but like parish brawls, which begin in mutual ignorance, intoxication, and boasting speech; which end in broken windows, damage, waste, and bloody noses; and which one hopes the general good sense is now in the way towards putting down in some measure.—*Carlyle.*

" Yet here, as elsewhere, not absurdly does ' Metaphysic call for aid on Sense.' The physical science of war may do more to abolish war than all our good and growing sense of its folly, wickedness, and extreme discomfort. For what State would be at the expense of drilling and feeding Dumdrudges to be annihilated by the first discharge of the COMING GUN ? "

LOVE

WITHOUT END HATH NO END.

No wheedler loves.—*Lavater.*'
Il y a dans la jalousie plus d'amour-propre que d'amour.

Il n'y a point de déguisement qui puisse longtemps cacher l'amour où il est, ni le feindre où il n'est pas.—*Rochefoucauld.*

"LOVE ASKS FAITH, AND FAITH FIRMNESS."

OUR TIME.

Is like our money : when we change a guinea, the shillings escape as things of small account : when we break a day by idleness in the morning, the rest of the hours lose their importance in our eyes.—*Sir W. Scott.*

EXPENSE.

COMMONLY it is less dishonourable to abridge petty charges than to stoop to petty gettings. A man ought warily to begin charges, which once begun will continue ; but in matters that return not, he may be more magnificent.—*Bacon.*

Fuller says, " Occasional entertainment of men greater than thyself is better than solemn inviting them ; " and a proverb bids us beware of taking for servant one who has waited on our betters. In both cases we shall have to spend beyond our means, and be despised to boot.

TRUTH AND JUSTICE.

ARE all one ; for Truth is but Justice in our knowledge ; and Justice is but Truth in our practice.—*Milton.*

RICHES.

THESE times strike money'd worldlings with dismay:
  Ev'n rich men, brave by nature, taint the air
  With words of apprehension and despair ;
While tens of thousands looking on the fray,
Men unto whom sufficient for the day,
  And minds not stinted or untill'd are given,
  Sound healthy children of the God of heaven,
Are cheerful as the rising sun in May.

What do we gather hence but firmer faith
That every gift of nobler origin
  Is breathed upon with Hope's perpetual breath;
That Virtue, and the faculties within,
Are vital; and that Riches are akin
  To fear, to change, to cowardice, and death?
—*Wordsworth.*

" Ah! Davy," said Johnson to Garrick, who was showing off his fine grounds at Twickenham, " it is these things that make us fear to die."

CHOICE OF A CALLING.

IN all things, to serve from the lowest station upwards is necessary. To restrict yourself to a Trade is best. For the narrow mind, whatever he attempts is still a Trade; for the higher, an Art; and the highest, in doing one thing, does all; or, to speak less paradoxically, in the one thing which he does rightly, he sees the likeness of all that is done rightly.—*Goethe.*

" ANY ROAD LEADS TO THE END OF THE WORLD."

Whatever a young man at first applies to is commonly his delight afterwards.—*Hartley.*

" Whatever a man delights in he will do best: and that he had best do."

" Themistocles said he could not fiddle, but he could rule a city. If a man can rule a city well, let him: but it is better to play the fiddle well than to rule a city ill."

ENVY.

LA plus véritable marque d'être né avec de grandes qualités, c'est d'être né sans envie.—*Rochefoucauld.*

Genius may coexist with idleness, wildness, folly, and even crime; but not long, believe me, with selfishness, and the indulgence of an envious disposition. Envy is κάκιστος καὶ δικαιότατος θεός— it dwarfs and withers its worshippers.—*Coleridge.*

Therefore when you are next sitting down to your epic or your tragedy, pause, and look within, and if you recognize there any grudge against A so praised in the *Quarterly* or B so fêted in America, you may, if you please, save yourself a deal of laborious composition.

A fine brazen statue was accidentally reduced by fire into a shapeless mass. This was re-cast by another artist into another statue, quite different from the former, but as beautiful.

" It is well," said Envy; " but he could not have turned out even this middling piece of work, had not the stuff of the old statue run of itself into shape."—*German*.

ART DIPLOMATIC.

THE sure way to make a foolish Ambassador is to bring him up to it. What can an Englishman abroad really want but an honest and bold heart, a love for his country, and the Ten Commandments? Your art diplomatic is stuff—no truly great man would negotiate upon such shallow principles.—*Coleridge*.

Certainly the ablest men that ever were have had an openness and frankness of dealing, and a name of urbanity and veracity.—*Bacon*.

How often (says the *Tatler*) I have wished, for the good of the nation, that several good Politicians could take any pleasure in feeding ducks. I look upon an able statesman out of business like a huge whale, that will endeavour to overturn the ship unless he has an empty cask to play with.

SICKNESS.

QUAND on se porte bien, on ne comprend pas comment on pourroit faire si on étoit malade : et quand on l'est, on prend médicine gaiement : le mal y résout. On n'a plus les passions et les désirs des divertissements et des promenades que la santé donnoit, et qui sont incompatibles avec les nécessités de la maladie. La nature donne alors des passions et des désirs conformes à l'état présent. Ce ne sont que les craintes que nous nous donnons nous-mêmes, et non pas la nature, qui nous troublent ; parce qu'elles joignent à l'état où nous sommes les passions de l'état où nous ne sommes pas.—*Pascal.*

Sir C. Bell records the general cheerfulness of the sick and dying at hospitals.

GOD TEMPERS THE WIND TO THE SHORN LAMB.

TEACHING.

I HOLD that a man is only fit to teach so long as he is himself learning daily. If the mind once becomes stagnant, it can give no fresh draught to another mind; it is drinking out of a pond instead of from a spring.

A schoolmaster's intercourse is with the young, the strong, and the happy; and he cannot get on with them unless in animal spirits he can sympathize with them, and show that his thoughtfulness is not connected with selfishness and weakness.—*Arnold.*

You may put poison, if you please, in an earthen pitcher, said Socrates, and the pitcher be washed after, and none the worse. But you can take nothing into the soul that does not indelibly infect it whether for good or for evil.

TORY.

TACITUS wrote (says Luther) that by the ancient Germans it was held no shame at all to drink and swill four-and-twenty hours together. A gentlemen of the Court asked, "How long ago it was since Tacitus wrote this?" He was answered, "Almost 1,500 years." Whereupon the gentlemen said, "Forasmuch as drunkenness is so ancient a custom, let us not abolish it."

An old ruinous tower which had harboured innumerable jackdaws, sparrows, and bats, was at length repaired. When the masons left it, the jackdaws, sparrows, and bats came back in search of their old dwellings. But these were all filled up. "Of what use now is this great building?" said they; "come, let us forsake this useless stone-heap."—*German.*

HOW TO WRITE A GOOD BOOK.

"HE THAT BURNS MOST SHINES MOST."

A LOVING heart is the beginning of all knowledge. This it is that opens the whole mind, quickens every faculty of the intellect to do its work—that of knowing; and therefrom, by sure consequence, of vividly uttering forth. Other secret for being "graphic" is there none, worth having; but this is an all-sufficient one. •See, for example, what a small Boswell can do! Hereby, indeed, is the whole man made a living mirror, wherein the wonders of this ever-wonderful universe are in their true light (which is ever a magical, miraculous one) represented and reflected back on us. It has been said, "the heart sees further than the head." But indeed without the seeing heart, there is no true seeing for the head so much as possible; all is mere *oversight*, hallucination, and vain superficial phantasmagories, which can permanently profit no one. Here too may we not pause for an instant, and make a practical reflection? Considering the multitude of mortals that handle the pen in these days, and can mostly spell, and write without glaring violations of grammar; the question naturally arises, How is it, then, that no work proceeds from them bearing any stamp of authenticity and permanence, of worth for more than one day? Shiploads of fashionable novels, sentimental rhymes, tragedies, farces, diaries of travel, tales by flood and field, are swallowed monthly into the bottomless pool; still does the press boil: innumerable paper-makers, compositors, printers' devils, bookbinders, and hawkers grown hoarse with loud proclaiming, rest not from their labour; and still, in torrents, rushes on the great array of publications, unpausing, to their final home; and still Oblivion, like the grave, cries, Give! give! How is it that of all these countless multitudes, no one can attain to the smallest mark of excellence, or produce aught that shall endure longer than the "snowflake on the river," or the foam of penny-beer? We answer, because they *are* foam: because there is no reality in them. These three thousand men, women, and children, that make up the army of British authors, do not, if we will consider it, *see* anything whatever; consequently *have* nothing that they can record and utter, only more or fewer things that they can plausibly pretend to record. The universe, of man and nature, is still quite shut up from them; the " open secret " still utterly a secret; because no sympathy with man or nature, no love and free simplicity of heart, has yet unfolded the same. Nothing but a pitiful image of their own pitiful self, with its vanities, and grudgings, and ravenous hunger of all kinds, hangs for ever painted in the retina of these unfortunate persons; so that the starry all, with whatsoever it embraces, does but appear as some expanded magic-lantern shadow of that same image, and naturally looks pitiful enough.

It is in vain for these persons to allege that they are naturally without gift, naturally stupid and sightless, and so *can* attain to no knowledge of anything; therefore, in writing of anything, must needs write falsehoods of it, there being in it no truth for them. Not so, good friends. The stupidest of you has a certain faculty; were it but that of articulate speech (say in the Scottish, the Irish, the cockney dialect, or even in " governess-English ") and of physically discerning what lies under your nose. The stupidest of you would perhaps grudge to be compared in faculty with James Boswell; yet see what he has produced! You do not use your faculty honestly: your heart is shut up—full of greediness, malice, discontent; so your intellectual sense cannot lie open. It is in vain also to urge that James Boswell had opportunities, saw great men and great things, such as you can never hope to look on. What make ye of Parson White of Selborne? He had not only no great men to look on, but not even men, merely sparrows and cockchafers; yet has he left us a biography of these, which, under its title, *Natural History of Selborne*, still remains valuable to us; which has copied a little sentence or two *faithfully* from the inspired volume of nature, and so is in itself not without inspiration. Go ye and do likewise. Sweep away utterly all frothiness and falsehood from your heart: struggle unweariedly to acquire, what is possible for every God-created man, a free, open, humble soul: *speak not at all in any wise till you have something to speak:* care not for the reward of your speaking, but simply, and with undivided mind, for the *truth* of your speaking; then be placed in what section of space and time soever, do but open your eyes and they shall actually *see*, and bring you real knowledge, wondrous, worthy of belief; and, instead of our Boswell and our White, the world will rejoice in a thousand—stationed on their thousand several watch-towers, to instruct us, by indubitable documents, of whatsoever in our so stupendous world comes to light and *is !—Carlyle*.

"And yet," says he again, "What of Books? Hast thou not already a Bible to write, and publish in print, that is eternal; namely—

A LIFE TO LEAD."

DATE AND DABITUR:

THERE is in Austria (said Luther) a Monastery, which was, in former times, very rich, and continued rich so long as it gave freely to the poor; but when it gave over that, then it became poor itself, and so remains to this day. Not long since, a poor man knocked at the gate and begged alms for God's sake: the porter said they were themselves too poor to give. "And do you know why?" said the other: "I will tell you. You had formerly in this monastery two Brethren, one named DATE, and the other DABITUR. DATE you thrust out; and DABITUR went away of himself soon after."

Γνῶθι Σεαυτόν

THIS famous "Know thyself," it does but say,
"Know thine own business," in another way.—*Menander*.

"Hence too," says a testy modern, "the folly of that impossible precept, 'Know thyself,' till it gets translated into this more possible one, 'Know what thou canst work at.'"

"It is true," says Harrington, "that men are no fit judges of themselves, because commonly they are partial in their own cause; yet it is as true, that he that will dispose himself to judge indifferently of himself, can do it better than anybody else, because a man can see further into his own mind and heart than any one else can."

"He," says Fuller, "who will not freely and sadly confess that he is *much* a fool, is *all* a fool."

Argenson's friend read a book many times over, and complained of the author's repeating himself a great deal.

Kettle called Pot—
You know what.

EAGLES NO FLY-CATCHERS.

THE slightness we see in Gainsborough's works cannot always be imputed to negligence. However they may appear to superficial observers, painters know very well that a steady attention to the general effect takes up more time, and is much more laborious to the mind, than any mode of high-finishing or smoothness, without such attention.—*Sir J. Reynolds*.

Sir Joshua said, "though Johnson did not write his *Discourses*, the general principles he laid down in morals and literature served as the groundwork of much propounded in them."

By way of requital, Opie used to relate how a clerical friend of his preached Sir Joshua's *Discourses* from the pulpit, only changing the terms of art to those of morals.

This might easily be done with the sentence quoted above. The "superficial observers" remain as they are, admiring the laborious finish of the model-man, whose every word is weighed and smile measured; but scandalized at him who, having laid down a large and noble design of life, is careless of the petty detail of behaviour —whose heart may run wild though it never goes astray.

SUPERSTITION.

SUPERSTITION is the religion of feeble minds; and they

must be tolerated in an intermixture of it, in some trifling or some enthusiastic shape or other, else you will deprive weak minds of a resource found necessary to the strongest.—*Burke*.

They that are against superstition oftentimes run into it of the wrong side. If I will wear all colours but black, then I am superstitious in not wearing black.—*Selden*.

"The guillotine was as much a superstition as the aristocracy and priestcraft it was set up to exterminate."

MODESTY.

BEING the case of chastity, it is to be feared that when the case is broken, the jewel is lost.—*Fuller*.

On peut trouver des femmes qui n'ont jamais eu de galanterie : mais il est rare de trouver qui n'en aient jamais eu qu'une.—*Rochefoucauld*.

"IL N'Y A QUE LE PREMIER PAS QUI COUTE."

NATURE AND HABIT.

LA vertu d'un homme ne doit pas se mesurer par ses efforts, mais par ce qu'il fait d'ordinaire.—*Pascal*.

All men are better than their ebullitions of evil, but also worse than their ebullitions of good.—*Richter*.

Nature is often hidden—sometimes overcome—seldom extinguished. Force maketh nature more violent in the return; doctrine and discourse maketh nature less importune; but custom only doth alter and subdue nature.—*Bacon*.

"Let him who would know how far he has changed the old Adam, consider his Dreams."

"HE THAT COMES OF A HEN MUST SCRAPE."

EVERY MAN JUDGES FROM HIMSELF.

WE measure the excellency of other men by some excellency we conceive to be in ourselves. Nash, a poet, poor enough (as poets used to be), seeing an alderman with a gold chain upon his great horse, by way of scorn said to one of his companions, "Do you see yon fellow—how goodly, how big he looks?—why, that fellow cannot make a blank verse."

Nay, we measure the goodness of God from ourselves: we measure His goodness, His justice, His wisdom, by something we call just, good, wise in ourselves. And in so doing, we judge proportionably to the country fellow in the play; who said, if he were a king, he would live like a lord, and have pease and bacon every day, and a whip that cried Slash.—*Selden.*

So Warburton says, the Bigot reverses the order of creation, and makes God in man's image; choosing the very ugliest pattern to model from—namely, himself.

SELF-LOVE.

It is the nature of self-lovers as they will set a house on fire and it were but to roast their eggs. Wisdom for a man's self is in many branches thereof a depraved thing. It is the wisdom of rats, that will be sure to leave a house somewhat before it fall.—*Bacon.*

"Enlighten self-interest," cries the philosopher, "do but sufficiently enlighten it!"—We ourselves have seen enlightened self-interests ere now; and truly, for the most part, their light was only as that of a horn-lantern; sufficient to guide the bearer himself out of various puddles —but to us and the world of comparatively small advantage. And figure the human species like an endless host seeking its way onwards through undiscovered Time, in black darkness, save that each had his horn-lantern and the van-guard some few of glass.—*Carlyle.*

IT IS A POOR CENTRE OF A MAN'S ACTIONS—HIMSELF.—*Bacon.*

PREJUDICES.

"No wise man can have a contempt for the prejudices of others; and he should stand in a certain awe of his own, as if they were aged instructors. They may in the end prove wiser than he."

Many of our men of speculation, instead of exploding general prejudices, employ their sagacity to discover the latent wisdom which prevails in them. If they find what they seek, and they seldom fail, they think it more wise to continue the prejudice, with the reason involved, than to cast away the coat of prejudice and leave the naked reason; because prejudice, with its reason, has a motive to give action to that reason, and an affection which will give it permanence. Prejudice is of ready application in the emergency: it previously engages the mind in a steady course of wisdom and virtue, and does not leave the man hesitating in the moment of decision, sceptical, puzzled, and unresolved. Prejudice renders a man's virtue his habit, and not a series of unconnected acts.—*Burke.*

MUSIC.

"MUCH music marreth men's manners," saith Galen. Although some men will say that it doth not so, but rather recreateth and maketh quick a man's mind; yet methinks, by reason, it doth as honey doth to a man's stomach, which at first receiveth it well, but afterward it maketh it unfit to abide any strong nourishing meat. And even so in a manner these instruments make a man's wit so soft and smooth, so tender and quaisy, that they be less able to brook strong and rough study. Wits be not sharpened, but rather made blunt, with such soft sweetness, even as good edges be blunted which men whet upon soft chalk-stones.—*R. Ascham.*

Plato allowed but of two kinds of music in his Republic: the Martial, and the Sedate. He forbad the luxurious, the doleful, the sentimental. And Aristophanes complains of the new intricate divisions that were in his day superseding the simple plain-song of more heroic times.

One may conceive that Handel is wholesomer for a people than Bellini.

GENIUS.

THE French were distressed that Dumont claimed to have supplied their Mirabeau with materials for his eloquence. "Good people," said Goethe, "as if their Hercules, or any Hercules, must not be well fed—as if the Colossus must not be made of parts. What is Genius but the faculty of seizing things from right and left—here a bit of marble, there a bit of brass—and breathing life into them?"

"If children," he says elsewhere, "grew up according to early indications, we should have nothing but Geniuses; but growth is not merely development: the various organic systems that constitute one man, spring from one another, follow each other, change into each other, supplant each other, and even consume each other; so that after a time scarce a trace is left of many aptitudes and abilities."

FORMS OF BEHAVIOUR.

To attain to good Forms it almost sufficeth not to despise them: for so shall a man observe them in others—and let him trust himself with the rest. For if he labour too much to express them he shall lose their grace; which is, to be natural and unaffected.

Some men's behaviour is like a verse wherein every syllable is weighed. How can a man comprehend great matters that breaketh his mind too much to small observation?

The sum of behaviour is—to retain a man's own dignity without intruding upon that of others.—*Bacon.*

DISPUTES.

"SOME have wondered that disputes about opinions should so often end in personalities: but the fact is, that such disputes *begin* with personalities; for our opinions are a part of ourselves."

Besides, "after the first contradiction it is ourselves, and not the thing, we maintain."

WHAT IS A MAN'S RELIGION?

Not the Church creed which he professes, the articles of faith which he will sign, and in words or deeds otherwise assert; not this wholly; in many cases not this at all. We see men of all kinds of professed creeds attain to almost all degrees of worth and worthlessness under each or any of them. This is not what I call religion, this profession and assertion, which is often only a profession and assertion from the outworks of man, from the mere argumentative region of him, if even so deep as that. But the thing a man does *practically believe* (and this is often enough without asserting it to himself, much less to others), the thing a man does practically lay to heart, and know for certain concerning his vital relations to this mysterious universe, and his duty and destiny there—that is in all cases the primary thing for him, and creatively determines all the rest. That is his religion; or, it may be, his mere scepticism and no religion.—*Carlyle.*

FAITH AND HOPE.

Just before Socrates drinks the poison, he relates to his friends the famous Mythus of Tartarus and Elysium—the final destination of the soul after death according to its deeds in the life. A Mythus, if not exact in details, he says, yet true in the main; and while men cannot get at TRUTH itself, they are bound to seize upon the MOST TRUE, and on that, as on a raft, float over the dangerous sea of life.

" If a man have not Faith, he has surely Hope; and he is bound to act on his highest Hope as on a certainty. Whence does that Hope spring? And he may well embody it in any innocent form of public Faith, which, if not wholly to his mind, is yet a sufficient symbol of what he desires, and at least mixes him up in wholesome communion with his fellow-men."

When at the last hour, says Richter, all other hopes and fears die within us, and knowledge and confidence vanish away, Religion alone survives and blossoms as the night of death closes round.

STUDIES.

STUDIES serve for delight, for ornament, and for ability. Their chief use for delight is in privateness and retiring; for ornament, is in discourse; and for ability, is in the judgment and disposition of business. For expert men can execute, and perhaps judge of particulars one by one; but the general counsels, and the plots and marshallings of affairs, come best from those that are learned. To spend too much time in studies, is sloth, to use them too much for ornament, is affectation; to make judgment wholly by their rules, is the humour of a scholar. They perfect nature, and are perfected by experience: for natural abilities are like natural plants, that need pruning by study; and studies themselves do give forth directions too much at large except they be bounded in by experience. Crafty men contemn studies, simple men admire them, and wise men use them; for they teach not their own use; but that is a wisdom without them, above them, born by observation. Read not to confute and contradict, nor to believe and take for granted; but to weigh and consider.

Reading maketh a full man; conference, a ready man; and writing, an exact man.—*Bacon.*

THE GENTLEMAN'S CALLING.

MEN ought to know that, in the theatre of human life, it is only for God and angels to be Spectators.—*Bacon.*

To make some nook of God's creation a little fruitfuller, better, more worthy of God: to make some human hearts a little wiser, manfuller, happier; more blessed, less accursed!—It is work for a God.—*Carlyle.*

"I lived myself like a Pauper," said Pestalozzi, "to try if I could teach Paupers to live like Men."

"THE ROLLING STONE GATHERS NO MOSS."

OH unwise mortals, that for ever change and shift, saying, "Yonder—not here"—wealth richer than both the Indies lies everywhere for man, if he will endure. Nor his oaks only, and his fruit trees, his very Heart roots itself wherever he will abide; roots itself, draws nourishment from the deep fountains, of universal being! Vagrant Sam Slicks, who rove over the earth " doing strokes of trade "—what wealth have these? Horseloads, shiploads, of white or yellow metal—in very truth, what are these? Slick rests no where—he is homeless! he can build stone or marble houses; but to continue in them is denied him. The wealth of a man is the number of things which he loves and blesses —which he is loved and blessed by. The herdsman in his clay shealing, where his very cow and dog are friends to him, and not a cataract but carries memories for him, and not a mountain-top but nods old recognition; his life, all-encircled as in blessed mother's arms, is it poorer than Slick's, with ass-loads of yellow metal on his back?—*Carlyle.*

Coalescere otio non potes, nisi desinas circumspicere et errare.—*Seneca.*

FRIENDSHIP.

A PRINCIPAL fruit of Friendship is the ease and discharge of the fulness and swelling of the heart, which passions of all kinds do cause and induce. We know diseases of stoppings and suffocations are the most dangerous to the body; and it is not otherwise in the mind. You may take sarza to open the liver; steel to open the spleen; flour of sulphur for the lungs; castoreum for the brain. But no receipt openeth the heart but a true Friend; to whom you may impart griefs, joys, fears, hopes, suspicions, counsels, and whatsoever lieth upon the heart to oppress it, in a kind of civil shift or confession.—*Bacon.*

On ne sauroit conserver longtemps les sentiments qu'on doit avoir pour ses amis et pour ses bienfaiteurs si on se laisse la liberté de parler de leurs défauts.—*Rochefoucauld.*

A modern Greek proverb says

"LOVE YOUR FRIEND WITH HIS FOIBLE."

And finally, beware of long silence and long absence.

Πολλὰς δὴ φιλίας ἀπροσηγορία διέλυσεν.

"OUT OF SIGHT, OUT OF MIND!"

AND so, what we never can replace, the mirror of our former selves, is broken!"

"Old friends," says Selden, "are best. King James used to call for his old shoes, they were easiest to his feet."

Those that have loved longest love best. A sudden blaze of kindness may, by a single blast of coldness, be extinguished: but that fondness which length of time has connected with many circumstances and occasions, though it may be for a while suppressed by disgust and resentment, with or without a cause, is hourly revived by accidental recollection. To those who have lived long together, everything heard, and everything seen, recalls some pleasure communicated, or some benefit conferred; some petty quarrel, or some slight endearment. Esteem of great powers, or amiable qualities newly discovered, may embroider a day or a week; but a friendship of twenty years is interwoven with the texture of life. A friend may be often found and lost; but an *old friend* never can be found, and nature has provided that he cannot easily be lost.—*Johnson.*

AVARICE.

"DREAM OF GOLD, AND WAKE HUNGRY."

WRETCHED are those who in pursuit of gold
Come to mistake the evil for the good:
For getting blinds the inward eye of thought.
—*From the Greek.*

Luther thought that love of money, besides being in other ways unprosperous, foreboded a man's death. "I hear that the Prince Elector George begins to be Covetous, which is a sign of his death very shortly. When I saw Dr. Gode begin to tell his puddings hanging in his chimney, I told him he would not live long, and so it fell out."

But Misers, unfortunately, live long,—their hard habit of mind not affected perhaps by the wear and tear of other passions and affections; perpetually soothed by the sight of increasing wealth, preserved by the very temperance their avarice prescribes.

Goethe defined Italian industry—" not to make Riches, but to live free from Care "—an amiable contrast to much of ours.

THE SOUL IS THE MAN.

WE were indeed

πάντα κόνις καὶ πάντα γέλως, καὶ πάντα τὸ μηδέν,

if we did not feel that we were so.—*Coleridge.*

Man is but a reed—the feeblest thing in nature. But then he is a reed that *thinks*. It needs no gathering up of the powers of nature to crush him: a vapour, a drop of water, will do it. But if the whole universe should fall upon him and crush him, man would yet be more noble than that which slew him, because he *knows* he is dying; and the universe knows it not. Therefore it is that our whole dignity lies but in this—the faculty of Thinking. By this only do we rise in the scale of being; not by any extension of space and duration.

Let us therefore strive to Think Well.—*Pascal.*

FAME.

PRAISE is the reflection of virtue; but it is as the glass or body which giveth reflection. If it be from the common people, it is commonly false and nought; and rather followeth vain persons than virtuous. For the common people understand not many excellent virtues: the lowest virtues draw praise from them; the middle virtues work in them astonishment or admiration; but of the highest virtues they have no sense or perceiving at all; but shows, and *species virtutibus similes*, do best with them.—*Bacon*.

Thus indeed is it always, or nearly always, with true Fame. The heavenly luminary rises amid vapours; stargazers enough must scan it with critical telescopes; it makes no blazing; the world can either look at it, or forbear looking at it. Not until after a time and times does its celestial nature become indubitable. Pleasant, on the other hand, is the blazing of a Tar-barrel: the crowd dance merrily round it with loud huzzaing, universal three times three, and, like Homer's peasants, " bless the useful light." But unhappily it so soon ends in darkness, foul choking smoke, and is kicked into the gutters, a nameless imbroglio of charred staves, pitch cinders, and " *vomissement du diable.*"—*Carlyle*.

THE LIGHTING OF THE TORCH.

THE human mind is so much clogged and borne downward by the strong and early impressions of Sense, that it is wonderful how the ancients should have made such a progress, and seen so far into intellectual matters, without some glimmering of a Divine tradition. Whoever considers a parcel of rude savages left to themselves, how they are sunk and swallowed up in sense and prejudice, and how unqualified by their natural force to emerge from this state, will be apt to think that the first spark of philosophy was derived from heaven, and that it was, as a heathen writer expresses it, θεοπαράδοτος φιλοσοφία.—*Berkeley*.

THE LOOKING-GLASS.

SHE neglects her heart who studies her glass. He who avoids the glass, aghast at the caricature of morally debased features, feels mighty strife of virtue and vice—*Lavater*.

SOLOMON'S SEAL.

THE Sultan asked Solomon for a Signet motto, that should hold good for Adversity or Prosperity. Solomon gave him

"THIS ALSO SHALL PASS AWAY."

"QUID PRO QUO."

IF the doing of Right depends on the receiving of it; if our fellow-men in this world are not Persons, but mere Things, that for services bestowed will return services—Steam-engines that will manufacture calico if we put in coals and water—then, doubtless, the calico ceasing, our coals and water may also rationally cease. But if, on the other hand, our fellow-man is no Steam-engine, but a Man, united with us and with all men in sacred, mysterious, indissoluble bonds, in an all-embracing love that encircles at once the seraph and the glowworm, then will our duties to him rest on quite another basis than this very humble one of Quid pro Quo.—*Carlyle.*

LOVE IS THE TRUE PRICE OF LOVE.

THE WORLD WE LIVE IN.

ALTHOUGH the misery on earth is great indeed, yet the foundation of it rests, after deduction of the partly bearable and partly imaginary evil of the natural world, entirely and alone on the moral dealings of Man.—*Coleridge, from the German.*

Could the world unite in the practice of that despised train of virtues which the divine ethics of our Saviour hath so inculcated upon us, the furious face of things must disappear; Eden would be yet to be found, and the Angels might look down not with pity but joy upon us.—*Sir T. Browne.*

And how are we to set about passing this greatest REFORM BILL?

To two bad verses which I write
Two good shall be appended:
IF EVERY MAN WOULD MEND A MAN,
THEN ALL MANKIND WERE MENDED.

"HAVE AT IT, AND HAVE IT."

One might add many capital English proverbs of this kind, all so characteristic of the activity and boldness of our forefathers.

The Romans had the same. "Vetus proverbium est, Gladiatorem in arenâ capere consilium."

"Not to resolve, is to resolve," says Bacon. "Necessity, and this same '*Jacta est Alea*,' hath many times an advantage, because it awaketh the powers of the mind, and strengtheneth endeavour—'*caeteris pares, necessitate certè superiores.*'"

It has been said, the English are wise in action, not in thought. It has been also said by the head of a people of thought, that, "Doubt *of any kind* can only be removed by action."

While we sit still, we are never the wiser; but going into the river, and moving up and down, is the way to discover its depths and shallows.—*Bacon.*

Men, till a matter be done, wonder that it can be done; and as soon as it is done, wonder again that it was no sooner done.—*Bacon.*

When you tell a man at once, and straight forward, the purpose of any object, he fancies there is nothing in it.—*Goethe.*

"I am persuaded, that if the majority of mankind could be made to see the order of the Universe, such as it is,—as they would not remark in it any virtues attached to certain numbers, nor any properties inherent in certain planets, nor fatalities in certain times and revolutions of these; they would not be able to restrain themselves, on the sight of this admirable regularity and beauty, from crying out with astonishment—What! is this all?"

OMNE IGNOTUM PRO MAGNIFICO.

ANGER.

Is certainly a kind of baseness, as it appears well in the weakness of those subjects in whom it reigns—Children, women, old folks, sick folks.—*Bacon.*

While Sir Gareth of Orkney is disguised as a servant, the kitchen-wench calls out—" Oh Jhesu, merveille have I what manner a man be ye, for it may never ben otherwise but that ye be comen of a noble blood, for so foule ne shamefully dyd never woman rule a knyghte as I have done you, and ever curtoisly ye have suffred me ; and that cam never but of a gentyl blood."—*K. Digby.*

Ung chevalier, n'en doubtez pas,
Doigt ferir hault, et parler bas.

A Gallant man is above ill words. An example we have in the old Lord Salisbury, who was a great wise man. Stone had called some Lord about Court, "*Fool ;* " the Lord complains, and has Stone whipt. Stone cries, " I might have called my Lord of Salisbury *"Fool"* often enough before he would have had me whipt."—*Selden.*

" FAST BIND, FAST FIND."

DIDEROT has convinced himself, and indeed, as above became plain enough, acts on the conviction, that Marriage, contract it, solemnize it, in what way you will, involves a solecism which reduces the amount of it to simple Zero. It is a suicidal covenant ; annuls itself in the very forming. " Thou makest a vow," says he, twice or thrice, as if the argument were a clencher—" Thou makest a vow of Eternal constancy under a rock which is even then crumbling away." True, O Denis : the rock crumbles away ; all things are changing ; man changes faster than most of them: Man changes, and will change : the question then arises, Is it wise in him to tumble forth in headlong obedience to this love of change ; is it so much as possible for him ? Among the dualisms of man's wholly dualistic state, this we might fancy was an observable one ; that along with his unceasing tendency to Change, there is a no less ineradicable tendency to Preserve. How in this world of perpetual flux shall man secure himself the smallest foundation, except hereby alone : that he take pre-assurance of his fate ; that in this and the other high act of his life, his *will,* with all solemnity, abdicate its right to Change ; voluntarily become involuntary, and say once for all—'
—Be there no further dubitation on it !—*Carlyle.*

NOBLES and heralds, by your leave,
　Here lie the bones of Matthew Prior;
He was the son of Adam and Eve—
　Let Nassau or Bourbon go higher.

No Prince, how great soever, begets his Predecessors; and the noblest rivers are not navigable to the Fountain. Even the Parentage of the Nile is yet in obscurity, and 'tis a dispute among authors whether Snow be not the head of his pedigree.—*A. Marvell.*

CURIOSITY.

A MAN that is busy and inquisitive is commonly Envious; for to know much of other men's matters cannot be because all that ado may concern his own estate; therefore it must needs be that he taketh a kind of play-pleasure in looking upon the fortunes of others. Neither can he that mindeth but his own business find much matter for envy; for envy is a gadding passion, and walketh the streets, and doth not keep house. "*Non est Curiosus quin idem sit Maleficus.*"—*Bacon.*

POLEMICS.

Fallacia alia aliam trudit.

"ONE NAIL DRIVES OUT ANOTHER."

THE Polemic annihilates his opponent; but in doing so annihilates himself too; and both are swept away to make room for something other and better.—*Carlyle.*

Generally, when truth is communicated *polemically* (that is, not as it exists in its own inner Simplicity, but as it exists in external relations to error), the temptation is excessive to use those arguments which will tell at the moment upon the crowd of by-standers, in preference to those which will approve themselves ultimately to enlightened disciples. If a man denied himself all specious arguments and all artifices of dialectic subtlety, he must renounce the hopes of a *present* triumph; for the light of absolute truth, on moral or on spiritual themes, is too dazzling to be sustained by the diseased optics of those habituated to darkness, etc.—*Blackwood*, 49.

"Such are the folios of Schoolmen and Theologians. Let us preserve them in our libraries, however, out of reverence for men who fought well in their day with the weapons then in use; and also, as perpetual monuments of what has been thoroughly tried, and found to fail. These folios do very well to block up one of the roads that lead to nothing."

THE TIME OF DAY.

IN the youth of a State, Arms do flourish; in the middle age of a state, Learning; and then both of them together for a time; *in the declining age of a State, mechanical arts and merchandise.—Bacon.*

CRATES saw a young man walking alone, and asked him what he was about. "Conversing with myself." "Take care," said Crates, "you may have got into very bad company."

"Eagles may fly alone; but I believe all the wiser animals live in societies and ordered communities."

"BE NOT SOLITARY, BE NOT IDLE."

"TOUCH PITCH AND BE DAUBED."

NEVER wholly separate in your mind the merits of any political question from the Men who are concerned in it. You will be told, that if a measure is good, what have you to do with the character and views of those who bring it forward? But designing men never separate their plans from their interests, and if you assist them in their schemes, you will find the pretended good in the end thrown aside, or perverted, and the interested object alone compassed; and this perhaps through your means.—*Burke.*

'THE DEVIL CAN QUOTE SCRIPTURE," ETC.

"HE IS WISE THAT FOLLOWS THE WISE."

" WHAT can the incorruptiblest Bobuses elect, if it be not some Bobissimus, should they find such ? "

The Gods, when they appeared to men, were commonly unrecognized of them.—*Goethe.*

THE EYE FOR HISTORY.

THE difference between a great mind's and a little mind's use of History is this: the latter would consider, for instance, what Luther did, taught, or sanctioned; the former, what Luther—a Luther—would *now* do, teach, and sanction.—*Coleridge.*

Some persons are shocked at the cruelty of Walton's Angler, as if the most humane could be expected to trouble themselves about fixing a worm on a hook at a time when they burnt men at a stake in conscience and tender heart. We are not to measure the feelings of one age by those of another. Had Walton lived in our day, he would have been the first to cry out against the cruelty of angling. As it was, his flies and baits were only a part of his tackle.—*Hazlitt.*

" So from the failings of the good to the vices of the bad. ' Give the devil his due.' Henry the Eighth, had he lived now, might be little more than the ' First Gentleman in Europe.' He would but cheat his subjects (if he could), and tease his wives to death, without murdering either. He could not have done what he did had not his people, in some measure, approved it : they were as ready to burn heretics, and disembowel traitors, as he ; and ready to be burned and disembowelled themselves when their turn came. We are surprised to read of Henry's victims praying for him on the scaffold ; but religion and loyalty were one, and men's bodies and souls were stouter."

LEARNING.

WE have to bear in mind what was said after the revival

of letters by men of all creeds, that Learning is the fruit of Piety; in order that, by the sincerity of our hearts, by knowledge of ourselves, and by a conscientious walk in the sight of God, we may guard ourselves against the desire to appear what we are not; that we may never forgive ourselves the slightest desertion from Truth; and that we may never consider as Truth any result of our investigations that flatters our wishes, so long as there is in our conscience the slightest feeling of its being wrong.—*Niebuhr.*

Each man, who has no gift for producing first-rate works, should entirely abstain from the pursuit of Art, and seriously guard himself against any deception on that subject. For it must be owned that in all men there is a certain vague desire to imitate whatever is presented to them; and such desires do not prove at all that we possess the force within us necessary for such enterprises. Look at boys, how, whenever any rope-dancers have been visiting the town, they go scrambling up and down, and balancing on all the planks and beams within their reach, till some other charm calls them off to other sports, for which, perhaps, they are as little suited. Hast thou never marked it in the circle of our friends? No sooner does a Dilettante introduce himself to notice, than numbers of them set themselves to learn playing on his instrument. How many wander back and forward on this bootless way! Happy they who soon detect the chasm that lies between their Wishes and their Powers.—*Wilhelm Meister.*

Nothing in prose or verse was ever yet worth a wisp to rub down the writer with, produced in a " fit of sympathetic admiration."—*Christopher North.*

" SAY-WELL AND DO-WELL END WITH ONE LETTER :
SAY-WELL IS GOOD ; BUT DO-WELL IS BETTER."

PLATO, et Aristoteles, et omnis in diversum itura sapientium turba, plus ex Moribus quam ex Verbis Socratis traxit.—*Seneca.*

Preachers say, " Do as I *say,* not as I *do.*" But if a

physician had the same disease on him that I have, and he should bid me do one thing, and he do another, could I believe him?—*Selden.*

FAMILY TIES.

CERTAINLY, Wife and Children are a kind of discipline of humanity; and single men, though they be many times more Charitable, because their means are less exhaust, on the other side, they are more Cruel and hard-hearted—good to make severe inquisitors, because their tenderness is not so often called upon.—*Bacon.*

A PERSIAN LEGEND.

" A CERTAIN man of Bagdad dreamed one night that in a certain house in a certain street in Cairo he should find a treasure. To Egypt accordingly he set forth, and met in the Desert with one who was on his road from Cairo to Bagdad, having dreamt that in a certain house in a certain street there *he* should find a treasure : and lo, each of these men had been directed to the other's house to find a treasure that only needed looking for in his own."

The error of a lively rake lies in his Passions, which may be reformed; but a dry rogue, who sets up for Judgment, is incorrigible.—*Berkeley.*

Nothing is more unsatisfactory than a mature judgment adopted by an immature mind.—*Goethe.*

ORATORY.

QUESTION was asked of Demosthenes, what was the chief part of an Orator ? He answered, Action. What next ? Action. What next again ? Action. He said it that knew it best; and had by nature himself no advantage in that he commended. A strange thing, that that part of an Orator, which is but superficial, and rather the virtue of a Player, should be placed so high above those other noble parts of invention, elocution, and the rest; nay, almost as if it were all in all. But the reason is plain.

There is in human nature, generally, more of the Fool than of the Wise; and therefore those faculties by which the Foolish part of men's minds is taken, are most potent.—*Bacon.*

Fox used to say, that if a speech *read* very well it was not a good *speech.*

Burke, whose rising emptied the House, is the only one of the Orators of that day who now can be said to survive. The rest were wise in their generation, and are gone with it.

"NEVER SIGH, BUT SEND."

ONE secret act of self-denial, one sacrifice of inclination to duty, is worth all the mere good thoughts, warm feelings, passionate prayers, in which idle people indulge themselves. It will give us more comfort on our death-bed to reflect on one deed of self-denying mercy, purity, or humility, than to recollect the shedding of many tears, and the recurrence of frequent transports, and much spiritual exaltation.

I would have a man disbelieve he can do one jot or tittle more than he has already done; refrain from borrowing aught on the hope of the future, however good a security he seems to be able to show; and never to take his good feelings and wishes in pledge for one single untried deed.

NOTHING BUT PAST ACTS ARE VOUCHERS FOR FUTURE.—*Newman.*

VANITY—BY A FRENCHMAN.

IL n'y a que ceux qui sont Méprisables qui craignent d'être Méprisés.

Si nous ne Flattions pas nous-mêmes la Flatterie des autres ne nous pourroit nuire.

Si nous n'avions point d'Orgueil, nous ne nous plaindrions pas de celui des autres.

Les passions les plus violentes nous laissent quelquefois du relâche; mais la Vanité nous agite toujours.

M.W.

PREJUDICE.

No one has a right to congratulate his neighbour that a deep-rooted Conviction has departed out of his mind, unless a Truth has replaced it. Earnest feelings may have been entwined about it, and may perish with it—how likely that the void in the heart will be supplied with worse vanities than those which have been abandoned.—*Eustace Connay.*

HYPOCRISY.

THERE is no vice, says Rochefoucauld, that is not better than the means we take to conceal it.

A vice, determining outwardly, is nearer to extinction than that which smoulders inwardly.

It is not in human nature to deceive Others, for any long time, without, in a measure, deceiving Ourselves.—*Newman.*

The Mask grows one with the Face, and so we see it in the glass.

The beginning of self-deception is when we begin to find *reasons* for our *propensities.*

The chief stronghold of Hypocrisy is to be always judging one another.—*Milton.*

To those to whom it is of no moment to say, "Do all as if God were looking at thee," Seneca's rule may apply. "Do all as if some Man were looking at thee."

Finally, Xenophon says the easiest way to *seem* good is to *be* good.

NO FABLE.

AN ancient Oak being cut down, and split through the midst, out of the very heart of the tree crept a large Toad, and walked away with all the speed he could. Now how long, may we probably imagine, had this creature continued there? It is not unlikely it might have remained in its nest above a hundred years. It is not improbable it was nearly, if not altogether, coeval with the oak ; having been, some way or other, enclosed therein at the time of planting.

This poor animal had organs of sense, yet it had not any sensation. It had eyes, yet no ray of light ever entered its black abode. There was nothing to hear, nothing to taste or smell, for there was no air to circulate, there was no space to move. From the very first instant of its existence, there it was shut up in impenetrable darkness. It was shut up from the sun, moon, and stars, and from the beautiful face of nature ; indeed, from the whole visible world, as much as if it had no being.

He who lives "without God in the world" is, in respect to the Invisible world, as this toad was in respect to the Visible world.—*J. Wesley.*

THE ART OF GOVERNING.

To learn Obeying is the fundamental art of Governing How much would any Serene Highness have learned, had he travelled through the world with water jug and empty wallet, *sine omni impensâ*, and at his victorious return sat down, not to newspaper paragraphs and city illuminations, but at the foot of St. Edmund's shrine, to shackles and bread and water ! He that cannot be servant of many, will never be master, true guide, and deliverer, of many ; that is the true meaning of mastership. Heavens ! had a Duke of Logwood, now rolling sumptuously to his place in the Collective Wisdom, but himself happened to plough daily, at one time with 7s. 6d. a week, with no out-door relief—what a light, unquenchable by logic, and statistic, and arithmetic, would he have thrown on several things for him.—*Carlyle.*

The hall was the place where the great lord used to eat (wherefore else were the halls made so large ?), where he saw his tenants about him. He never ate in private, except in time of sickness. When once he became a thing cooped up, all his greatness was spoiled. Nay, the king himself used to eat in the hall, and his lords sat with him—and thus he understood Men.—*Selden.*

"THE FAT SOW KNOWS NOT WHAT THE LEAN ONE THINKS."

MELANCHOLY AND MADNESS.

LET him not be alone or idle, in any kind of melancholy, but still accompanied with such friends and familiars he most affects, neatly drest, washt, and combed, according to his ability, at least in clean linen, spruce, handsome, decent, sweet, and good apparel; for nothing sooner dejects a man than want, squalor, and nastiness, foul or old clothes out of fashion.—*Burton.*

If I could get his beard and hood removed I should reckon it a weighty point; for nothing more exposes us to madness than distinguishing ourselves from others, and nothing more contributes to maintain our common sense than living in the universal way with multitudes of men.—*Goethe.*

BE NOT SOLITARY, BE NOT IDLE.

TOSSING THE THOUGHTS.

WHOSOEVER hath his mind fraught with many Thoughts, his wits and understanding do clarify and break up in the communication and discoursing with another; he tosseth his thoughts more easily; he marshalleth them more orderly; he seeth how they look when they are turned into words: finally, he waxeth wiser than himself; and that more by an hour's Discourse than by a day's Meditation. It was well said by Themistocles to the king of Persia, "that Speech was like cloth of Arras opened and put abroad; whereby the imagery doth appear in figure; whereas in Thoughts they lie but in packs."

Neither is this second fruit of Friendship in opening the understanding restrained only to such friends as are able to give a man counsel (they indeed are best), but even without that, a man learneth of himself, and bringeth his own thoughts to light, and whetteth his wits as against a stone, which itself cuts not. In a word, a man were better relate himself to a picture or a statue, than to suffer his thoughts to pass in smother.—*Bacon.*

POLONIUS
PETIT À PETIT
L'OISEAU FAIT SON NID.

LET him take heart who does but, even the least little, advance.—*Plato*.

   And I must work through months of toil,
    And years of cultivation,
  Upon my proper patch of soil,
   To grow my own plantation :
  I'll take the showers as they fall,
    I will not vex my bosom ;
  Content if at the end of all
   A little garden blossom.—*A. Tennyson*.

A HANDFUL OF ARROWS.

EVERY new institution should be but a fuller development of, addition to, what already exists.—*Niebuhr*.

He that changes his party from Humour is not more virtuous than he who changes it for Interest; he loves Himself better than Truth.—*Johnson*.

Opposition to Authority is a good reason, not for suppressing a theory, but for delivering it in modest and tolerant language.—*Goethe*.

" He who tells *all* he knows, will also tell *more* than he knows."

Show me a man who loves no one place better than another, and I will show you a man who loves nothing but himself.—*Southey*.

The great Art now to be learned is the Art of staying at Home.

Upon the same Man, as upon a vineyard planted on a mount, there grow more kinds of wine than one : on the south side, something little worse than Nectar ; on the north, something little better than Vinegar.—*Richter*.

What has Life to show us but the glass-door of heaven ?

Through it we see the highest beauty and the highest bliss—but it is not open.[1]—*Richter.*

The grand basis of Christianity is broad enough for the whole bulk of Mankind to stand on, and join hands, as children of one family.—*Lancaster.*

Who hunt the World's delight too late their hunting rue,
When it a Lion proves the hunter to pursue.
Sin not until 'tis left will truly sinful seem;
A man must be Awake ere he can tell his Dream.—*Trench.*

AESTHETICS.

MEMORABLE—because of the high Office of the speaker, and the Place he spoke in—was the praise addressed by Lord Palmerston to an English Gentleman, who had been visiting Naples, not to explore volcanoes and excavated cities, but to go down into the prisons and declare to all Europe the horrors of Tyranny and misgovernment.

OH would " YOUNG ENGLAND " half the study thrown
Into Greek annals turn upon our own;
Would spell the Actual Present's open book
Where men may read strange matters—learn that Cook,
Tailor, and Dancer, are ill Heraldry,
Compared with LIVING PLAIN AND THINKING HIGH:
That Fools enough have travell'd up the Rhine;
Discuss'd Italian Operas, French Wine,
Gaped at the Pope, call'd Raffaelle "*divine*"—
Yea, could the Nation with one single will
Renounce the Arts she only bungles still,
And stick to that which of all nations best
She knows, and which is well worth all the rest,

---

[1] " Even that vulgar and tavern music, which makes one man Merry and another Mad, strikes in me a deep fit of Devotion, and a profound contemplation of the FIRST COMPOSER; there is something in it of Divinity more than the Ear discovers: it is an Hieroglyphical and shadowed lesson of the Whole World, and creatures of God; such a Melody to the Ear, as the whole world, well understood, would afford the Understanding—a sensible fit of that Harmony which Intellectually sounds in the Ears of God."
—*Sir T. Browne.*

Just Government—by the ancient Three-fold Cord
Faster secured than by the point of Sword—
Would we but teach THE PEOPLE, from whom Power
Grows slowly up into the Sovereign Flower,
By all just dealing with them, head and heart
Wisely and religiously to do their part;
And heart and *hand*, whene'er the hour may come,
Answer Brute force, that will not yet be dumb.—
Lest, like some mighty ship that rides the sea,
Old England, one last refuge of the Free,
Should, while all Europe Thunders with the waves
Of war, which shall be Tyrants, Czars, or Slaves,
Suddenly, with sails set and timbers true,
Go down, betrayed by a degenerate crew!

"SECOND THOUGHTS ARE BEST."

"No," says the Guesser at Truth, "*First* Thoughts are best, being those of Generous Impulse; whereas *Second* Thoughts are those of Selfish Prudence; *best* in worldly wisdom; but, in a higher economy, *worst*."

The proverb, in fact, as so many of its kind are said to do, tells just *half* the truth;—needing its converse to complete the whole.

For, if a man be Generous by nature, then it may be as the Guesser at Truth says. But if he be *un*generous by nature, then the order is reversed, and the proverb will hold even in that better economy adverted to—his First Thoughts will be those of Selfish Policy; but his Second may be those, not Generous Impulse indeed, but of a Generous Religion or Philosophy.

LOT IN LIFE.

"EVERY PATH HAS A PUDDLE."

WHATSOEVER is under the moon is subject to corruption—alteration; and so long as thou livest upon earth look not for other. Thou shalt not here find peaceable and cheerful days, quiet times; but rather clouds, storms, calumnies

—such is our fate. And as those errant planets in their distinct orbs have their several motions, sometimes direct, stationary, retrograde, in apogeo, perigeo, oriental, occidental, combust, feral, free, and (as our astrologers will) have their fortitudes and debilities, by reason of those good and bad irradiations, conferred to each other's site in the heavens, in their terms, houses, cases, detriments, etc. ;—so we rise and fall in this world, ebb and flow, in and out, reared and dejected; lead a troublesome life, subject to many accidents and casualties of fortunes, infirmities, as well from ourselves as others.

Yea, but thou thinkest thou art more miserable than the rest ; other men are happy in respect of thee ; their miseries are but flea-bitings to thine ; thou alone art unhappy, none so bad as thyself. Yet if, as Socrates said, all men in the world should come and bring their grievances together, of body, mind, fortune, sores, ulcers, madness, epilepsies, agues, and all those common calamities of beggary, want, servitude, imprisonment—and lay them on a heap to be equally divided—wouldst thou share alike, and take thy portion, or be as thou art ? Without question thou wouldst be as thou art.

Every man knows his own, but not others' defects and miseries ; and 'tis the nature of all men still to reflect upon themselves, their own misfortunes ; not to examine or consider other men's ; not to confer themselves with others ; to recount their own miseries, but not their good gifts, fortunes, benefits, which they have ; to ruminate on their adversity, but not once to think on their prosperity —not what they have, but what they want ; to look still on those that go before, but not on those infinite numbers that come after. Whereas many a man would think himself in heaven, a petty prince, if he had but the least part of that fortune which thou so much repinest at, abhorrest, and accountest a most vile and wretched estate. How many thousands want that which thou hast! How many myriads of poor slaves, captives, of such as work day and night in coal-pits, tin-mines, with sore toil to maintain a poor living ; of such as labour in body and mind, live in extreme anguish and pain ; all which thou are freed from! "*O fortunatos nimium sua si bona nôrint!*" Thou art most happy, if thou couldst be content and acknowledge thy happiness; *rem carendo, non fruendo, cognoscimus;* when thou shalt hereafter come to want that which thou now loathest, abhorrest, and art weary of and tired with, when 'tis past, thou wilt say thou wert most happy; and after a little miss, wish with all thine heart thou hadst the same content again—mightest lead but such a life—a world for such a life! The remembrance of it is pleasant. Be silent then; rest satisfied—*desine; intuensque in aliorum infortunia solare mentem;* comfort thyself with other men's misfortunes; and as the mouldi-warp in Aesop told the fox, complaining for want of a tail, and the rest of his companions—*Tacete, quando me oculis captum videtis*—" You complain of toys; but I am blind—be quiet "—I say to thee, Be satisfied. It is recorded of the hares, that with a general consent they went to drown themselves, out of a feeling of their misery; but when they saw a company of frogs more fearful than they were, they began to take courage and comfort again. Confer thine estate with others. *Similes aliorum respice casus, Mitius ista feres.* Be content, and rest satisfied, for thou art well in respect of others: be thankful for that thou hast; that God hath done for thee; He hath not made thee a monster, a beast, a base creature, as He might; but a Man, a Christian—such a man.—Consider aright of it, thou art full well as thou art.—*Burton.*

> FOR EVERY ILL BENEATH THE SUN
> THERE IS SOME REMEDY, OR NONE.
> SHOULD THERE BE ONE, RESOLVE TO FIND IT;
> IF NOT, SUBMIT, AND NEVER MIND IT.

INDEX TO "POLONIUS"

A
Action and Aspiration, 132, 159
Aesthetics, 166
Anger, 154
Art, 137
Atheism, 120
Avarice, 150

B
Best in the Barrel, 119
Building, 109

C
Calling—Choice of, 136
Chivalry—New, 113
Content, 113, 137
Conversation, etc., 114, 126
Cure or Endure, 99
Curiosity, 156

D
Date and Dabitur, 141
Diplomacy, 137
Disputes, 146
Dives, 111

E
Eagles no Fly-Catchers, 142
Envy, 136
Everybody's Fable, 97
Expense, 135
Eye—what it Sees, 102

F
Fame, 151
Family Ties, 160
Faust, 118
Forgive and Forget, 104
Forms and Ceremonies, 109
  „ of Behaviour, 146
Found by one's Sin, 106
Friendship, 149
Fun in the Fiddle, 101

G
Genius, 146
Gentleman, 115, 148
Giving and Asking, 130
Government—Art of, 163
Guile and Guilelessness, 120, 122
Guilt, 128

H
Handful of Arrows, 165
Have at it, have it, 154
History—Eye for, 158
Honesty, 100
Humanity, 127
Hypocrisy, 162

I
Idleness, 109
Ignotum Magnificum, 154
Imaginary Evils, 132
Inconstancy, 104
Indifference, 110

K
Knowledge, Opinion, Ignorance, 116
Knowledge and Half-knowledge, 110

L
Lavater—Chapter from, 123
Learning 123, 158
Liberty, 129
Life. 98, 131
Lighting the Torch, 152
Looking-Glass, 152
Lot in Life, 167
Love, 134

M
Melancholy and Madness, 164
Mercy and Valour, 99
Mimicry, 125
Modesty, 143
Music, 145

INDEX

N
Native Air, 127
Nature and Habit, 143
Never Sigh, but Send, 161

O
Old Age, 121
Oratory, 160
Our Time, 135

P
Pedigree, 156
Pegasus in Harness, 116
Penny wise, etc., 99
Persian Legend, 160
Petit à petit, 165
Philosopher, 98
Plain Living and High Thinking, 115
Poetry, 127
Polemics, 156
Poor—the, 105
Poverty and Riches, 126, 135
Power and Place, 104, 114, 137
Precedence, 131
Prejudice, 144, 162

Q
Quid pro Quo, 153

R
Religion, 147
River—the Great, 107, 136
Rolling Stone, 126, 148

S
Satiety, 122
Say Well and Do Well, 159
Second Thoughts, 167
Seed-sowing, 101
Self-Contemplation, 110

Self-Knowledge, 97
„ Love, 144
„ Judging of others, 143
„ Isolation, 118
Sickness, 137
Socratis Paternoster, 130
Solitude, 157, 164
Solomon s Seal, 153
Soul is the Man, 151
Studies, 148
Superstition, 142

T
Taste, 112
Teaching, 138
Three Races, 106
Time of Day, 157
Thought-tossing, 164
To-day and To-morrow, 119
Tory, 138
Touch Pitch——, 157
Travel, 117
Truth and Justice, 135

V
Vanity, 127, 161
Vent au Visage, 131

W
War, 134
Weakness and Falsity, 103, 113
Weight and Worth, 119
When the Cup is fullest, 97
Will and Reason, 125
Will and Wish, 102
Wit, 96, 122
Words and Deeds, 115
World we live in, 153
World's Pulse, 112
Writing Well, 139

SALÁMÁN AND ABSÁL

I

Prologue

    O Thou, whose Memory quickens Lovers' Souls,
Whose Fount of Joy renews the Lover's Tongue,
Thy Shadow falls across the World, and They
Bow down to it; and of the Rich in Beauty
Thou art the Riches that make Lovers mad.
Not till thy Secret Beauty through the cheek
Of Laila smite doth she inflame Majnún;[1]
And not till Thou have sugar'd Shírín's Lip
The Hearts of those Two Lovers fill with Blood.[1]
For Lov'd and Lover are not but by Thee,
Nor Beauty; Mortal Beauty but the Veil
Thy Heavenly hides behind, and from itself
Feeds, and our Hearts yearn after as a Bride
That glances past us Veil'd—but ever so
As none the Beauty from the Veil may know.
How long wilt thou continue thus the World
To cozen[2] with the Fantom of a Veil
From which Thou only peepest?—Time it is
To unfold thy perfect Beauty. I would be
Thy Lover, and Thine only—I, mine Eyes
Seal'd in the Light of Thee to all but Thee,
Yea, in the Revelation of Thyself
Self-Lost, and Conscience-quit of Good and Evil.
Thou movest under all the Forms of Truth,

---

[1] All well-known types of Eastern Lovers. Shirin and her Suitors figure in Section xx.
[2] The Persian Mystics also represent the Deity Dice-ing with Human Destiny behind the curtain.

Under the Forms of all created things;
Look whence I will, still nothing I discern
But Thee in all the Universe, in which
Thyself Thou dost invest, and through the Eyes
Of MAN, the subtle Censor[1] scrutinize.
To thy Harîm DIVIDUALITY
No Entrance finds—no Word of THIS and THAT;
Do Thou my separate and Derivéd Self
Make one with thy Essential! Leave me room
On that Diván which leaves no room for Two:[2]
Lest, like the simple Kurd of whom they tell,
I grow perplext, O God! 'twixt " I " and " Thou ":
If I—this Dignity and Wisdom whence?
If THOU—then what this abject Impotence?

> *A Kurd perplext by Fortune's Frolics*
> *Left his Desert for the City.*
> *Sees a City full of Noise and*
> *Clamour, agitated People,*
> *Hither, Thither, Back and Forward*
> *Running, some intent on Travel,*
> *Others home again returning,*
> *Right to Left, and Left to Right,*
> *Life-disquiet everywhere!*
> *Kurd, when he beholds the Turmoil,*
> *Creeps aside, and, Travel-weary,*
> *Fain would go to Sleep; " But," saith he,*
> *" How shall I in all this Hubbub*
> *Know myself again on waking?"*
> *So by way of Recognition*
> *Ties a Pumpkin round his Foot,*

---

[1] "The Apollonius of Keats' *Lamia*."
[2] This Súfi identification with Deity (further illustrated in the story of Section xx) is shadowed in a parable of Jelaladdin, of which here is an outline. "One knocked at the Beloved's Door; and a Voice asked from within, 'Who is there?' And he answered, 'It is I.' Then the Voice said, 'This House will not hold Me and Thee.' And the Door was not opened. Then went the Lover into the Desert, and fasted and prayed in solitude. And after a Year he returned, and knocked again at the Door. And again the Voice asked, 'Who is there?' And he said, 'It is Thyself!'—and the Door was opened to him."

*And turns to Sleep. A Knave that heard him
Crept behind, and slyly watching
Slips the Pumpkin off the Sleeper's
Ancle, ties it round his own,
And so down to sleep beside him.
By-and-by the Kurd awaking
Looks directly for his Signal—
Sees it on another's Ancle—
Cries aloud, " O Good-for-Nothing
Rascal to perplex me so !
That by you I am bewilder'd,
Whether I be I or no !
If I—the Pumpkin why on You ?
If You—then Where am I, and Who ? "*

II

O God ! this poor bewildered Kurd am I,
Than any Kurd more helpless !—Oh, do Thou
Strike down a Ray of Light into my Darkness !
Turn by Thy Grace these Dregs into pure Wine,
To recreate the Spirits of the Good !
Or if not that—yet as the little Cup
Whose name I go by [1] not unworthy found
To pass thy salutary Vintage round !
I listen in the Tavern of Sweet Songs,
And catch no echo of their Harmony :
The Guests have drunk the Wine and are departed,
Leaving their empty Bowls behind—not one
To carry on the Revel Cup in hand !
Up, Jámi, then ! And whether Lees or Wine
To offer—boldly offer it in Thine !
And yet, how long, Jámi, in this Old House
Stringing thy Pearls upon a Harp of Song ?
Year after year striking up some new Song,
The Breath of some old Story ? [2] Life is gone,

---

[1] The poet's name " *Jámi* " also signifies " *A Cup.*" The poet's Yúsuf and Zulaikha opens also with this Divine Wine, the favourite Symbol of Hafiz and other Persian Mystics. The Tavern spoken of is The World.

[2] *Yúsuf and Zulaikha, Layla and Majnún,* etc.

And yet the Song is not the last; my Soul
Is spent—and still a Story to be told!
And I, whose Back is crookéd as the Harp
I still keep tuning through the Night till Day!
That Harp untun'd by Time—the Harper's hand
Shaking with Age—how shall the Harper's hand
Repair its cunning, and the sweet old Harp
Be modulated as of old ? Methinks
'Twere time to break and cast it in the Fire ;
Yea, sweet the Harp that can be sweet no more,
To cast it in the Fire—the vain old Harp
That can no more sound Sweetness to the Ear,
But burn'd may breathe sweet Attar to the Soul,
And comfort so the Faith and Intellect,
Now that the Body looks to Dissolution.
My teeth fall out—my two Eyes see no more
Till by Feringhí Glasses turn'd to Four ; [1]
Pain sits with me sitting behind my knees,
From which I hardly rise unhelpt of hand ;
I bow down to my root, and like a Child
Yearn, as is likely, to my Mother Earth,
Upon whose bosom I shall cease to moan and weep,
And on my Mother's Bosom fall asleep.

The House in Ruin, and its Music heard
No more within, nor at the Door of Speech,
Better in Silence and Oblivion
To fold me Head and Foot, remembering
What that BELOVED to the Master whisper'd :—
" No longer think of Rhyme, but Think of ME "—
Of Whom ?—Of Him whose Palace THE SOUL is,
And Treasure-house—who notices and knows
Its Income and Out-going, and *then* comes
To fill it when the Stranger is departed.
Yea ; but Whose Shadow being Kings—whose Attributes
The Type of Theirs—their Wrath and Favour His—
Lo ! in the celebration of His Glory

---

[1] First notice of Spectacles in Oriental Poetry, perhaps.

The KING himself comes on me unaware,
And suddenly arrests me for his own.
Wherefore once more I take—best quitted else—
The Field of Verse, to chaunt that double Praise,
And in that Memory, refresh my Soul
Until I grasp the Skirt of Living Presence.

> *One who travel'd in the Desert*
> *Saw* MAJNÚN *where he was sitting*
> *All alone like a Magician*
>   *Tracing Letters in the Sand.*
> *" O distracted Lover ! writing*
> *What the Sword-Wind of the Desert*
> *Undecyphers soon as written*
> *So that none who travels after*
> *Shall be able to interpret ! "—*
> MAJNÚN *answer'd—" I am writing*
> *Only for myself, and only*
>   *'* LAILA,*' were it only '* LAILA,*'*
> *Yet a* BOOK *of Love and Passion ;*
> *And, with but her Name to doat on,*
> *Amorously I caress it*
> *As it were Herself, and sip*
> *Her Presence till I drink her Lip."*

III

When Night had thus far brought me with my Book
In middle Thought Sleep robb'd me of myself;
And in a Dream Myself I seem'd to see,
Walking along a straight and even Road,
And clean as is the Soul of the Sufí;
A road whose spotless Surface neither Breeze
Lifted in Dust, nor mix'd the Rain to Mire.
There I, methought, was pacing tranquilly,
When, on a sudden, the tumultuous Shout
Of Soldiery behind broke on mine Ear,
And took away my Wit and Strength for Fear.
I look'd about for Refuge, and Behold !

A Palace was before me; whither running
For Refuge from the coming Soldiery,
Suddenly from the Troop a Shâhzemân,[1]
By Name and Nature HASAN—on the Horse
Of Honour mounted—robed in Royal Robes,
And wearing a White Turban on his Head,
Turn'd his Rein tow'rd me, and with smiling Lips
Open'd before my Eyes the Door of Peace.
Then, riding up to me, dismounted; kiss'd
My hand, and did me Courtesy; and I,
How glad of his Protection, and the Grace
He gave it with!—Who then of gracious Speech
Many a Jewel utter'd; but of these
Not one that in my Ear till Morning hung,
When waking on my Bed, my waking Wit
I question'd what the Vision meant, it answered;
" This Courtesy and Favour of the Shah
Foreshows the fair Acceptance of thy Verse,
Which lose no moment pushing to Conclusion."
This hearing, I address'd me like a Pen
To steady Writing; for perchance, I thought,
From the same Fountain whence the Vision grew
The Interpretation also may come True.

Breathless ran a simple Rustic
To a Cunning Man of Dreams;
" Lo, this morning I was dreaming—
And, methought, in yon deserted
Village wander'd—all about me
Shattered Houses—and, Behold!
Into one, methought, I went—and
Search'd —and found a Hoard of Gold!"
Quoth the Prophet in Derision,
" O Thou Jewel of Creation,
Go and sole your feet like Horses,

[1] " Lord of the World, SOVEREIGN; HASAN, BEAUTIFUL, GOOD."
HASAN BEG of Western Persia, famous for his Beauty, had helped
Jámi with Escort in a dangerous Pilgrimage. He died (as History
and a previous line in the Original tell) before *Salámán* was written,
and was succeeded by his son, YÁCÚB.

*And returning to your Village
Stamp and scratch with Hoof and Nail,
And give Earth so sound a Shaking,
She must hand you something up."
Went at once the unsuspecting
Countryman ; with hearty Purpose
Set to work as he was told ;
And, the very first Encounter,
Struck upon his Hoard of Gold !*

Until Thou hast thy purpose by the Hilt,
Catch at it boldly—or Thou never wilt.

IV

THE STORY

A SHAH there was who ruled the realm of YUN,[1]
And wore the Ring of Empire of Sikander ;
And in his reign a SAGE, who had the Tower
Of Wisdom of so strong Foundation built
That Wise Men from all Quarters of the World,
To catch the Word of Wisdom from his Lip
Went in a girdle round him.—Which THE SHAH
Observing, took him to his Secresy ;
Stirr'd not a Step, nor set Design afoot,
Without that SAGE'S sanction ; till, so counsell'd,
No Nation of the World or Nation's Chief
Who wore the Ring but under span of his
Bow'd down the Neck ; then rising up in Peace
Under his Justice grew, and knew no Wrong,
And in their strength was his Dominion strong.

The Sháh that has not Wisdom in Himself,
Nor has a Wise Man for his Counsellor,

---

[1] Or " Yavan," Son of Japhet, from whom the country was called " Yúnan "— Ionia, meant by the Persian to express GREECE generally. Sikander is, of course, Alexander the Great, of whose Ethics Jámi wrote, as Nizami of his Deeds.

The Wand of his Authority falls short,
And his dominion crumbles at the Base.
For he, discerning not the Characters
Of Tyranny and Justice, confounds both,
Making the World a Desert, and the Fount
Of Justice and Seráb.[1] Well was it said,
"*Better just Kafir than Believing Tyrant.*"

God said to the Prophet David,—
"*David, speak, and to the Challenge
Answer of the Faith within Thee.
Even Unbelieving Princes,
Ill-reported if Unworthy,
Yet, if They be Just and Righteous,
Were their Worship of* THE FIRE—
*Even These unto Themselves
Reap Glory and redress the World.*"

V

One night THE SHAH of Yúnan, as his wont,
Consider'd of his Power, and told his State,
How great it was, and how about him sat
The Robe of Honour, of Prosperity;
Then found he nothing wanted to his Heart
Unless a Son, who his Dominion
And Glory might inherit after him.
And then he turn'd him to THE SAGE, and said;
"O Thou, whose wisdom is the Rule of Kings—
(Glory to God who gave it!) Answer me;
Is any Blessing better than a Son?
Man's prime Desire; by which his Name and He
Shall live beyond Himself; by whom his Eyes
Shine living, and his Dust with Roses blows;
A Foot for thee to stand on he shall be,
A Hand to stop thy Falling; in his Youth

---

[1] "Mirâge; but, of two Foreign Words, why not the more original Persian? Identical with the Hebrew Shárâb; as in Isaiah xv. 7, 'The *Shárâb* (or *Mirâge*) shall become a Lake'; rather, and better, than our Version, "The parched Ground shall become a Pool." See Gesenius.

Thou shalt be Young, and in his Strength be Strong;
Sharp shall he be in Battle as a Sword,
A Cloud of Arrows on the Enemy's Head;
His voice shall cheer his Friends to better Plight,
And turn the Foeman's Glory into Flight."

Thus much of a Good Son, whose wholesome growth
Approves the Root he grew from; but for one
Kneaded of Evil—well, could one undo
His generation, and as early pull
Him and his Vices from the String of Time.
Like Noah's, puff'd with Ignorance and Pride,
Who felt the Stab of "HE IS NONE OF THINE!"
All perish'd in the Deluge.[1] And because
All are not Good, be slow to pray for One,
Whom having you may have to pray to lose.

> *Crazy for the Curse of Children,*
> *Ran before the Sheikh a Fellow,*
> *Crying out, " Oh, hear and help me!*
> *Pray to Allah from my Clay*
> *To raise me up a fresh young Cypress,*
> *Who my Childless Eyes may lighten,*
> *With the Beauty of his Presence."*

[1] In the *Kurán* God engages to save Noah and his Family,—meaning all who believed in the Warning. One of Noah's Sons (Canaan or Yam, some think) would not believe. "And the Ark swam with them between waves like Mountains, and Noah called up to his Son, who was separated from him, saying, 'Embark with us, my Son, and stay not with the unbelievers.' He answered, 'I will get on a Mountain which will secure me from the Water.' Noah replied, 'There is no security this Day from the Decree of God, except for him of whom he shall have Mercy.' And a wave passed between them, and he became one of those who were drowned. And it was said, 'Oh Earth, swallow up thy Waters, and Thou, Oh Heaven, withhold thy Rain!' And immediately the Water obeyed and the Decree was fulfilled, and the Ark rested on the mountain Al Judi, and it was said, 'Away with the ungodly People!' Noah called upon his Lord and said, 'O Lord, verily my Son is of my Family, and Thy Promise is True, for Thou art of those who exercise Judgment.' God answered, 'O Noah, verily he is not of thy Family; this intercession of thine for him is not a righteous work.'"
—*Sale's Kurán*, vol. ii. p. 21.

Said the Skeikh, " Be wise, and leave it
Wholly in the Hand of Allah,
Who, whatever we are after,
Understands our Business best."
But the man persisted, saying,
" Sheikh, I languish in my Longing ;
Help, and set my Prayer a-going !"
Then the Sheikh held up his Hand—
Pray'd—his Arrow flew to Heaven—
From the Hunting-ground of Darkness
Down a musky Fawn of China
Brought a Boy—who, when the Tender
Shoot of Passion in him planted
Found sufficient Soil and Sap,
Took to drinking with his Fellows ;
From a Corner of the House-top
Ill affronts a Neighbour's Wife,
Draws his Dagger on the Husband,
Who complains before the Justice,
And the Father has to pay.
Day and Night the Youngster's Doings
Such—the talk of all the City ;
Nor, Entreaty, Threat, or Counsel
Held him; till the Desperate Father
Once more to the Sheikh a-running,
Catches at his Garment, crying,
" Sheikh, my only Hope and Helper !
One more Prayer ! That God who laid,
Will take that trouble from my Head !"
But the Sheikh replied : " Remember
How that very day I warn'd you
Better not importune Allah ;
Unto whom remains no other
Prayer, unless to pray for Pardon.
When from this World we are summon'd
On to bind the pack of Travel
Son or Daughter ill shall help us ;
Slaves we are and unencumber'd,
But may do the Master's mind ;
And, whatever he may order,
Do it with a Will Resign'd."

VI

When the Sharp-witted SAGE
Had heard these sayings of the SHAH he said :
" O SHAH, who would not be the Slave of Lust
Must still endure the sorrow of no Son.
—Lust that makes blind the Reason ; Lust that makes
A Devil's self seem Angel to our Eyes ;
A Cataract that, carrying havoc with it,
Confounds the prosperous House ; a Road of Mire
Where whoso falls he rises not again ;
A Wine of which whoever tastes shall see
Redemption's face no more—one little Sip
Of that delicious and unlawful drink,
Making crave much, and hanging round the Palate
Till it become a Ring to lead thee by [1]
(Putting the rope in a Vain Woman's hand),
Till thou thyself go down the Way of Nothing."
For what is Woman ? A foolish, Faithless Thing—
To whom the Wise Self-subjected himself,
Deep sinks beneath the folly he sets up.
A very Káfir in Rapacity :
Clothe her a hundred Years in Gold and Jewel,
Her Garment with Brocade of Susa braided,
Her very Night-gear wrought in Cloth of Gold,
Dangle her Ears with Ruby and with Pearl,
Her house with Golden Vessels all a-blaze,
Her tables loaded with the Fruit of Kings,
Ispahan Apples, Pomegrantes of Yazd ;
And, be she thirsty, from a Jewell'd Cup
Drinking the Water of the Well of Life—
One little twist of Temper,—all you've done
Goes all for nothing. ' Torment of my life ! '
She cries, ' What have you ever done for me ! '—
Her brows' white Tablet—Yes—'tis uninscrib'd
With any Letter of Fidelity ;

---

[1] "*Mihar*"—a piece of Wood put through a Camel's Nose to guide him by.

Who ever read it there? Lo, in your Bosom
She lies for Years—you turn away a moment,
And she forgets you—worse, if, as you turn,
Her eyes should light on any Younger Lover."

> *Once upon the Throne of Judgment,*
> *Telling one another Secrets,*
> *Sate* SULAYMAN *and* BALKÍS;[1]
> *The Hearts of Both were turn'd to Truth,*
> *Unsullied by Deception.*
> *First the King of Faith* SULAYMAN
> *Spoke—" Though mine the Ring of Empire,*
> *Never any Day that passes*
> *Darkens any one my Door-way*
> *But into his Hand I look—*
> *And he who comes not empty-handed*
> *Grows to honour in mine Eyes."*
> *After this,* BALKÍS *a Secret*
> *From her hidden Bosom utter'd,*
> *Saying: " Never Night or Morning*
> *Comely Youth before me passes*
> *Whom I look not longing after;*
> *Saying to myself, ' Oh were he*
> *Comforting of my Sick Soul!'"*

" If this, as wise Ferdúsi says, the Curse
Of Better Women, what should be the Worse?"

VII

THE SAGE his Satire ended; and THE SHAH
With Magic-mighty WISDOM his pure WILL
Leaguing, its Self-fulfilment wrought from Heaven.
And lo! from Darkness came to Light A CHILD,
Of Carnal Composition Unattaint —
A Rosebud blowing on the Royal Stem,—
A perfume from the realm of Wisdom wafted;
The Crowning Jewel of the Crown; a Star
Under whose augury triumph'd the Throne.
For whose auspicious Name they clove the Words

[1] Solomon and the Queen of Sheba.

" SALÁMAT "—Incolumity from Evil—
And " AUSEMÁN "—the Heav'n from which he came—
And hail'd him by the title of SALÁMÁN.
And whereas from no Mother Milk he drew,
They chose for him a Nurse—her name ABSÁL—
Her Years not twenty—from the Silver Line
Dividing the Musk-Harvest of her Hair
Down to her foot that trampled Crowns of Kings,
A Moon of Beauty Full : who thus elect
SALÁMÁN of Auspicious Augury,
Should carry in the Garment of her Bounty,
Should feed him with the Flowing of her Breast.
As soon as she had opened Eyes on him,
She closed those Eyes to all the World beside,
And her Soul crazed, a-doting on her Jewel,—
Her Jewel in a Golden Cradle set ;
Opening and shutting which her Day's Delight,
To gaze upon his heart-inflaming Cheek—
Upon the Darling whom, could she, she would
Have cradled as the Baby of her eye.[1]
In Rose and Musk she wash'd him—to his Lips
Press'd the pure Sugar from the Honeycomb ;
And when, Day over, she withdrew her Milk,
She made, and having laid him in, his Bed,
Burn'd all Night like a Taper o'er his Head.

Then still as Morning came, and as he grew,
She dress'd him like a Little Idol up ;
On with his robe—with fresh Collyrium Dew
Touch'd his Narcissus Eyes—the Musky Locks
Divided from his Forehead—and embraced
With Gold and Ruby Girdle his fine Waist.

So rear'd she him till full Fourteen his years,
Fourteen-day full the Beauty of his Face,
That rode high in a Hundred Thousand Hearts.
Yea, when SALÁMÁN was but Half-lance high,

---

[1] Literally, *Mardumak*—the *Mannikin*, or *Pupil*, of the Eye, corresponding to the Image so frequently used by our old Poets.

Lance-like he struck a wound in every One,
And burn'd and shook down Splendour like a Sun.

VIII

Soon as the Lord of Heav'n had sprung his Horse
Over the Horizon into the Blue Field,
SALÁMÁN rose, drunk with the Wine of Sleep,
And set himself a-stirrup for the Field;
He and a Troop of Princes—Kings in Blood,
Kings too in the Kingdom-troubling Tribe of Beauty,
All young in years and Courage,[1] Bat in hand,
Gallop'd a-field, toss'd down the Golden Ball
And chased, so many Crescent Moons a Full;
And, all alike Intent upon the Game,
SALÁMÁN still would carry from them all
The Prize, and shouting "Hal!" drive Home the Ball.[2]

This done, SAL MÁN bent him as a Bow
To Shooting—from the Marksmen of the World
Call'd for an unstrung Bow—himself the Cord
Fitted unhelpt,[3] and nimbly with his Hand
Twanging made cry, and drew it to his Ear:
Then fixing the Three-feather'd Fowl, discharged.
No point in Heaven's Azure but his Arrow
Hit; nay, but Heaven were made of Adamant,
Would overtake the Horizon as it roll'd;
And whether aiming at the Fawn a-foot,

[1] The same Persian Word serving for Both.
[2] The game of Chúgán, for Centuries the Royal Game of Persia, and adopted (Ouseley thinks) under varying modifications of Name and Practice by other Nations, was played by Horsemen, who, suitably habited, and armed with semicircular-headed Bats or Sticks so short the Player must stoop below the Saddle-bow to strike, strove to drive a Ball through a Goal of upright Pillars.
[3] Bows being so gradually stiffened to the Age and Strength of the Archer, as at last to need five Hundredweight of Pressure to bend, says an old Translation of Chardin, who describes all the Process up to bringing up the String to the Ear, "*as if to hang it there,*" before Shooting. Then the First Trial was, who could shoot highest; then the Mark, etc.

SALÁMÁN AND ABSÁL

Or Bird on wing, his Arrow went away
Straight—like the true Soul that cannot go astray.

When night came, that releases Man from Toil,
He play'd the Chess of Social Intercourse;
Prepar'd his Banquet Hall like Paradise,
Summon'd his Houri-faced Musicians,
And, when his Brain grew warm with Wine, the Veil
Flung off him of Reserve. Now Lip to Lip
Concerting with the Singer he would breathe
Like a Messias Life into the Dead;
Now made of the Melodious-moving Pipe
A Sugar-cane between his Lips that ran
Men's Ears with Sweetness: Taking up a Harp,
Between its dry String and his Finger fresh
Struck Fire; or lifting in his arms a Lute
As if a little Child for Chastisement,
Pinching its Ear, such cries of Sorrows wrung
As drew Blood to the Eyes of older men.
Now sang be like the Nightingale alone,
Now set together Voice and Instrument;
And this with his Associates Night he spent.

His Soul rejoiced in Knowledge of all kinds;
The fine Edge of his Wit would split a Hair,
And in the Noose of Apprehension catch
A Meaning ere articulate in Word;
His Verse was like the PLEIADS;[1] his Discourse
The MOURNERS OF THE BIER; his Penmanship,
(Tablet and running Reed his worshippers,)
Fine on the Lip of Youth as the First Hair,
Drove Penmen, as that Lovers, to Despair.

His Bounty was as Ocean's—nay, the Sea's
Self but the Foam of his Munificence,

---

[1] i.e.—Compactly strung, as opposed to Discursive Rhetoric which is compared to the scattered Stars of THE BIER AND ITS MOURNERS, or what we call THE GREAT BEAR. This contrast is otherwise prettily applied in the *Anvari Soheili*—" When one grows poor, his Friends, heretofore compact as THE PLEIADS, disperse, wide asunder as THE MOURNERS."

For it threw up the Shell, but he the Pearl;
He was a Cloud that rain'd upon the World
Dirhems for Drops; the Banquet of whose Bounty
Left Hátim's [1] Churlish in Comparison—

IX

SUDDENLY that Sweet Minister of mine
Rebuked me angrily; "What Folly, Jámi,
Wearing that indefatigable Pen
In celebration of an alien SHÁH
Whose Throne, not grounded in the Eternal World,
YESTERDAY was, TO-DAY is not!" [2] I answer'd;
"Oh Fount of Light!—under an Alien Name
I shadow One upon whose Head the Crown
Both WAS and IS TO-DAY; to whose Firmán
The Seven Kingdoms of the World are subject,
And the Seas Seven but droppings of his Largess.
Good luck to him who under other Name
Taught us to Veil the Praises of a Power
To which the Initiate scarce find open Door."

> *Sat a Lover solitary*
> *Self-discoursing in a Corner,*
> *Passionate and ever-changing*
> *Invocation pouring out;*
> *Sometimes Son and Moon; and sometimes*
> *Under Hyacinth half-hidden*
> *Roses; or the lofty Cypress,*
> *And the little Weed below.*
> *Nightingaling thus a Noodle*
> *Heard him, and, completely puzzled,—*
> *"What!" quoth he, "and you, a Lover,*
> *Raving not about your Mistress,*
> *But about the Moon and Roses!"*

---

[1] The Persian Type of Liberality, infinitely celebrated.
[2] The Hero of the Story being of YÚNAN—IONIA, or GREECE generally (the Persian Geography not being very precise)—and so not of THE FAITH.

Answer'd he: "O thou that aimest
Wide of Love, and Lover's Language
Wholly misinterpreting;
Sun and Moon are but my Lady's
Self, as any Lover knows;
Hyacinth I said, and meant her
Hair—her Cheek was in the Rose—
And I myself the wretched Weed
That in her Cypress Shadow grows."

X

Now was Salámán in his Prime of Growth,
His Cypress Stature risen to high Top,
And the new-blooming Garden of his Beauty
Began to bear; and Absál long'd to gather;
But the Fruit grew upon too high a Bough,
To which the Noose of her Desire was short.
She too rejoiced in Beauty of her own
No whit behind Salámán, whom she now
Began enticing with her Sorcery.
Now from her Hair would twine a musky Chain,
To bind his Heart—now twist it into Curls
Nestling innumerable Temptations;
Doubled the Darkness of her Eyes with Surma
To make him lose his way, and over them
Adorned the Bows[1] that were to shoot him then;
Fresh Rose, and then a Grain of[2] Musk lay there,
The bird of the Beloved Heart to snare.
Now to the Rose-leaf of her Cheek would add,
Now with a laugh would break the Ruby Seal
That lockt up Pearl; or busied in the Room
Would smite her Hand perhaps—on that Pretence
To lift and shew the Silver in her Sleeve;
Or hastily rising clash her Golden Anclets
To draw the Crownéd Head under her Feet.

[1] With dark Indigo-Paint, as the Archery Bow with a thin Papyrus-like Bark.
[2] A *Patch*, sc.—"*Noir comme le Musc.*" De Sacy.

Thus by innumerable Bridal wiles
She went about soliciting his Eyes,
Which she would scarce let lose her for a Moment;
For well she knew that mainly by THE EYE
Love makes his Sign, and by no other Road
Enters and takes possession of the Heart.

> *Burning with desire* ZULAIKHA
> *Built a Chamber, Wall and Ceiling*
> *Blank as an untarnisht Mirror,*
> *Spotless as the Heart of* YÚSUF.
> *Then she made a cunning Painter*
> *Multiply her Image round it;*
> *Not an inch of Wall but echoed*
> *With the Reflex of her Beauty.*
> *Then amid them all in all her*
> *Glory sat she down, and sent for*
> *YÚSUF—she began a tale*
> *Of Love—and Lifted up her Veil.*
> *From her Look he turn'd, but turning*
> *Wheresoever, ever saw her*
> *Looking, looking at him still.*
> *Then Desire arose within him—*
> *He was almost yielding—almost*
> *Laying Honey on her Lip—*
> *When a Signal out of Darkness*
> *Spoke to him—and he withdrew*
> *His hand, and dropt the Skirt of Fortune.*

XI

THUS day by day did ABSÁL tempt SALÁMÁN,
And by-and-by her Wiles began to work.
Her Eyes Narcissus stole his sleep—their Lashes
Pierc'd to his Heart—out from her Locks a Snake
Bit him—and bitter, bitter on his Tongue
Became the Memory of her Honey Lip.
He saw the Ringlet restless on her Cheek,
And he too quiver'd with Desire; his Tears
Turn'd Crimson from her Cheek, whose musky spot
Infected all his soul with Melancholy.

Love drew him from behind the Veil, where yet
Withheld him better Resolution—
" Oh, should the Food I long for, tasted, turn
Unwholesome, and if all my Life to come
Should sicken from one momentary Sweet ! "

On the Sea-shore sat a Raven
Blind, and from the bitter Cistern
Forc'd his only Drink to draw.
Suddenly the Pelican
Flying over Fortune's Shadow
Cast upon his Head,[1] *and calling*
" Come, poor Son of Salt, and taste of
Sweet, sweet Water from my Maw."
Said the Raven, " If I taste it
Once, the Salt I have to live on
May for ever turn to Loathing;
And I sit a Bird accurst
Upon the Shore to die of Thirst."

XII

Now when SALÁMÁN's Heart turned to ABSÁL,
Her Star was happy in the Heavens—Old Love
Put forth afresh—Desire doubled his Bond :
And of the running Time she watch'd an Hour
To creep into the Mansion of the Moon
And satiate her soul upon his Lips,
And the Hour came, she stole into his Chamber—
Ran up to him, Life's offer in her Hand—
And falling like a Shadow at his Feet,
She laid her Face beneath. SALÁMÁN then
With all the Courtesies of Princely Grace
Put forth his Hand—he raised her in his Arms—
He held her trembling there—and from that Fount
Drew first Desire; then Deeper from her Lips,
That, yielding, mutually drew from his
A Wine that ever drawn from never failed—

[1] Alluding to the Phœnix, the Shadow of whose wings foretold a Crown upon the Head it passed over.

So through the Day—so through another still—
The Day became a Seventh—the Seventh a Moon—
The Moon a Year—while they rejoiced together,
Thinking their pleasure never was to end.
But rolling Heaven whisper'd from his Ambush,
" So in my License is it not set down.
Ah for the sweet Societies I make
At Morning and before the Nightfall break;
Ah for that bliss that with the Setting Sun
I mix, and, with his Rising, all is done!"

> *Into Baghdad came a hungry*
> *Arab—after many days of waiting*
> *In to the Khalifah's Supper*
> *Push'd and got before a Pasty*
> *Luscious as the Lip of Beauty,*
> *Or the Tongue of Eloquence.*
> *Soon as seen, Indecent Hunger*
> *Seizes up and swallows down;*
> *Then his mouth undaunted wiping—*
> *" O Khalifah, hear me Swear,*
> *Not of any other Pasty*
> *Than of Thine to sup or dine."*
> *The Khalifah laughed, and answer'd:*
> *" Fool! who thinkest to determine*
> *What is in the Hands of Fate—*
> *Take and thrust him from the Gate!"*

XIII

WHILE a Full Year was counted by the Moon,
Sáláman and Absál rejoiced together,
And for so long he stood not in the face
Of SAGE or SHAH, and their bereavéd hearts
Were torn in twain with the Desire of Him.
They question'd those about him, and from them
Heard something: then Himself in presence summon'd,
And, subtly sifting on all sides, so plied
Interrogation till it hit the mark,
And all the Truth was told, Then SAGE and SHÁH
Struck out with Hand and Foot in his Redress.

And First with REASON, which is also Best;
REASON that rights the Retrograde—completes
The Imperfect—REASON that unites the Knot
Of either world, and sees beyond the Veil.
For REASON is the Fountain from of old
From which the Prophets drew, and none beside.
Who boasts of other Inspiration lies—
There are no other Prophets than THE WISE.

XIV

FIRST spoke THE SHAH:—" Salámán, O my Soul,
O Taper of the Banquet of my House,
Light of the Eyes of my Prosperity,
And making bloom the Court of Hope with Rose;
Years Rose-bud-like my own Blood I devour'd
Till in my hand I carried thee, my Rose;
Oh, do not tear my Garment from my Hand,
Nor wound thy Father with a Dagger Thorn.
Years for thy sake the Crown has worn my Brow,
And years my Foot been growing to the Throne
Only for Thee—Oh, spurn then not with Thine;
Oh turn thy Face from Dalliance unwise,
Lay not thy Heart's hand on a Minion!
For what Thy Proper Pastime? Is it not
To mount and manage RAKHSH [1] along the Field;
Not, with no stouter weapon than a Love-lock,
Idly reclining on a Silver Breast.
Go, fly thine Arrow at the Antelope
And Lion—let me not my Lion see
Slain by the Arrow eyes of a Ghazál.
Go, flash thy steel among the Ranks of Men,
And smite the Warriors' Necks; not, flying them,
Lay down thine own beneath a Woman's Foot.
Leave off such doing in the Name of God,
Nor bring thy Father weeping to the Ground;
Years have I held myself aloft, and all
For Thee. Oh, Shame if thou prepare my FALL!"

---

[1] "Lightning." The name of RUSTAM's famous Horse in the *Shah-Nameh*.

When before SHIRÚEH's *Feet,*
Drencht in Blood fell KAI KHUSRAÚ [1]
He declared this Parable—
"*Wretch! There was a branch that, waxing*
Wanton o'er the Root he drank from,
At a draught the Living Water
Drain'd wherewith Himself to crown ;
Died the Root—and with it died
The Branch—and barren was brought down!"

XV

SALÁMÁN heard—the Sea of his Soul was mov'd,
And bubbled up with Jewels, and he said:
"O SHAH, I am the Slave of thy Desire,
Dust of thy Throne ascending Foot am I;
Whatever thou Desirest I would do,
But sicken of my own Incompetence;
Not in the Hand of my infirmer Will
To carry into Deed mine own Desire.
Time upon Time I torture mine own Soul,
Devising liberation from the Snare
I languish in. But when upon that Moon
I think, my Soul relapses—and when *look—*
I leave both Worlds behind to follow her!"

XVI

THE SHAH ceased Counsel, and THE SAGE began:
"O thou new Vintage of a Garden old,
Last Blazon of the Pen of ' LET THERE BE,' [2]
Who read'st the SEVEN and FOUR ; [3] interpretest
The writing on the Leaves of Night and Day—

---

[1] Khusrau Parviz (Chosroe The Victorious), Son of NOSHIRAVAN The Great ; slain, after Thirty Years of Prosperous Reign, by his Son, SHIRÚEH, who, according to some, was in Love with his Father's Mistress, SHÍRÍN. *See* further, section xxi, for one of the most dramatic Tragedies in Persian History.

[2] The Pen of " Kún "—" Esto ! ".—the famous Passage of Creation stolen from Genesis by the *Kurán*.

[3] Planets ?—adding Sun, Moon, and the Nodal Dragon's Head and Tail ; according to the Sanscrit astronomy adopted by Persia.

Archetype of the Assembly of the World,
Who hold'st the Key of Adam's Treasury—
(Know thine own Dignity and slight it not,
For Thou art Greater yet than all I tell)—
The Almighty Hand that mix'd thy Dust inscribed
The Character of Wisdom on thy Heart;
Oh, Cleanse thy Bosom of Material Form,
And turn the Mirror of the Soul to SPIRIT,
Until it be with SPIRIT all possest,
Drown'd in the Light of Intellectual Truth.
Oh, veil thine Eyes from Mortal Paramour,
And follow not her Step! For what is She?—
What is She but a Vice and a Reproach,
Her very Garment-hem Pollution!
For such Pollution madden not thine Eyes,
Waste not thy Body's Strength, nor taint thy Soul,
Nor set the Body and the Soul in Strife!
Supreme is thine Original Degree,
Thy Star upon the Top of Heaven; but Lust
Will fling it down even unto the Dust!"

Quoth a Muezzin unto Crested
Chanticleer—" O Voice of Morning,
Not a Sage of all the Sages
Prophesies of Dawn, or startles
At the wing of Time, like Thee.
One so wise methinks were fitter
Perching on the Beams of Heaven,
Than with these poor Hens about him,
Raking in a Heap of Dung."
And," replied the Cock, " in Heaven
Once I was; but by my evil
Lust am fallen down to raking
With my wretched Hens about me
On the Dunghill. Otherwise
I were even now in Eden
With the Bird of Paradise."

XVII

WHEN from THE SAGE these words Salámán heard,

The breath of Wisdom round his Palate blew;
He said: "O darling of the Soul of Plato,
To whom a hundred Aristotles bow;
O Thou that an Eleventh to the Ten
Original INTELLIGENCES addest,[1]
I lay my Face before thee in the Dust,
The humblest Scholar of thy Court am I;
Whose every word I find a Well of Wisdom,
And hasten to imbibe it in my Soul.
But clear unto thy clearest Eye it is,
That choice is not within oneself—To Do,
Not in THE WILL, but in THE POWER, to Do.
From that which I originally am
How should I swerve ? or how put forth a Sign
Beyond the Power that is by Nature Mine ?"

XVIII

UNTO the Soul that is confused by Love
Comes Sorrow after Sorrow—most of all
To Love whose only Friendship is Reproof,
And overmuch of Counsel—whereby Love
Grows stubborn, and increases the Disease.
Love unreproved is a delicious food;
Reproved, is feeding on one's own Heart's Blood.

SALÁMÁN heard; his Soul came to his Lips;
Reproaches struck not ABSÁL out of him,
But drove Confusion in; bitter became
The Drinking of the sweet Draught of Delight,
And wan'd the Splendour of his Moon of Beauty.
His Breath was Indignation, and his Heart
Bled from the Arrow, and his anguish grew—
How bear it ? Able to endure one wound,
From Wound on Wound no remedy but Flight;
Day after Day, Design upon Design,
He turned the Matter over in his Heart,
And after all, no Remedy but Flight.
Resolved on that, he victuall'd and equipp'd

[1] This passage finds its explanation in the last section.

A Camel, and one Night he led it forth,
And mounted—he and ABSÁL at his side,
The fair SALÁMÁN and ABSÁL the Fair,
Together on one Camel side by side,
Twin Kernels in a single Almond packt.
And true Love murmurs not, however small
His Chamber—nay, the straitest best of all.

> *When the Moon of Canaan YÚSUF*
> *Darken'd in the Prison of Ægypt,*
> *Night by Night ZULAIKHA went*
> *To see him—for her Heart was broken.*
> *Then to her said One who never*
> *Yet had tasted of Love's Garden:*
> *" Leavest Thou thy Palace-Chamber*
> *For the Felon's narrow Cell ? "*
> *Answer'd She, " Without my Lover,*
> *Were my Chamber Heaven's Horizon,*
> *It were closer than an Ant's eye,*
> *And the Ant's eye wider were*
> *Than Heaven, my Lover with me there ! "*

XIX

SIX days SALÁMÁN on the Camel rode,
And then Remembrance of foregone Reproach
Abode not by him; and upon the Seventh
He halted on the Seashore, and beheld
An Ocean boundless as the Heaven above,
That reaching its Circumference from Káf
To Káf, down to the Back of GAU and MAHI [1]
Descended, and its Stars were Creatures' Eyes.
The Face of it was as it were a Range
Of moving Mountains; or as endless Hosts

---

[1] The Bull and Fish—the lowest Substantial Base of Earth. "He first made the Mountains; then cleared the Face of the Earth from Sea; then fixed it fast on Gau; Gau on Mahi; Mahi on Air; and Air on what?—on NOTHING; Nothing upon Nothing, all is Nothing —Enough." *Attar*; quoted in De Sacy's *Pendnamah*, xxxv.

Of Camels trooping from all Quarters up,
Furious, with the Foam upon their Lips.
In it innumerable glittering Fish
Like Jewels polish-sharp, to the sharp Eye
But for an Instant visible, glancing through
As Silver Scissors slice a blue Brocade;
But should the Dragon from its Hollow roused,
The Dragon of the Stars [1] would stare Aghast.
SALÁMÁN eyed the Sea, and cast about
To cross it—and forthwith upon the Shore
Devised a Shallop like a Crescent Moon,
Wherein that Sun and Moon in happy Hour
Enter'd as into some Celestial Sign;
That, figured like a Bow, but Arrow-like
In Flight, was feather'd with a little Sail,
And, pitcht upon the Water like a Duck,
So with her Bosom Sped to her Desire.

When they had Sail'd their Vessel for a Moon,
And marr'd their Beauty with the wind o' th' Sea,
Suddenly in mid Sea reveal'd itself
An Isle, beyond Description beautiful;
An Isle that all was Garden; not a Bird
Of Note or Plume in all the World but there;
There as in Bridal Retinue array'd
The Pheasant in his Crown, the Dove in her Collar;
And those who tuned their Bills among the Trees
That Arm in Arm, from Fingers paralyz'd
With any Breath of Air, Fruit moist and dry
Down scatter'd in Profusion to their Feet,
Where Fountains of Sweet Water ran, and round
Sunshine and Shadow chequer-chased the Ground.
Here Iram Garden seem'd in Secresy
Blowing the Rosebud of its Revelation;

---

[1] The Sidereal Dragon, whose Head, according to the Pauránic (or Poetic) Astronomers of the East, devoured the Sun and Moon in Eclipse. "But we know," said Ramachandra to Sir W. Jones, "that the supposed Head and Tail of the Dragon mean only the *Nodes*, or Points formed by intersections of the Ecliptic and the Moon's Orbit."—Sir W. Jones' *Works*, vol. iv. p. 74.

Or Paradise, forgetful of the Day
Of Audit, lifted from her Face the Veil.

SALÁMÁN saw the Isle, and thought no more
Of Further—there with ABSÁL he sat down,
ABSÁL and He together side by side
Rejoicing like the Lily and the Rose,
Together like the Body and the Soul.
Under its Trees in one another's Arms
They slept—they drank its Fountains hand in hand—
Sought Sugar with the Parrot—or in Sport
Paraded with the Peacock—raced the Partridge—
Chased the green Parrot with his stolen fruit,
Or fell a-talking with the Nightingale.
There was the Rose without a Thorn, and there
The Treasure and no Serpent to beware—
What sweeter than your Mistress at your side
In such a Solitude, and none to Chide?

> *Whisper'd one to* WÁMIK,[1] *" O Thou*
> *Victim of the Mound of* AZRA,
> *What is it like that a Shadow*
> *Movest thou about in Silence*
> *Meditating Night and Day?"*
> WÁMIK *answer'd: " Even this—*
> *To fly with* AZRA *to the Desert:*
> *There by so remote a Fountain*
> *That, whichever way one travell'd,*
> *League on League, one yet should never,*
> *Never meet the Face of Man—*
> *There to pitch my Tent—for ever*
> *There to gaze on my Belovéd;*
> *Gaze, till Gazing out of Gazing*
> *Grew to* BEING *Her I gaze on,*
> SHE *and I no more, but in One*
> *Undivided Being blended.*
> *All that is not* ONE *must ever*
> *Suffer with the Wound of Absence;*

[1] Another Typical LOVER of AZRA, A VIRGIN.

*And whoever in Love's City
Enters, finds but Room for* ONE,
And but in ONENESS *Union."*

XX

WHEN by-and-by THE SHAH was made aware
Of that Soul-wasting absence of his Son,
He reach'd a Cry to Heav'n—his Eyelashes
Wept blood—Search everywhere he set afoot,
But none would tell the hidden Mystery.
Then bade he bring a Mirror that he had,
A mirror, like the Bosom of the Wise,
Reflecting all the World,[1] and lifting up
The Veil from all its Secret, Good and Evil.
That Mirror bade he bring, and, in its Face
Looking, beheld the Face of his Desire.
He saw those Lovers in the Solitude,
Turn'd from the World, and all its ways and People,
And looking only in each other's Eyes,
And never finding any Sorrow there.
THE SHAH beheld them as they were, and Pity
Fell on his Eyes, and he reproach'd them not;
And, gathering all their Life into his hand,
Not a Thread lost, disposed in Order all.
Oh for the Noble Nature, and Clear Heart,
That, seeing Two who draw one breath, together
Drinking the Cup of Happiness and Tears,[2]

---

[1] Mythically attributed by the East—and in some wild Western Avatar—to this Shah's Predecessor, Alexander the Great. Perhaps (V. Hammer thinks) the Concave Mirror upon the Alexandrian Pharos, which by night projected such a Fiery Eye over the Deep as not only was fabled to exchange Glances with that on the Rhodian Colossus, and in Oriental Imagination and Language to penetrate "The WORLD," but by Day to Reflect it to him who looked therein with Eyes to see The Cup of their own JAMSHED had, whether Full or Empty, the same Property, And that Silver Cup found in Benjamin's Sack. "Is not this it in which my Lord drinketh, and whereby indeed he *Divineth?*" Genesis xliv. 5. Our Reflecting Telescope is going some way to realize the Alexandrian Fable.

[2] κρατῆρα μακρὸν ἡδονῆς καὶ δακρύων κιρνῶντες ἐξέπινον ἄχρις ἐς μέθην.

Unshatter'd by the Stone of Separation,
Is loth their sweet Communion to destroy,
Or cast a Tangle in the Skein of Joy.
The Arrows that assail the Lords of Sorrow
Come from the Hand of Retribution.
Do Well, that in thy Turn Well may betide Thee;
And turn from Ill, that Ill may turn beside Thee.

FARHÁD, Moulder of the Mountain
Love-distracted look'd to SHÍRÍN,
And SHÍRÍN the Sculptor's Passion
Saw, and turn'd her Heart to Him.

Then the Fire of Jealous Frenzy
Caught and carried up the Harvest
Of the Might of KAI KHUSRAU.

Plotting with that ancient Hag
Of Fate, the Sculptor's Cup he poison'd,
And remained the Lord of Love.

So—But Fate that Fate avenges
Arms SHIRÚEH with the dagger,
That at once from SHÍRÍN tore him,
Hurl'd him from the Throne of Glory.[1]

XXI

BUT as the days went on, and still THE SHAH
Beheld SALÁMÁN how sunk in ABSÁL,
And yet no hand of better Effort lifted;
But still the Crown that should adorn his Head,
And still the Throne that waited for his Foot,

---

[1] One story is that Khusrau had promised if Firhád cut through a Mountain and brought a Stream through, Shírín should be his. Firhád was on the point of achieving his work, when Khusrau sent an Old Woman (here, perhaps, purposely confounded with Fate) to tell him Shírín was dead; whereon Firhád threw himself headlong from the Rock. The Sculpture at Beysitún (or Besitún), where Rawlinson has decyphered Darius and Xerxes, was traditionally called Firhád's.

Trampled from Memory by a Base Desire,
Of which the Soul was still unsatisfied—
Then from the Sorrow of THE SHAH fell Fire;
To Gracelessness Ungracious he became,
And, quite to shatter his rebellious Lust,
Upon SALÁMÁN all his WILL discharged.[1]

And lo! SALÁMÁN to his Mistress turn'd,
But could not reach her—look'd and look'd again,
And palpitated tow'rd her—but in Vain!
Oh Misery! what to the Bankrupt worse
Than Gold he cannot reach! To one Athirst
Than Fountain to the Eye and Lip forbid!—
Or than Heaven opened to the Eyes in Hell!—
Yet, when SALÁMÁN's Anguish was extreme,
The Door of Mercy open'd in his Face;
He saw and knew his Father's Hand outstretcht
To lift him from Perdition—timidly,
Timidly tow'rd his Father's Face his own
He lifted, Pardon-pleading, Crime-confest,
As the stray Bird one day will find her Nest.

A Disciple ask'd a Master,
" By what token should a Father
Vouch for his reputed Son?"
Said the Master, " By the Stripling,
Howsoever Late or Early,
Like to the reputed Father,
Growing—whether Wise or Foolish."

" Lo the disregarded Darnel
With itself adorns the Wheat-field,
And for all the Early Season
Satisfies the Farmer's Eye;
But come once the Hour of Harvest,
And another Grain shall answer,
' Darnel and no Wheat, am I.' "

---

[1] He Mesmerizes Him! See also further on this Power of the Will in Sections xxiii and xxvi.

XXII

WHEN THE SHAH saw Salámán's face again,
And breathed the Breath of Reconciliation,
He laid the Hand of Love upon his Shoulder,
The Kiss of Welcome on his Cheek, and said:
"O Thou, who lost, Love's Banquet lost its Salt,
And Mankind's Eye its Pupil! Thy Return
Is as another Sun to Heaven; a new
Rose blooming in the Garden of the Soul.
Arise, O Moon of Majesty unwaned!
The Court of the Horizon is thy Court,
Thy Kingdom is the Kingdom of the World!
Lo! Throne and Crown await Thee—Throne and Crown
Without thy Impress but uncurrent Gold,
Not to be stamp'd by one not worthy Them;
Behold! The Rebel's Face is at thy Door;
Let him not triumph—Let the Wicked dread
The Throne under thy Feet, the Crown upon thy Head.
Oh, Spurn them not behind Thee! O my Son,
Wipe thou the Woman's Henna from thy Hand:
Withdraw Thee from the Minion who from Thee
Dominion draws;[1] the Time is come to choose,
Thy Mistress or the World to hold or lose."

Four are the Signs of Kingly Aptitude;
Wise Head—clean Heart—strong Arm—and open Hand.
Wise is he not—Continent cannot be—
Who binds himself to an unworthy Lust;
Nor Valiant, who submits to a weak Woman;
Nor Liberal, who cannot draw his Hand
From that in which so basely he is busied.
And of these Four who misses All or One
Is not the Bridegroom of Dominion.

XXIII

AH the poor Lover! In the changing Hands
Of Day and Night no wretcheder than He!

[1] "*Shâh*" and "*Shâhid*" (Mistress)—a sort of Punning the Persian Poets are fond of.

No Arrow from the Bow of Evil Fate
But reaches him—one Dagger at his Throat,
Another comes to wound him from behind.
Wounded by Love—then wounded by Reproof
Of Loving—and, scarce stauncht the Blood of Shame
By flying from his Love—then, worst of all,
Love's back-blow of Revenge for having fled!
SALÁMÁN heard—he rent the Robe of Peace—
He came to loathe his Life, and long for Death
(For better Death itself than Life in Death)—
He turned his Face with ABSÁL to the Desert—
Enter'd the deadly Plain; Branch upon Branch
Cut down, and gathered in a lofty Pile,
And fired. They look'd upon the Flames, those Two—
They look'd and they rejoic'd; and hand in hand
They sprang into the Fire. THE SHAH who saw,
In secret all had order'd; and the Flame
Directed by his Self-fulfilling WILL,
Devouring utterly ABSÁL, pass'd by
SALÁMÁN harmless—the pure Gold return'd
Entire, but all the baser Metal burn'd.

XXIV

HEAVEN'S Dome is but a wondrous House of Sorrow,
And Happiness therein a lying Fable,
When first they mixed the Clay of Man, and cloth'd
His Spirit in the Robe of Perfect Beauty,
For Forty Mornings did an Evil Cloud
Rain Sorrows over him from Head to Foot;
And when the Forty Mornings pass'd to Night,
Then came one Morning-Shower—one Morning-Shower
Of Joy—to Forty of the Rain of Sorrow!—
And though the better Fortune came at last
To seal the Work, yet every Wise Man knows
Such Consummation never can he here!

SALÁMÁN fired the Pile; and in the Flame
That, passing him, consumed ABSÁL like straw,
Died his Divided Self, and there survived

His Individual; and like a Body
From which the Soul is parted, all alone.
Then rose his Cry to Heaven—his Eyelashes
Dropt Blood—his Sighs stood like a Smoke in Heaven,
And Morning rent her Garments at his Anguish.[1]
He tore his Bosom with his Nails—he smote
Stone on his Bosom—looking then on hands
No longer lockt in hers, and lost their Jewel,
He tore them with his Teeth, and when came Night,
He hid him in some Corner of the House,
And communed with the Fantom of his Love.
" O Thou whose presence so long sooth'd my Soul,
Now burnt with Thy Remembrance! Oh, so long
The Light that fed these Eyes now dark with Tears!
Oh, Long, Long Home of Love now lost for Ever!
We were Together—that was all Enough—
We Two rejoicing in each other's Eyes,
Infinitely rejoicing—all the World
Nothing to Us, nor We to all the World—
No road to Reach us, nor an Eye to watch—
All Day we whispered in each other's Ears,
All night we slept in one another's arms—
All seem'd to our Desire, as if the Hand
Of unjust Fortune were for once too short.
Oh, would to God that when I lit the Pyre
The Flame had left Thee Living and me Dead,
Not Living worse than Dead, depriv'd of Thee!
Oh, were I but with Thee!—at any Cost
Stript of this terrible self-Solitude!
Oh, but with Thee Annihilation—lost,
Or in Eternal Intercourse renew'd!"

Slumber-drunk an Arab in the
Desert off his Camel tumbled,
Who the lighter of her Burden
Ran upon her road rejoicing.
When the Arab woke at morning

[1] "When the Cloud of Spring beheld the Evil Disposition of Time Its weeping fell upon the Jessamine and Hyacinth and Wild Rose."—HAFIZ.

Rubb'd his Eyes and look'd about him—
" Oh my Camel! Oh my Camel!"
Quoth he, " Camel of my Soul!—
That Lost with Her I lost might be,
Or found, She might be found with Me!"

XXV

WHEN in this Plight THE SHAH SALÁMÁN saw,
His Soul was struck with anguish, and the vein
Of Life within was strangled—what to do
He knew not. Then he turn'd him to THE SAGE—
"O Altar of the World, to whom Mankind
Directs the Face of Prayer in Weal or Woe,
Nothing but Wisdom can untie the Knot;
And art not Thou the Wisdom of the World,
The Master-Key of all its Difficulties?
ABSÁL is perisht; and, because of Her,
SALÁMÁN dedicates his Life to Sorrow;
I cannot bring back Her, nor comfort Him,
Lo, I have said! My Sorrow is before Thee;
From thy far-reaching Wisdom help Thou Me
Fast in the Hand of Sorrow! Help Thou Me,
For I am very wretched!" Then THE SAGE—
"O Thou that err'st not from the Road of Right,
If but SALÁMÁN have not broke my Bond,
Nor lies beyond the Noose of my Firmán,
He quickly shall unload his Heart to me,
And I will find a Remedy for all."

XXVI

THEN THE SAGE counsell'd, and SALÁMÁN heard,
And drew the Wisdom down into his Heart;
And, sitting in the Shadow of the Perfect,
His Soul found quiet under; sweet it seem'd,
Sweeping the Chaff and Litter from his own,
To be the very Dust of Wisdom's Door,
Slave of the Firmán of the Lord of Life.
Then THE SAGE marvelled at his Towardness,
And wrought in Miracle in his behalf.

He poured the Wine of Wisdom in his Cup,
He laid the Dew of Peace upon his Lips;
And when Old Love return'd to Memory,
And broke in Passion from his Lips, THE SAGE,
Under whose waxing WILL Existencce rose,
Responsive, and, relaxing, waned again,
Raining a Fantom Image of ABSÁL,
Set it awhile before SALÁMÁN's Eyes,
Till, having sow'd the Seed of Quiet there,
It went again down to Annihilation.
But ever, for the Sum of his Discourse,
THE SAGE would tell of a Celestial Love;
"Zuhrah,"[1] he said, "the Lustre of the Stars—
'Fore whom the Beauty of the Brightest wanes;
Who were she to reveal her perfect Beauty,
The Sun and Moon would craze; ZUHRAH," he said,
"The Sweetness of the Banquet—none in Song
Like her—her Harp filling the Ear of Heaven,
That Dervish-dances to her Harmony."

SALÁMÁN listen'd and inclined—again
Entreated, Inclination ever grew;
Until THE SAGE beholding in his Soul
The SPIRIT[2] quicken, so effectually
With ZUHRAH wrought, that she reveal'd herself
In her pure Beauty to SALÁMÁN's Soul,
And washing ABSÁL's Image from his Breast,
There reign'd instead. Celestial Beauty seen,
He left the Earthly; and, once come to know
Eternal Love, he let the Mortal go.

XXVII

THE Crown of Empire how supreme a Lot!
The Throne of the Sultan how high!—But not
For All—None but the Heaven-ward Foot may dare
To mount—the Head that touches Heaven to wear!—

[1] "ZUHRAH." The Planetary and Celestial Venus.
[2] "*Maany.*" The Mystical pass-word of the Súfís, to express the Transcendental New Birth of the Soul.

When the Belov'd of Royal Augury
Was rescued from the Bondage of ABSÁL,
Then he arose, and shaking off the Dust
Of the lost Travel, girded up his Heart,
And look'd with undefiléd robe to Heaven.
Then was His Head worthy to wear the Crown,
His Foot to mount the Throne. And then THE SHAH
S immon'd the Chiefs of Cities and of States,
S.immon'd the Absolute Ones who wore the Ring,
And such a Banquet order'd as is nȏt
For Sovereign Assemblement the like
In the Folding of the Records of the World.
No arméd Host, nor Captain of a Host,
From all the Quarters of the World, but there;
Of whom not one but to SALÁMÁN did
Obeisance, and lifted up his Neck
To yoke it under his Supremacy.
Then THE SHÁH crown'd him with the Golden Crown,
And set the Golden Throne beneath his Feet,
And over all his Heads of the Assembly,
And in the Ears of all of them, his Jewels
With the Diamond of Wisdom cut, and said:

XXVIII

" MY SON,[1] the Kingdom of the World is not
Eternal, nor the Sum of right Desire;
Make thou the Faith-preserving Intellect
Thy Counsellor; and considering TO-DAY
TO-MORROW'S Seed-field, ere That come to bear,
Sow with the Harvest of Eternity.
All Work with Wisdom hath to do—by that
Stampt current only; what Thyself to do
Art wise, that *Do*; what not, consult the Wise.
Turn not thy Face away from the Old Ways,
That were the Canon of the Kings of Old;
Nor cloud with Tyranny the Glass of Justice;

---

[1] One sees Jámi taking Advantage of his Allegorical Sháh to read a Lesson to the Real—whose Ears Advice, unlike Praise, scarce ever reached, unless obliquely. The warning (and doubtless with good Reason) is principally aimed at the Minister.

But rather strive that all Confusion
Change by thy Justice to its opposite.
In whatsoever Thou shalt Take or Give,
Look to the *How*; Giving and Taking still,
Not by the backward Counsel of the Godless,
But by the Law of FAITH increase and Give.
Drain not thy People's purse—the Tyranny
Which Thee enriches at thy Subject's cost,
Awhile shall make Thee strong; but in the End
Shall bow thy Neck beneath a Double Burden.
The Tyrant goes to Hell—follow not Him—
Become not Thou the Fuel of its Fires.
Thou art a Shepherd, and thy Flock the People,
To save and not destroy; nor at their Loss
To lift thyself above the Shepherd's calling.
For which is for the other, Flock or Shepherd?
And join with thee True men to keep the Flock—
Dogs, if you will—but Trusty—head in leash,
Whose Teeth are for the Wolf, not for the Lamb,
And least of all the Wolf's Accomplices,
Their Jaws Blood-dripping from the Tyrant's Shambles.
For Shahs must have Vizírs—but be they Wise
And Trusty—knowing well the Realm's Estate—
(For who eats Profit of a Fool? and least
A wise King girdled by a Foolish Council—)
Knowing how far to Shah and Subject bound
On either Hand—not by Extortion,
Not Usury wrung from the People's purse,
Their Master's and their own Estates (to whom
Enough is apt enough to make them Rebel),
Feeding to such a surplus as feeds Hell.
Proper in Soul and Body be they—pitiful
To Poverty—hospitable to the Saint—
Their sweet Access a Salve to wounded Hearts;
Their Vengeance terrible to the Evil Doer,
Thy Heralds through the Country, bringing Thee
Report of Good or Ill—which to confirm
By thy peculiar eye—and least to all
Suffering Accuser also to be Judge,
By surest steps builds up Prosperity."

XXIX

Epilogue

Under the Outward Form of any Story
An Inner Meaning lies.—This Story now
Completed, do Thou of its Mystery,
(Whereto the wise hath found himself a way)
Have thy Desire—No Tale of *I* and *THOU*
Though *I* and *THOU* be its Interpreters.[1]
What signifies The Shah ? and what The Sage ?
And what Salámán not of Woman born ?
And what Absál who drew him to Desire ?
And what the Kingdom that awaited him
When he had drawn his Garment from her Hand ?
What means that Fiery Pile ? And what The Sea ?
And what that Heavenly Zuhrah who at last
Clear'd Absál from the Mirror of his Soul ?
Learn part by part the Mystery from me ;
All Ear from Head to Foot and Understanding be.

XXX

The Incomparable Creator, when this World
He did create, created first of All
The First Intelligence [2]—First of a Chain

---

[1] The Story is of *Generals*, though enacted by *Particulars*.

[2] " These Intelligences are only another Form of the Neo-Platonic Daemones. The Neo-Platonists held that Matter and Spirit could have no Intercourse—they were, as it were, *incommensurate*. How then, granting this premise, was Creation possible ? Their answer was a kind of gradual Elimination. God, the "Actus Purus," created an Oeon ; this Oeon created a Second ; and so on, until the Tenth Oeon was sufficiently Material (as the Ten were in a continually descending Series) to affect Matter, and so cause the Creation by giving to Matter the Spiritual Form.

Similarly we have in Sufiism these Ten Intelligences in a corresponding series, and for the same End.

There are ten Intelligences, and Nine Heavenly Spheres, of which the Ninth is the Uppermost Heaven, appropriated to the First Intelligence ; the Eighth, that of the Zodiac, to the Second ; the Seventh, Saturn, to the Third ; The Sixth, Jupiter, to the Fourth ; the Fifth, Mars, to the Fifth ; the fourth, The Sun, to the Sixth ; the Third, Venus, to the Seventh ; the Second, Mercury, to the

Of Ten Intelligences, of which the Last
Sole Agent is in this our Universe,
ACTIVE INTELLIGENCE so call'd; The One
Distributor of Evil and of Good,
Of Joy and Sorrow. Himself apart from MATTER,
In Essence and in Energy—His Treasure
Subject to no such Talisman—He yet
Hath fashion'd all that is—Material Form,
And Spiritual, sprung from HIM—by HIM
Directed all, and in His Bounty drown'd.
Therefore is He that Firmán-issuing SHAH
To whom the World was subject. But because
What He distributes to the Universe
Himself from still a Higher Power receives,
The Wise, and all who comprehend aright,
Will recognize that Higher in THE SAGE.

HIS, the PRIME SPIRIT that, spontaneously,
Projected by the TENTH INTELLIGENCE,
Was from no Womb of MATTER reproduced:
A Special Essence called THE SOUL—a CHILD
Fresh sprung from Heaven in Raiment undefiled
Of Sensual Taint, and therefore call'd SALÁMÁN.

And who ABSÁL?—The Lust-adoring Body
Slave to the Blood and Sense—through whom THE SOUL,
Although the Body's very Life it be,
Does yet imbibe the knowledge and Desire
Of things of SENSE; and these united thus
By such a Tie God only can unloose,
Body and Soul are Lovers Each of other.

What is the Sea on which they sail'd?—The Sea
Of Animal Desire—the Sensual Abyss,
Under whose waters lies a World of Being
Swept far from God in that Submersion.

Eighth; the First, The Moon, to the Ninth; and The Earth is the peculiar Sphere of the TENTH, or lowest Intelligence, called THE ACTIVE."

And wherefore was it ABSÁL in that Isle,
Deceived in her Delight, and that SALÁMÁN
Fell short of his Desire?—That was to show
How Passion tires, and how with Time begins
The Folding of the Carpet of Desire.

And what the turning of SALÁMÁN's Heart
Back to THE SHAH, and looking to the Throne
Of Pomp and Glory? What but the Return
Of the lost SOUL to its true Parentage,
And back from Carnal Error looking up
Repentant to its Intellectual Throne?

What is THE FIRE?—Ascetic Discipline,
That burns away the Animal Alloy,
Till all the Dross of MATTER be consumed,
And the Essential Soul, its raiment clean
Of Mortal Taint, be left. But forasmuch
As any Life-long Habit so consumed,
May well recur a Pang for what is lost,
Therefore THE SAGE set in SALÁMÁN's Eyes
A soothing Fantom of the Past; but still
Told of a better Venus, till his Soul
She fill'd, and blotted out his Mortal Love.
For what is ZUHRAH?—That Divine Perfection
Wherewith the Soul inspired and all array'd
In Intellectual Light is Royal blest,
And mounts THE THRONE, and wears THE CROWN, and Reigns,
Lord of the Empire of Humanity.

This is the Meaning of this Mystery,
Which to know wholly ponder in thy Heart
Till all its ancient Secret be enlarged.
Enough—The written Summary I close,
And set my Seals:

THE TRUTH GOD ONLY KNOWS.

MEMOIR OF BERNARD BARTON

(*From a Letter of Bernard Barton*)
" 2 mo. 11, 1839.

"THY cordial approval of my brother John's hearty wish to bring us back to the simple habits of the olden time induces me to ask thee if I mentioned in either of my late letters the curious old papers he stumbled on in hunting through the repositories of our late excellent spinster sister ? I quite forget whether I did or not ; so I will not at a venture repeat all the items. But he found an inventory of the goods and chattels of our great-grandfather, John Barton of Ive-Gill, a little hamlet about five or seven miles from Carlisle ; by which it seems our progenitor was one of those truly patriarchal personages, a Cumbrian statesman—living on his own little estate, and drawing from it all things needful for himself and his family. I will be bound for it my good brother was more gratified at finding his earliest traceable ancestor such an one than if he had found him in the college of heralds with *gules purpure* and argent emblazoned as his bearings. The total amount of his stock, independent of house, land, and any money he might have, seems by the valuation to have been £61 6s., and the copy of his admission to his little estate gives the fine as £5, so that I suppose its annual value was then estimated at £2 15s. This was about a century back. Yet this man was the chief means of building the little chapel in the dale, still standing. (He was a Churchman.) I doubt not he was a fine simple-hearted noble-minded yeoman, in his day, and I am very proud of him. Why did his son, my grandfather, after whom I was named, ever leave that pleasant dale, and go and set up a manufactory in Carlisle ; inventing a piece of machinery[1] for which he had a medal from the Royal Society ?—so says Pennant. Methinks he had better have abode in the old grey stone, slate-covered homestead on the banks of that pretty brooklet the Ive ! but I bear his name, so I will not quarrel with his memory."

Thus far Bernard Barton traces the history of his family. And it appears that, as his grandfather's mechanical genius drew him away from the pastoral life at Ive-Gill, so his father, who was of a literary turn, reconciled himself with difficulty to the manufactory he inherited at Carlisle. " I always," he wrote, " perused a Locke, an Addison, or a Pope, with delight,[2] and ever sat down to my ledger with a sort of disgust ; " and he at one time determined to quit a business in which he had been " neither successfully nor agreeably engaged," and become a " minister of some sect of religion—it will *then* be time," he says, " to determine of what sect when I am enabled to judge of their respective merits. But this I will freely confess to you, that if there be any one of them, the tenets of which are more favourable to rational religion than the one in which I have been brought up, I shall be so far from thinking it a crime, that I cannot but consider it my duty to embrace it." This' however, was written when he was very young. He never gave up business, but changed one business for another, and shifted the scene of its transaction. His religious inquiries led to a more decided result. He very soon left the Church of England, and became a member of the Society of Friends.

About the same time he married a Quaker lady, Mary Done, of a Cheshire family, She bore him several children ; but only three lived to maturity : two daughters, of whom

---

[1] The manufactory was one of calico-printing. The " piece of machinery " is thus described by Pennant : " Saw at Mr. Bernard Barton's a pleasing sight of twelve little girls spinning at once at a horizontal wheel, which set twelve bobbins in motion ; yet so contrived, that should any accident happen to one, the motion of that might be stopped without any impediment to the others."

[2] See an amusing account of his portrait, with his favourite books about him, painted about this time, Letter I of this Collection.

the elder, Maria, distinguished herself, afterward, as the author of many useful children's books under her married name, Hack; and one son, Bernard, the poet, who was born on January 31, 1784.

Shortly before Bernard's birth, however, John Barton had removed to London, where he engaged in something of the same business he had quitted at Carlisle, but where he probably found society and interests more suited to his taste. I do not know whether he ever acted as minister in his Society; but his name appears on one record of their most valuable endeavours. The Quakers had from the very time of George Fox distinguished themselves by their opposition to slavery: a like feeling had gradually been growing up in other quarters of England; and in 1787 a mixed committee of twelve persons was appointed to promote the Abolition of the Slave-trade; Wilberforce engaging to second them with all his influence in Parliament. Among these twelve stands the name of John Barton, in honourable companionship with that of Thomas Clarkson.

"I lost my mother," again writes B. B., "when I was only a few days old; and my father married again in my infancy so wisely and so happily, that I knew not but his second wife was my own mother, till I learned it years after at a boarding school." The name of this amiable step-mother was Elizabeth Horne; a Quaker also; daughter of a merchant, who, with his house in London and villa at Tottenham was an object of B. B.'s earliest regard and latest recollection. "Some of my first recollections," he wrote fifty years after, "are, looking out of his parlour windows at Bankside on the busy Thames, with its ever-changing scene, and the dome of St. Paul's rising out of the smoke on the other side of the river. But my most delightful recollections of boyhood are connected with the fine old country-house in a green lane diverging from the high road which runs through Tottenham. I would give seven years of life as it now is, for a week of that which I then led. It was a large old house, with an iron palisade and a pair of iron gates in front, and a huge stone eagle on each pier. Leading up to the steps by which you went up to the hall door was a wide gravel walk, bordered in summer-time by huge tubs, in which were orange and lemon trees, and in the centre of the grass-plot stood a tub yet larger, holding an enormous aloe. The hall itself to my fancy then lofty and wide as a cathedral would seem now, was a famous place for battledore and shuttlecock; and behind was a garden, equal to that of old Alcinous himself. My favourite walk was one of turf by a long strait pond, bordered with lime trees. But the whole demesne was the fairy ground of my childhood; and its presiding genius was grandpapa. He must have been a handsome man in his youth, for I remember him at nearly eighty, a very fine-looking one, even in the decay of mind and body. In the morning a velvet cap; by dinner, a flaxen wig; and features always expressive of benignity and placid cheerfulness. When he walked out into the garden, his cocked hat and amber-headed cane completed his costume. To the recollection of this delightful personage I am, I think, indebted for many soothing and pleasing associations with old age."

John Barton did not live to see the only child—a son—that was born to him by this second marriage. He had some time before quitted London, and taken partnership in a malting business at Hereford, where he died, in the prime of life. After his death his widow returned to Tottenham, and there with her son and step-children continued for some time to reside.

In due time Bernard was sent to a much-esteemed Quaker school at Ipswich: returning always to spend his holidays at Tottenham. When fourteen years old, he was apprenticed to Mr. Samuel Jesup, a shopkeeper at Halstead in Essex. "There I stood," he writes, "for eight years behind the counter of the corner shop at the top of Halstead Hill, kept to this day" (November 9, 1828) "by my old master, and still worthy uncle, S. Jesup."

In 1806 he went to Woodbridge; and a year after married Lucy Jesup, the niece of his former master, and entered into partnership with her brother as coal and corn merchant. But she died a year after marriage, in giving birth to the only child, who now survives them both; and he, perhaps sickened with the scene of his blighted love,[1] and finding, like his father, that he had less taste for the ledger than for literature, almost directly quitted Woodbridge, and engaged himself as private tutor in the family of Mr. Waterhouse, a merchant in Liverpool. There Bernard Barton had some family connexions; and there also he was kindly received and entertained by the Roscoe family, who were old acquaintances of his father and mother.

After a year's residence in Liverpool, he returned to Woodbridge, and there became clerk in Messrs. Alexander's bank—a kind of office which secures certain, if small, remuneration, without any of the anxiety of business; and there he continued for forty years, working till within two days of his death.

He had always been fond of books; was one of the most active members of a Woodbridge Book Club, which he only quitted a month or two before he died; and had written and sent to his friends occasional copies of verse. In 1812 he published his first volume of Poems, called *Metrical Effusions*, and began a correspondence with Southey, who continued to give him most kind and wise

[1] The following verses were published in his first volume—

O thou from earth for ever fled!
Whose reliques lie among the dead,
With daisied verdure overspread,
    My Lucy!

For many a weary day gone by,
How many a solitary sigh
I've heaved for thee, no longer nigh,
    My Lucy!

And if to grieve I cease awhile,
I look for that enchanting smile
Which all my cares could once beguile,
    My Lucy!

But ah! in vain—the blameless art
Which used to soothe my troubled heart
Is lost with thee, my better part,
    My Lucy!

Thy converse, innocently free,
That made the fiends of fancy flee,
Ah, then I feel the want of thee,
    My Lucy!

advice for many years. A complimentary copy of verses which he had addressed to the author of the *Queen's Wake* (just then come to notice), brought him long and vehement letters from the Ettrick Shepherd, full of thanks to Barton and praises of himself; and along with all this, a tragedy " that will astonish the world ten times more than the *Queen's Wake* has done," a tragedy with so many characters in it of equal importance " that justice cannot be done it in Edinburgh," and therefore the author confidentially entrusts it to Bernard Barton to get it represented in London. Theatres, and managers of theatres, being rather out of the Quaker poet's way, he called into council Capel Lofft, with whom he also corresponded, and from whom he received flying visits in the course of Lofft's attendance at the county sessions. Lofft took the matter into consideration, and promised all assistance, but on the whole dissuaded Hogg from trying London managers;

> Nor is it for myself alone
> That I thy early death bemoan ;
> *Our* infant now is *all my own,*
>   My Lucy !
>
> Couldst thou a guardian angel prove
> To the dear offspring of our love,
> Until it reach the realms above,
>   My Lucy !
>
> Could thy angelic spirit stray,
> Unseen companion of my way,
> As onward drags the weary day,
>   My Lucy !
>
> And when the midnight hour shall close
> Mine eyes in short unsound repose,
> Couldst thou but whisper off my woes,
>   My Lucy !
>
> Then, though thy loss I must deplore,
> Till next we meet to part no more
> I'd wait the grasp that from me tore
>   My Lucy !
>
> For, be my life but spent like thine,
> With joy shall I that life resign,
> And fly to thee, for ever mine,
>   My Lucy !

he himself having sent them three tragedies of his own; and others by friends of "transcendent merit, equal to Miss Baillie's," all of which had fallen on barren ground.[1]

In 1818 Bernard Barton published by subscription a thin 4to volume—*Poems by an Amateur*,—and shortly afterward appeared under the auspices of a London publisher in a volume of *Poems*, which, being favourably reviewed in the *Edinburgh*, reached a fourth edition by 1825. In 1822 came out his *Napoleon*, which he managed to get dedicated and presented to George the Fourth. And now being launched upon the public with a favouring gale, he pushed forward with an eagerness that was little to his ultimate advantage. Between 1822 and 1828 he published five volumes of verse. Each of these contained many pretty poems; but many that were very hasty, and written more as task-work, when the mind was already wearied with the desk-labours of the day;[2] not waiting for the occasion to suggest, nor the impulse to improve. Of this he was warned by his friends, and of the danger of making himself too cheap with publishers and the public. But the advice of others had little weight in the hour of success with one so inexperienced and so hopeful as himself. And there was in Bernard Barton a certain boyish impetuosity in pursuit of anything he had at heart, that age itself scarcely could subdue. Thus it was with his correspondence; and thus it was with his poetry. He wrote always with great facility, almost unretarded by that worst labour of correction; for he was not fastidious himself about exactness of thought or of harmony of numbers, and he could scarce comprehend why the public should be less easily satisfied. Or if he did labour—and labour

---

[1] This was not B. B.'s nearest approach to theatrical honours. In 1822 (just after the review on him in the *Edinburgh*) his niece Elizabeth Hack writes to him: "Aunt Lizzy tells us, that when one of the Sharps was at Paris some little time ago, there was a party of English actors performing plays. One night he was in the theatre, and an actor of the name of Barton was announced, when the audience called out to inquire if it was the Quaker poet."

[2] The *Poetic Vigils*, published in 1824, have (he says in the Preface) "at least this claim to the title given them, that they are the production of hours snatched from recreation or repose."

he did at that time—still it was at task-work of a kind he liked. He loved poetry for its own sake, whether to read or to compose, and felt assured that he was employing his own talent in the cause of virtue and religion,[1] and the blameless affections of men. No doubt he also liked praise; though not in any degree proportional to his eagerness in publishing; but inversely, rather. Very vain men are seldom so careless in the production of that from which they expect their reward. And Barton soon seemed to forget one book in the preparation of another; and in time to forget the contents of all except a few pieces that arose more directly from his heart, and so naturally attached themselves to his memory. And there was in him one great sign of the absence of any inordinate vanity—the total want of envy. He was quite as anxious others should publish as himself; would never believe there could be too much poetry abroad; would scarce admit a fault in the verses of others, whether private friends or public authors, though after a while (as in his own case) his mind silently and unconsciously adopted only what was good in them. A much more likely motive for this mistaken activity of publication is the desire to add to the slender income of his clerkship. For Bernard Barton was a generous and not a provident man; and, few and modest as were his wants, he did not usually manage to square them to the still narrower limit of his means.

But apart from all these motives, the preparation of a book was amusement and excitement to one who had little enough of it in the ordinary routine of daily life; treaties with publishers—arrangements of printing—correspondence with friends on the subject—and, when the little volume was at last afloat, watching it for a while somewhat as a boy watches a paper boat committed to the sea.

His health appears to have suffered from his exertions. He writes to friends complaining of low spirits, headache, etc., the usual effect of sedentary habits, late hours, and

---

[1] The *Devotional Verses* (1827) were begun with a very serious intention, and seem written carefully throughout, as became the subject.

overtasked brain. Charles Lamb advises after his usual fashion : some grains of sterling available truth amid a heap of jests.[1] Southey replies more gravely, in a letter that should be read and marked by every student.

"*Keswick*, 27 *Jan*., 1822.

"I am much pleased with the *Poet's Lot*—no, not with his lot, but with the verses in which he describes it. But let me ask you—are you not pursuing your studies intemperately, and to the danger of your health ? To be 'writing long after midnight' and 'with a miserable headache' is what no man can do with impunity ; and what no pressure of business, no ardour of composition, has ever made me do. I beseech you, remember the fate of Kirke White ;—and remember that if you sacrifice your health (not to say your life) in the same manner, you will be held up to your own community as a warning — not as an example for imitation. The spirit which disturbed poor Scott of Amwell in his last illness will fasten upon your name ; and your fate will be instanced to prove the incon-

---

[1] "You are too much apprehensive about your complaint. I know many that are always ailing of it, and live on to a good old age. I know a merry fellow (you partly know him) who, when his medical adviser told him he had drunk away all *that part*, congratulated himself (now his liver was gone) that he should be the longest liver of the two. The best way in these cases is to keep yourself as ignorant as you can—as ignorant as the world was before Galen—of the entire inner constructions of the animal man ; not to be conscious of a midriff ; to hold kidneys (save of sheep and swine) to be an agreeable fiction ; not to know whereabouts the gall grows ; to account the circulation of the blood a mere idle whim of Harvey's ; to acknowledge no mechanism not visible. For once fix the seat of your disorder, and your fancies flux into it like so many bad humours. Those medical gentry choose each his favourite part, one takes the lungs—another the aforesaid liver, and refers to that whatever in the animal economy is amiss. Above all, use exercise, take a little more spirituous liquors, learn to smoke, continue to keep a good conscience, and avoid tamperings with hard terms of art—viscosity, scirrosity, and those bugbears by which simple patients are scared into their graves. Believe the general sense of the mercantile world, which holds that desks are not deadly. It is the mind, good B. B., and not the limbs, that taints by long sitting. Think of the patience of tailors—think how long the Lord Chancellor sits—think of the brooding hen."

sistency of your pursuits with that sobriety and evenness of mind which Quakerism requires, and is intended to produce.

"You will take this as it is meant, I am sure.

"My friend, go early to bed; and if you eat suppers, read afterwards, but never compose, that you may lie down with a quiet intellect. There is an intellectual as well as a religious peace of mind;—and without the former, be assured there can be no health for a poet. God bless you,
"Yours very truly,
"R. SOUTHEY."

Mr. Barton had even entertained an idea of quitting the bank altogether, and trusting to his pen for subsistence.— An unwise scheme in all men: most unwise in one who had so little tact with the public as himself. From this, however, he was fortunately diverted by all the friends to whom he communicated his design.[1] Charles Lamb thus wrote to him :—

[1] So long ago as the date of his first volume he had written to Lord Byron on the subject; who thus answered him :—

"SIR,—   "*St. James's Street, June* 1, 1812.
"The most satisfactory answer to the concluding part of your letter is, that Mr. Murray will republish your volume if you still retain your inclination for the experiment, which I trust will be successful. Some weeks ago my friend Mr. Rogers showed me some of the Stanzas in MS., and I then expressed my opinion of their merit, which a further perusal of the printed volume has given me no reason to revoke. I mention this as it may not be disagreeable to you to learn that I entertained a very favourable opinion of your power before I was aware that such sentiments were reciprocal. —Waiving your obliging expressions as to my own productions, for which I thank you very sincerely, and assure you that I think not lightly of the praise of one whose approbation is valuable; will you allow me to talk to you candidly, not critically, on the subject of yours ?—You will not suspect me of a wish to discourage, since I pointed out to the publisher the propriety of complying with your wishes. I think more highly of your poetical talents than it would perhaps gratify you to hear expressed, for I believe, from what I observe of your mind, that you are above flattery.—To come to the point, you deserve success; but we knew before Addison wrote his *Cato*, that desert does not always command it. But suppose it attained—

"*9th January*, 1823.

"Throw yourself on the world without any rational plan of support beyond what the chance employ of booksellers would afford you ! ! !

"Throw yourself rather, my dear Sir, from the steep Tarpeian rock, slap-dash headlong upon iron spikes. If you have but five consolatory minutes between the desk and the bed, make much of them, and live a century in them, rather than turn slave to the booksellers. They are Turks and Tartars when they have poor authors at their beck. Hitherto you have been at arm's length from them. Come not within their grasp. I have known many authors want for bread—some repining—others enjoying the best security of a counting-house —all agreeing they had rather have been tailors, weavers,—what not ?—rather than the things they were. I have known some starved, some to go mad, one dear friend literally dying in a workhouse. You know not what a rapacious, dishonest set these booksellers are. Ask even Southey, who (a single case almost) has made a fortune by book-drudgery, what he has found them. O you know not, may you never know ! the miseries of subsisting by authorship ! 'Tis a pretty appendage to a situation like yours or mine ; but a slavery worse than all

"You know what ills the author's life assail,
Toil, envy, want, the *patron*, and the jail.—

Do not renounce writing, but never trust enrirely to authorship. If you have a profession, retain it, it will be like Prior's fellowship, a last and sure resource.—Compare Mr. Rogers with other authors of the day ; assuredly he is among the first of living poets, but is it to that he owes his station in society and his intimacy in the best circles ? No, it is to his prudence and respectability. The world (a bad one I own) courts him because he has no occasion to court it.—He is a poet, nor is he less so because he was something more.— I am not sorry to hear that you are not tempted by the vicinity of Capel Lofft, Esq., though if he had done for you what he has for the Bloomfields I should never have laughed at his rage for patronizing.—But a truly well-constituted mind will ever be independent. —That you may be so is my sincere wish ; and if others think as well of your poetry as I do, you will have no cause to complain of your readers.——Believe me,

"Your obliged and obedient Servant,
"BYRON."

slavery, to be a bookseller's dependant, to dradge your brains for pots of ale and breasts of mutton, to change your free thoughts and voluntary numbers for ungracious taskwork. The booksellers hate us. The reason I take to be, that, contrary to other trades, in which the master gets all the credit (a jeweller or silversmith, for instance), and the journeyman, who really does the fine work, is in the background: in *our* work the world gives all the credit to *us*, whom *they* consider as *their* journeymen, and therefore do they hate us, and cheat us, and oppress us, and would wring the blood of us out, to put another sixpence in their mechanic pouches.

* * * * *

"Keep to your bank, and the bank will keep you. Trust not to the public: you may hang, starve, drown yourself for anything that worthy personage cares. I bless every star that Providence, not seeing good to make me independent, has seen it next good to settle me upon the stable foundation of Leadenhall. Sit down, good B. B., in the banking office: what! is there not from six to eleven, P.M., six days in the week, and is there not all Sunday? Fie, what a superfluity of man's time, if you could think so! Enough for relaxation, mirth, converse, poetry, good thoughts, quiet thoughts. O the corroding, torturing, tormenting thoughts that disturb the brain of the unlucky wight who must draw upon it for daily sustenance! Henceforth I retract all my fond complaints of mercantile employment—look upon them as lovers' quarrels. I was but half earnest. Welcome dead timber of a desk that gives me life. A little grumbling is a wholesome medicine for the spleen, but in my inner heart do I approve and embrace this our close but unharassing way of life. I am quite serious.

"Yours truly,
"C. Lamb."

In 1824, however, his income received a handsome addition from another quarter. A few members of his Society, including some of the wealthier of his own family, raised £1,200 among them for his benefit. Mr. Sherwell of Ipswich, who was one of the main contributors to this fund, writes to me that the scheme originated with Joseph John Gurney :—" one of those innumerable acts of kindness and beneficence which marked his character, and the *measure* of which will never be known upon the earth." Nor was the measure of it known in this instance ; for of the large sum that he handed in as the subscription of several, Mr. Sherwell thinks he was " a larger donor than he chose to acknowledge." The money thus raised was vested in the name of Mr. Sherwell, and its yearly interest paid to Bernard Barton ; till, in 1839, the greater part of it was laid out in buying that old house and the land round it, which Mr. Barton so much loved as the habitation of his wife's mother, Martha Jesup.

It seems that he felt some delicacy at first in accepting this munificent testimony which his own people offered to his talents. But here again Lamb assisted him with plain, sincere, and wise advice.

" DEAR B. B.,—   " *March 24th*, 1824.
" I hasten to say that if my opinion can strengthen you in your choice it is decisive for your acceptance of what has been so handsomely offered. I can see nothing injurious to your most honourable sense. Think that you are called to a poetical ministry—nothing worse—the minister is worthy of his hire.

" The only objection I feel is founded on a fear that the acceptance may be a temptation to you to let fall the bone (hard as it is) which is in your mouth, and must afford tolerable pickings, for the shadow of independence. You cannot propose to become independent on what the low state of interest could afford you from such a principal as you mention ; and the most graceful excuse for the acceptance would be, that if left you free to your voluntary functions : that is the less *light* part of the scruple. It has no darker shadow. I put in *darker*, because of the ambiguity of the word light, which Donne, in his admirable poem on the Metempsychosis, has so ingeniously illustrated in his invocation—

'Make my *dark heavy* poem *light* and *light*—'

where the two senses of *light* are opposed to different opposites. A trifling criticism.—I can see no reason for any scruple then but what arises from your own interest; which is in your own power, of course, to solve. If you still have doubts, read over Sanderson's *Cases of Conscience* and Jeremy Taylor's *Ductor Dubitantium;* the first a moderate octavo, the latter a folio of nine hundred close pages; and when you have thoroughly digested the admirable reasons *pro* and *con* which they give for every possible case, you will be—just as wise as when you began, Every man is his own best casuist; and, after all, as Ephraim Smooth, in the pleasant comedy of *Wild Oats*, has it, 'There is no harm in a guinea.' *A fortiori*, there is less in two thousand.

"I therefore most sincerely congratulate with you, excepting so far as excepted above. If you have fair prospects of adding to the principal, cut the bank; but in either case, do not refuse an honest service. Your heart tells you it is not offered to bribe you *from* any duty, but *to* a duty which you feel to be your vocation.

"Farewell heartily,
"C. L."

While Mr. Barton had been busy publishing, his correspondence with literary people had greatly increased. The drawers and boxes which at last received the overflowings of his capacious Quaker pockets (and he scarcely ever destroyed a letter) contain a multitude of letters from literary people, dead or living. Beside those from Southey and Lamb, there are many from Charles Lloyd—simple, noble, and kind, telling of his many Poems—of a Romance in six volumes he was then copying out with his own hand for the seventh time; from old Lloyd, the father, into whose hands Barton's letters occasionally fell by mistake, telling of his son's many books, but "that it is easier to write them than to gain numerous readers;" from old Mr. Plumptre, who mourns the insensibility of publishers to his castigated editions of Gay and Didbin—leaving one letter midway, to go to his "spring task of pruning the gooseberries and currants." There are also girlish letters from

L. E. L., and feminine ones from Mrs. Hemans. Of living authors there are many letters from Mitford, Bowring, Conder, Mrs. Opie, C. B. Taylor, the Howitts, etc.

Owing to Mr. Barton's circumstances, his connexion with most of these persons was solely by letter. He went indeed ocasionally to Hadleigh, where Mr. Drake then flourished, and Mr. Taylor was curate; to Mr. Mitford's at Benhall;[1] and he visited Charles Lamb once or twice in London and at Islington. He once also met Southey at Thomas Clarkson's at Playford, in the spring of 1824. But the rest of the persons whose letters I have just mentioned I believe he never saw. And thus perhaps he acquired a habit of writing that supplied the place of personal intercourse. Confined to a town where there was but little stirring in the literary way, he naturally travelled out of it by letter, for communication on those matters; and this habit gradually extended itself to accquaintances not literary, whom he seemed as happy to converse with by letter as face to face. His correspondence with Mr. Clemesha arose out of their meeting once and once only, by chance, in the commercial room of an inn. And with Mrs. Sutton, who, beside other matters of interest, could tell him about the "North Countrie," from which his ancestors came, and which he always loved in fancy (for

[1] Here is one of the notes that used to call B. B. to Benhall in those days.

"MY DEAR POET,— "*Benhall*, 1820.

"We got your note to-day. We are at home and shall be glad to see you, but hope you will not swim here; in other words, we think it better that you should wait, till we can seat you under a chestnut and listen to your oracular sayings. We hope that, like your sister of the woods, you are in full song; she does not print, I think; we hope you do; seeing that you beat her in sense, though she has a little the advantage in melody. Together you will make a pretty duet in our groves. You have both your defects: she devours glowworms, you take snuff; she is in a great hurry to go away, and you are prodigious slow in arriving; she sings at night, when nobody can hear her, and you write for Ackermann, which nobody thinks of reading. In spite of all this, you will get a hundred a year from the king, and settle at Woodbridge; in another month, she will find no more flies, and set off for Egypt.

"Truly yours,
"J. M."

he never saw it), he kept up a correspondence of nearly thirty years, though he and she never met to give form and substance to their visionary conceptions of one another.

From the year 1828 his books, as well as his correspondence with those "whose talk was of" books, declined; and soon after this he seemed to settle down contentedly into that quiet course of life in which he continued to the end. His literary talents, social amiability, and blameless character made him respected, liked, and courted among his neighbours. Few, high or low, but were glad to see him at his customary place in the bank, from which he smiled a kindly greeting, or came down with friendly open hand, and some frank words of family inquiry—perhaps with the offer of a pinch from his never-failing snuff-box— or the withdrawal of the visitor, if more intimate, to see some letter or copy of verses, just received or just composed, or some picture just purchased. Few, high and low, but were glad to have him at their tables; where he was equally pleasant and equally pleased, whether with the fine folks at the Hall or with the homely company at the Farm; carrying everywhere indifferently the same good feeling, good spirits, and good manners; and by a happy frankness of nature, that did not too precisely measure its utterance on such occasions, chequering the conventional gentility of the drawing-room with some humours of humbler life, which in turn he refined with a little sprinkling of literature.—Now too, after having long lived in a house that was just big enough to sit and sleep in, while he was obliged to board with the ladies of a Quaker school over the way,[1] he obtained a convenient house of his own, where he got his books and pictures about him. But, more than all this, his daughter was now grown up to be his housekeeper and companion. And amiable as Bernard Barton was in social life, his amiability in this little *tête-à-tête* household of his was yet a fairer thing to

---

[1] Where he writes a letter one day, but he knows not if intelligibly; "for all hands are busy round me to clap, to starch, to iron, to plait—in plain English, 'tis washing-day; and I am now writing close to a table in which is a bason of starch, caps, kerchiefs, etc., and busy hands and tongues round it."

behold; so completely was all authority absorbed into confidence and into love—

> A constant flow of love, that knew no fail,
> Ne'er roughen'd by those cataracts and breaks
> That humour interposed too often makes,

but gliding on uninterruptedly for twenty years, until death concealed its current from all human witness.

In earlier life Bernard Barton had been a fair pedestrian, and was fond of walking over to the house of his friend Arthur Biddell of Playford. There, beside the instructive and agreeable society of his host and hostess, he used to meet George Airy, now Astronomer Royal, then a lad of wonderful promise; with whom he had many a discussion about poetry, and Sir Walter's last new novel, a volume of which perhaps the poet had brought in his pocket. Mr. Biddell, at one time, lent him a horse to expedite his journeys to and fro, and to refresh him with some wholesome change of exercise. But of that Barton soon tired. He gradually got to dislike exercise very much; and no doubt greatly injured his health by its disuse. But it was not to be wondered at, that having spent the day in the uncongenial task of "figure-work," as he called it, he should covet his evenings for books, or verses, or social intercourse. It was very difficult to get him out even for a stroll in the garden after dinner, or along the banks of his favourite Deben on a summer evening. He would, after going a little way, with much humorous grumbling at the useless fatigue he was put to endure, stop short of a sudden, and, sitting down in the long grass by the riverside, watch the tide run past, and the well-known vessels gliding into harbour, or dropping down to pursue their voyage under the stars at sea, until his companions, returning from their prolonged walk, drew him to his feet again, to saunter homeward far more willingly than he set forth, with the prospect of the easy chair, the book, and the cheerful supper before him.

His excursions rarely extended beyond a few miles round Woodbridge—to the vale of Dedham, Constable's birthplace and painting-room; or to the neighbouring sea-coast,

loved for its own sake—and few could love the sea and
the heaths beside it better than he did—but doubly dear
to him from its association with the memory and poetry
of Crabbe. Once or twice he went as far as Hampshire
on his visit to his brother ; and once he visited Mr. W. B.
Donne, at Mattishall, in Norfolk, where he saw many
portraits and mementoes of his favourite poet Cowper,
Mr. Donne's kinsmen. That which most interested him
there was Mrs. Bodham, ninety years old, and almost
blind, but with all the courtesy of the old school about
her—once the " Rose " whom Cowper had played with at
Catfield parsonage when both were children together,
and whom until 1790, when she revived their acquaintance
by sending him his mother's picture, he had thought
" withered and fallen from the stalk." Such little excursions it might be absurd to record of other men ; but they
were some of the few that Bernard Barton could take, and
from their rare occurrence, and the simplicity of his nature,
they made a strong impression upon him.

He still continued to write verses, as well on private
occasions as for annuals ; and in 1836 published another
volume, chiefly composed of such fragments. In 1845
came out his last volume, which he got permission to
dedicate to the Queen. He sent also a copy of it to Sir
Robert Peel, then Prime Minister, with whom he had
already corresponded slightly on the subject of the income
tax, which Mr. Barton thought pressed rather unduly
on clerks, and others, whose narrow income was only for
life. Sir Robert asked him to dinner at Whitehall.—
" Twenty years ago," writes Barton, " such a summons
had elated and exhilarated me—now I felt humbled and
depressed at it. Why ?—but that I verge on the period
when the lighting down of the grasshopper is a burden,
and desire itself begins to fail."—He went, however, and
was sincerely pleased with the courtesy and astonished
at the social ease of a man who had so many and so
heavy cares on his shoulders. When the Quaker poet
was first ushered into the room, there were but three
guests assembled, of whom he little expected to know one.
But the mutual exclamations of " George Airy ! " and

"Bernard Barton!" soon satisfied Sir Robert as to his country guest's feeling at home at the great town dinner.

On leaving office a year after, Sir Robert recommended him to the Queen for an annual pension of £100 : one of the last acts, as the retiring Minister intimated, of his official career, and one he should always reflect on with pleasure.—B. Barton gratefully accepted the boon. And to the very close of life he continued, after his fashion, to send letters and occasional poems to Sir Robert, and to receive a few kind words in reply.

In 1844 died Bernard's eldest sister, Maria Hack. She was five or six years older than himself; very like him in the face; and had been his instructress ("a sort of oracle to me," he says) when both were children. "It is a heavy blow to me," he writes, "for Maria is almost the first human being I remembered to have fondly loved, or been fondly loved by—the only living participant in my first and earliest recollections. When I lose her, I had almost as well never have been a child; for she only knew me as such — and the best and brightest of memories are apt to grow dim when they can be no more reflected." "She was just older enough than I," he elsewhere says, "to recollect distinctly what I have a confused glimmering of —about our house at Hereford—even of hers at Carlisle."

Mr. Barton had for many years been an *ailing* man, though he never was, I believe, *dangerously* ill (as it is called) till the last year of his life. He took very little care of himself; laughed at all rules of diet, except temperance; and had for nearly forty years, as he said, "taken almost as little exercise as a milestone, and far less fresh air." Some years before his death he had been warned of a liability to disease in the heart, an intimation he did not regard, as he never felt pain in that region. Nor did he to that refer the increased distress he began to feel in exertion of any kind, walking fast or going upstairs, a distress which he looked upon as the disease of old age, and which he used to give vent to in half-humorous groans, that seemed to many of his friends rather expressive of his dislike to exercise than implying any serious inconvenience from it. But probably the disease that partly arose from inactivity now became the true apology for it. During the last year of his life, too, some loss of his little fortune, and some perplexity in his affairs, not so distressing because of any present inconvenience to himself as in the prospect of future evil to one whom he loved as himself, may have increased the disease within him, and hastened its final blow.

Towards the end of 1848 the evil symptoms increased much upon him; and, shortly after Christmas it was found that the disease was far advanced. He consented to have his diet regulated; protesting humorously against the small glass of small beer allowed him in place of the temperate allowance of generous port, or ale, to which he was accustomed. He fulfilled his daily duty in the bank,[1] only remitting (as he was peremptorily bid) his attendance there after his four o'clock dinner.[2] And though not able to go out to his friends, he was glad to see them at his own house to the last.

Here is a letter, written a few days before his death, to one of his kindest and most hospitable friends.

"2 mo. 14, 1849.

"MY DEAR OLD FRIEND—Thy home-brewed has been duly received, and I drank a glass yesterday with relish, but I must not indulge too often—for I make slow way, if any, toward recovery, and at times go on puffing, panting, groaning, and making a variety of noises, not unlike a loco-

---

[1] He had written of himself, some years before, "I shall go on making figures till Death makes me a cipher."
[2] For which he half accused himself as "*a skulker.*" And of late years, when the day account of the bank had not come quite right by the usual hour of closing, and it seemed necessary to carry on business late into the evening, he would sometimes come up wearied to his room, saying—"Well, we've got all right but a shilling, and I've left my boys" (as he called the younger clerks) "to puzzle that out." But even then he would get up from *Rob Roy* or the *Antiquary* every now and then, and go to peep through the curtain of a window that opens upon the back of the bank, and, if he saw the great gas-lamp flaming within, announce with a half comical sympathy, that "they were still at it;" or when the lamp was at last extinguished, would return to his chair more happily, now that his partners were liberated.

motive at first starting; more to give vent to my own discomfort than for the delectation of those around me. So I am not fit to go into company, and cannot guess when I shall. However, I am free from much acute suffering, and not so much hypp'd as might be forgiven in a man who has such trouble about his breathing that it naturally puts him on thinking how long he may be able to breathe at all. But if the hairs of one's head are numbered, so, by a parity of reasoning, are the puffs of our bellows. I write not in levity, though I use homely words. I do not think J—— sees any present cause of serious alarm, but I do not think he sees, on the other hand, much prospect of speedy recovery, if of entire recovery at all. The thing has been coming on for years, and cannot be cured at once, if at all. A man can't poke over desk or table for forty years without putting some of the machinery of the chest out of sorts. As the evenings get warm and light we shall see what gentle exercise and a little fresh air can do. In the last few days too I have been in solicitude about a little pet niece of mine dying, if not dead, at York: this has somewhat worried me, and agitation or excitement is as bad for me as work or quickness of motion. Yet, after all, I have really more to be thankful for than to grumble about. I have no very acute pain, a skeely doctor, a good nurse, kind solicitous friends, a remission of the worst part of my desk hours—so why should I fret? Love to the younkers.
"Thine,
"B."

On Monday, February 19, he was unable to get into the bank, having passed a very unquiet night—the first night of distress, he thankfully said, that his illness had caused him. He suffered during the day; but welcomed as usual the friends who came to see him as he lay on his sofa; and wrote a few *notes*—for his correspondence must now, as he had humorously lamented, become as short-breathed as himself. In the evening, at half-past eight, as he was yet conversing cheerfully with a friend, he rose up, went to his bedroom, and suddenly rang a bell. He was found by his daughter—dying. Assistance was sent for; but all assistance was vain. " In a few minutes more," says the note dispatched from the house of death that night, " all distress was over on *his* part—and that warm kind heart is still for ever."

The Letters and Poems that follow are very faithful revelations of Bernard Barton's soul; of the genuine piety to God, goodwill to men, and cheerful guileless spirit, which animated him, not only while writing in the undisturbed seclusion of the closet, but (what is a very different matter) through the walk and practice of daily life. They prove also his intimate acquaintance with the Bible, and his deep appreciation of many beautiful passages which might escape a common reader.

The Letters show that while he had well considered and well approved the pure principles of Quakerism, he was equally liberal in his recognition of other forms of Christianity. He could attend the *church* or the *chapel*, if the *meeting* were not at hand, and once assisted in raising money to build a new *Established Church* in Woodbridge. And while he was sometimes roused to defend Dissent from the vulgar attacks of High Church and Tory,[1] he could also

---

[1] Here are two little Epigrams showing that the quiet Quaker *could* strike, though he was seldom provoked to do so.

DR. E——
A bullying, brawling champion of the Church;
Vain as a parrot screaming on her perch;
And, like that parrot, screaming out by rote
The same stale, flat, unprofitable note;
Still interrupting all discreet debate
With one eternal cry of ' Church and State!'—
With all the High Tory's ignorance, increased
By all the arrogance that marks the priest;
One who declares upon his solemn word,
The voluntary system is absurd:
He well may say so;—for 'twere hard to tell
Who would support him, did not law compel.

On one who declared in a public speech—" This was the opinion he had formed of the Dissenters; he only saw in them wolves in sheep's clothing."

give the bishops a good word when they were unjustly assailed.

While duly conforming to the usages of his Society on all proper occasions, he could forget *thee* and *thou* while mixing in social intercourse with people of another vocabulary, and smile at the Reviewer who reproved him for using the heathen name *November* in his Poems. "I find," he said, "these names of the months the prescriptive dialect of *poetry*, used as such by many members of our Society before me—'*sans peur et sans reproche*'; and I use them accordingly, asking no questions for conscience' sake as to their origin. Yet while I do this, I can give my cordial tribute of approval to the scruples of our early friends, who advocate a simpler nomenclature. I can quite understand and respect their simplicity and godly sincerity; and I conceive that I have duly shown my reverence for their scruples in adhering *personally* to their dialect, and only using another *poetically*. Ask the British Friend the name of the planet with a belt round it, and he would say, Saturn; at the peril, and on the pain, of excommunication."

As to his politics, he always used to call himself "a Whig of the old school." Perhaps, like most men in easy circumstances, he grew more averse to change as he grew older. He thus writes to a friend in 1845, during the heats occasioned by the proposed Repeal of the Corn Laws:—
"Queer times these, and strange events. I feel most shamefully indifferent about the whole affair; but my political fever has long since spent itself. It was about its height when they sent Burdett to the Tower. It has cooled down wonderfully since then. He went there, to

"Wolves in sheep's clothing!" bitter words and big;
But who applies them? first *the speaker* scan;
A suckling Tory! an apostate Whig!
Indeed, a very silly, weak young man!

What such an one may either think or say,
With sober people matters not one pin;
In *their* opinion, his own senseless bray
Proves *him* the ASS WRAPT IN A LION'S SKIN.

the best of my recollection, in the character of Burns'
Sir William Wallace—

'Great patriot hero—ill-requited chief ;—'

and dwindled down afterward to 'Old Glory.' No more
patriots for me." But Bernard Barton did not trouble
himself much about politics. He occasionally grew interested when the interests of those he loved were at stake,
and his affections generally guided his judgments. Hence
he was always against a Repeal of the Corn Laws, because
he loved Suffolk farmers, Suffolk labourers, and Suffolk
fields. Occasionally he took part in the election of a friend
to Parliament—writing in prose or verse in the county
papers. And here also, though he more willingly sided
with the Liberal interest, he would put out a hand to help
the good old Tory at a pinch.

He was equally tolerant of men, and free of acquaintance.
So long as men were honest (and he was slow to suspect
them to be otherwise), and reasonably agreeable (and he
was easily pleased), he could find company in them. "My
temperament," he writes, " is, as for as a man can judge of
himself, eminently social. I am wont to live out of myself,
and to cling to anything or anybody lovable within my
reach." I have before said that he was equally welcome
and equally at ease, whether at the Hall or at the Farm ;
himself indifferent to rank, though he gave every one his
title, not wondering even at those of his own community,
who, unmindful perhaps of the military implication, owned
to the soft impeachment of *Esquire*. But nowhere was
he more amiable than in some of those humbler meetings—
about the fire in the *keeping-room* at Christmas, or under
the walnut tree in summer. He had his cheerful remembrances with the old ; a playful word for the young—
especially with children, whom he loved and was loved
by.—Or, on some summer afternoon, perhaps, at the little
inn on the heath, or by the riverside—or when, after a
pleasant picnic on the sea-shore, we drifted homeward up
the river, while the breeze died away at sunset, and the
heron, at last startled by our gliding boat, slowly rose from

the ooze over which the tide was momentarily encroaching.

By nature, as well as by discipline perhaps, he had a great dislike to most violent occasions of feeling and manifestations of it, whether in real life or story. Many years ago he entreated the author of *May You Like It*, who had written some tales of powerful interest, to write others "where the appeals for one's feelings were perhaps less frequent—I mean one's sympathetic feelings with suffering virtue—and the more pleasurable emotions called forth by the spectacle of quiet, unobtrusive domestic happiness more dwelt on." And when Mr. Tayler had long neglected to answer a letter, Barton humorously proposed to rob him on the highway, in hopes of recovering an interest by crime which he supposed every-day good conduct had lost. Even in Walter Scott, his great favourite, he seemed to relish the humorous parts more than the pathetic; Bailie Nicol Jarvie's dilemmas at Glennaquoich, rather than Fergus MacIvor's trial; and Oldbuck and his sister Grizel rather than the scenes at the fisherman's cottage. Indeed, many, I dare say, of those who only know Barton by his poetry, will be surprised to hear how much humour he had in himself, and how much he relished it in others. Especially, perhaps, in later life, when men have commonly had quite enough of " domestic tragedy," and are glad to laugh when they can.

With little critical knowledge of pictures, he was very fond of them, especially such as represented scenery familiar to him—the shady lane, the heath, the cornfield, the village, the sea-shore. And he loved after coming away from the bank to sit in his room and watch the twilight steal over his landscapes as over the real face of nature, and then lit up again by fire or candle light. Nor could any itinerant picture-dealer pass Mr. Barton's door without calling to tempt him to a new purchase. And then was B. B. to be seen, just come up from the bank, with broad-brim and spectacles on, examining some picture set before him on a chair in the most advantageous light; the dealer recommending and Barton wavering, until partly by money, and partly by exchange of some older favourites, with perhaps a snuff-box thrown in to turn the scale, a bargain was concluded—generally to B.'s great disadvantage and great content. Then friends were called in to admire; and letters written to describe; and the picture taken up to his bedroom to be seen by candle-light on going to bed, and by the morning sun on awaking; then hung up in the best place in the best room; till in time perhaps it was itself exchanged for some newer favourite.

He was not learned—in language, science, or philosophy. Nor did he care for the loftiest kinds of poetry—" the heroics," as he called it. His favourite authors were those that dealt most in humour, good sense, domestic feeling, and pastoral description—Goldsmith, Cowper, Wordsworth in his lowlier moods, and Crabbe. One of his favourite prose books was Boswell's *Johnson*; of which he knew all the good things by heart, an inexhaustible store for a country dinner-table.[1] And many will long remember him as he used to sit at table, his snuff-box in his hand, and a glass of genial wine before him, repeating some favourite passage, and glancing his fine brown eyes about him as he recited.

But perhaps his favourite prose book was Scott's Novels. These he seemed never tired of reading and hearing read. During the last four or five winters I have gone through several of the best of these with him—generally on one night in each week—Saturday night, that left him free to the prospect of Sunday's relaxation. Then was the volume taken down impatiently from the shelf almost before tea was over; and at last, when the room was clear, candles snuffed, and fire stirred, he would read out, or listen to, those fine stories, anticipating with a glance, or an impatient ejaculation of pleasure, the good things he knew were coming—which he liked all the better for knowing they were coming —relishing them afresh in the fresh enjoyment of his companion, to whom they were less familiar; until the modest supper coming in closed the book, and recalled him to his cheerful hospitality.

---

[1] He used to look with some admiration at an ancient fellow-townsman, who, beside a rich fund of Suffolk stories vested in him, had once seen Dr. Johnson alight from a hackney coach at the *Mitre.*

Of the literary merits of this volume, others, less biassed than myself by personal and local regards, will better judge. But the Editor, to whom, as well as the Memoir, the task of making any observations of this kind usually falls, has desired me to say a few words on the subject.

The letters, judging from internal evidence as well as from all personal knowledge of the author's habits, were for the most part written off with the same careless ingenuousness that characterized his conversation. "I have no alternative," he said, "between not writing at all and writing what first comes into my head." In both cases the same cause seems to me to produce the same agreeable effect.

The Letters on graver subjects are doubtless the result of graver "foregone conclusion,"—but equally spontaneous in point of utterance, without any effort at style whatever.

If the Letters here published are better than the mass of those they are selected from, it is because better topics happened to present themselves to one who, though he wrote so much, had perhaps as little of new or animating to write about as most men.

The Poems, if not written off as easily as the Letters, were probably as little elaborated as any that ever were published. Without claiming for them the highest attributes of poetry (which the author never pretended to), we may surely say they abound in genuine feeling and elegant fancy expressed in easy, and often very felicitous, verse. These qualities employed in illustrating the religious and domestic affections, and the pastoral scenery with which such affections are perhaps most generally associated, have made Bernard Barton, as he desired to be, a household poet with a large class of readers—a class who, as they may be supposed to welcome such poetry as being the articulate voice of those good feelings yearning in their own bosoms, one may hope will continue and increase in England.

While in many of these Poems it is the spirit within that redeems an imperfect form—just as it lights up the irregular features of a face into beauty—there are many which will surely abide the test of severer criticism. Such are several of the Sonnets; which, if they have not (and they do not aim at) the power and grandeur, are also free from the pedantic stiffness of so many English Sonnets. Surely that one "To my Daughter" is very beautiful in all respects.

Some of the lighter pieces—"To Joanna," "To a Young Housewife," etc., partake much of Cowper's playful grace. And some on the decline of life, and the religious consolations attending it, are very touching.

Charles Lamb said the verses "To the Memory of Bloomfield" were "sweet with Doric delicacy." May not one say the same of those "On Leiston Abbey," "Cowper's Rural Walks," "On Some Pictures," and others of the shorter descriptive pieces? Indeed, utterly incongruous as at first may seem the Quaker clerk and the ancient Greek Idyllist, some of these little poems recall to me the inscriptions in the Greek Anthology—not in any particualr passages, but in their general air of simplicity, leisurely elegance, and quiet unimpassioned pensiveness.

Finally, what Southey said of *one* of Barton's volumes—"there are many rich passages and frequent felicity of expression"—may modestly be said of these selections from ten. Not only is the fundamental thought of many of them very beautiful—as in the poems, "To a Friend in Distress," "The Deserted Nest," "Thoughts in a Garden," etc.—but there are many verses whose melody will linger in the ear, and many images that will abide in the memory. Such surely are those of men's hearts brightening us at Christmas "like a fire new stirred,"—of the stream that leaps along over the pebbles "like happy hearts by holiday made light"—of the solitary tomb showing from afar like a lamb in the meadow. And in the poem called "A Dream"—a dream the poet really had—how beautiful is that chorus of the friends of her youth who surround the central vision of his departed wife, and who, much as the dreamer wonders they do not see she is a spirit, and silent as she remains to their greetings, still with countenances of "blameless mirth," like some of Correggio's angel attendants, press around her without awe or hesitation, repeating "Welcome, welcome!" as to one suddenly returned to them from some earthly absence only, and not from beyond the dead—from heaven.   E. F. G.

DEATH OF BERNARD BARTON

(From the *Ipswich Journal*, February 24, 1849)

At Woodbridge, on the night of Monday last, February 19, between the hours of eight and nine, after a brief spasm in the heart, died Bernard Barton. He was born near London in 1784, came to Woodbridge in 1806, where he shortly after married, and was left a widower at the birth of his only child, who now survives him. In 1810 he entered as clerk in Messrs. Alexander's Bank, where he officiated almost to the day of his death. He had been for some months afflicted with laborious breathing which his doctor knew to proceed from disease in the heart, though there seemed no reason to apprehend immediate danger. But those who have most reason to lament his loss, have also most reason to be thankful that he was spared a long illness of anguish and suspense, by so sudden and easy a dismissal.

To the world at large Bernard Barton was known as the author of much pleasing, amiable, and pious poetry, animated by feeling and fancy, delighting in homely subjects, so generally pleasing to English people. He sang of what he loved—the domestic virtues in man, and the quiet pastoral scenes of Nature—and especially of his own county—its woods, and fields, and lanes, and homesteads, and the old sea that washed its shores; and the nearer to his own home the better he loved it. There was a true and pure vein of pastoral feeling in him. Thousands have read his books with innocent pleasure; none will ever take them up and be the worse for doing so. The first of these volumes was published in 1811.

To those of his own neighbourhood he was known beside as a most amiable, genial, charitable man—of pure, unaffected, unpretending piety—the good neighbour—the cheerful companion—the welcome guest—a hospitable host—tolerant of all men, sincerely attached to many. Few, high and low, but were glad to see him at his customary place in the bank; to exchange some words of kindly greeting with him—few but were glad to have him at their own homes; and there he was the same man and had the same manners to all; always equally frank, genial, and communicative, without distinction of rank. He had all George Fox's "better part"—thorough independence of rank, titles, wealth, and all the distinctions of haberdashery, without making any needless display of such independence. He could dine with Sir Robert Peel one day, and the next day sup off bread and cheese with equal relish at a farmhouse, and relate with equal enjoyment at the one place what he had heard and seen at the other.

He was indeed as free from vanity as any man, in spite of the attention which his books drew towards him. If he liked to write, and recite, and print his own occasional verses, it was simply that he himself was interested in them at the time—interested in the subject—in the composition, and amused with the very printing; but he was equally amused with anything his friends had said or written—repeating it everywhere with almost disproportionate relish. And this surely is not a usual mark of vanity. Indeed, had he had more vanity, he would have written much less instead of so much, would have altered and polished and condensed. Whereas it was all first impulse with him: he would never correct his own verses, though he was perfectly ready to let his friends alter what they chose in them—nay, ask them to do so, so long as he was not called on to assist.

It was the same with his correspondence, which was one great amusement of his later years. He wrote off as he thought and felt, never pausing to turn a sentence, or to point one; and he was quite content to receive an equally careless reply, so long as it came. He was content with a poem so long as it was good in the main, without minding those smaller beauties which go to make up perfection—content with a letter that told of health and goodwill, with very little other news—and content with a friend who had the average virtues and accomplishments of men, without being the faultless monster which the world never saw, but so many are half their lives looking for.

It was the same with his conversation. He never dressed himself for it, whatever company he was going into. He would quote his favourite poems in a farmhouse and tell his humorous Suffolk stories in the genteelest drawing-room—what came into his head at the impulse of the moment came from his tongue; a thing not in general commendable, but wholly pleasant and harmless in one so innocent, so kind, and so agreeable as himself.

He was excellent company in all companies; but in none more than in homely parties, in or out of doors, over the winter's fire in the farmhouse, or under the tree in summer. He had a cheery word for all; a challenge to good fellowship with the old—a jest with the young—enjoying all, and making all enjoyable and joyous. Many hereabouts will long look to that place in their rooms where this good, amiable, and pleasant man used to sit and spread good-humour around him. Nor can the present writer forget the last out-of-door party he enjoyed with this most amiable man: it was in last June, down his favourite river Deben to the sea. Though far from well, when once on board he would be cheerful; was as lively and hearty as any at the little inn at which we disembarked to refresh ourselves; and had a word of cheery salute for every boat or vessel that passed or met us as we drifted home again with a dying breeze at close of evening.

He was not learned, in languages, or in science of any kind. Even the loftier poetry of our own country he did not much affect. He loved the masters of the homely, the pathetic, and the humorous—Crabbe, Cowper, and Goldsmith—for it may surprise many readers of his poems that he had as great relish for humour—good-humoured humour—as any man. And few of his friends will forget him as he used to sit at table, his snuff-box in hand, and a glass of genial wine before him as he repeated some humorous passage from one of his favourites, glancing his fine brown eyes around the company as he recited. Amongst prose works, his great favourite was Sir Walter Scott—him he was never tired of reading. He would not allow that one novel was bad, and the best were to him the best of all books. For the last four winters, the present writer has gone through several of these masterpieces with him—generally one night in the week was so employed—Saturday night, which left him free to the prospect of the Sunday's relaxation. Then was the volume taken down impatiently from the shelf, almost before tea was over; and at last when all was ready, candle snuffed, and fire stirred, he would read out, or listen to, those fine stories, one after another, anticipating with a smile or a glance the pathetic or humorous turns that were coming—that he relished all the more because he knew they were coming—enjoying all as much the twentieth time of reading as he had done at the first—till supper coming in, closed the book, and recalled him to his genial hospitality, which knew no limit. It was only on Friday last we finished the *Heart of Midlothian*, which he enjoyed, however ill at ease; on Sunday he wanted to know when we should (begin another novel), and on Monday night, after a little mortal agony (to use the words of one who loved him best, and by him was best beloved of all the world), that warm kind heart was still for ever.

It would not be fitting to record in a public paper the domestic virtues of a private man, but Bernard Barton was a public man; and the public is pleased, or should be pleased, to know that a writer really is as amiable as his books pretend. No common case, especially in the poetic line, where the very sensibilities that constitute poetic feeling are most apt to revolt at the little rubs of common life. Scarce a year has elapsed since the death of one of his oldest and dearest friends—Major Moor—whose praise he justly celebrated in verse. Major Moor was also as well known to the public by his books, as much beloved by a large circle of friends. These two men were, perhaps, of equal abilities, though of a different kind; their virtues equal and the same. Long does the memory of such men haunt the places of their mortal abode; stirring within us, perhaps, at the close of many a day, as the sun sets over the scenes with which they were so long associated. It is surely not improper to endeavour to record something to the honour of such men in their own neighbourhoods. Nay, should we not, if we could, make their histories as public as possible? for surely none could honour them without loving them, and, perhaps, unconsciously striving to follow in their footsteps.

(From the *Ipswich Journal*, March 3, 1849)

WOODBRIDGE

FUNERAL OF BERNARD BARTON.—On Monday, February 26, the mortal remains of Bernard Barton were committed to the earth. A long train of members of the Society to which he belonged, and of old friends and fellow-townsmen, waited to follow him from the door from which he had so often been seen to issue alive and welcome to all eyes. Thus attended, the coffin was borne up the street to the cemetery of the Friends' Meeting-House; and there, surrounded by the grave and decent Brotherhood, and amid the affecting silence of their ceremonial, broken but once by the warning voice of one reverent elder, was lowered down into its final resting-place.

> Lay him gently in the ground,
>   The good, the genial, and the wise;
>   While Spring blows forward in the skies
> To breathe new verdure o'er the mound
>   Where the kindly Poet lies.
>
> Gently lay him in his place,
>   While the still Brethren round him stand;
> The soul indeed is far away,
> But he would reverence the clay,
> In which so long she made a stay,
> Beaming through the friendly face,
>   And holding forth the honest hand—
>
> Thou, that didst so often twine,
>   For other urns the funeral song,
>   One who has known and lov'd thee long
>   Would ere he mingles with the throng,
> Just hang his little wreath on thine.
>
> Farewell, thou spirit kind and true;
> Old Friend, for evermore Adieu!

DEATH OF THE REV. GEORGE CRABBE

SEPTEMBER 16. Of epilepsy, aged 72, the Rev. George Crabbe, Vicar of Bredfield, near Woodbridge, eldest son and biographer of the celebrated Poet.

He was born November 16, 1785, at Stathern in Leicestershire; educated at Ipswich Grammar School; took his degree in 1807, at Trinity College Cambridge; a year after was ordained deacon, and entered on the curacy of Allington in Lincolnshire, where he continued till 1811, when he went to reside at Trowbridge, in Wiltshire, to which Rectory his father had just been presented by the Duke of Rutland.

In 1815 he gave up his duty and took to residing mainly in London, taking various walking excursions through the kingdom. In 1817 he married Caroline Matilda Timbrell, of Trowbridge, and took the curacy of Pucklechurch, in Gloucestershire, where he continued eighteen years. It was in 1832 that, his father dying, and a complete edition of his Poems being called for, Mr. Crabbe contributed the volume containing the Poet's life, one of the most delightful memoirs in the language. In 1834 he was presented by Lord Chancellor Lyndhurst to the vicarages of Bredfield and Petistree, in Suffolk, in the former of which he built a parsonage, and continued residing till his death. Of his numerous family five children alone survived him, of which the eldest son, George, in Holy Orders, is Rector of Merton, Norfolk, and the second Thomas, is in Australia; the remaining three are daughters. Besides his father's biography, Mr. Crabbe was author of a volume of *Natural Theology*, on the plan and in the form of the *Bridgwater Treatises*, and of several Theological and Scientific Tracts published independently or in magazines.

To manhood's energy of mind, and great bodily strength, he united the boy's heart; as much a boy at seventy as boys need be at seventeen; as chivalrously hopeful, trustful, ardent, and courageous; as careless of riches, as intolerant of injustice and oppression, as incapable of all that is base, little and mean. With this heroic temper were joined the errors of that over-much affection, rashness in judgment and act, liability to sudden and violent emotions, to sudden and sometimes unreasonable like and dislike; and, in defiance of experience and probability, over-confidence—not in himself, for he was almost morbidly self-distrustful—but in the cause he had at heart, that it *must* bring about the result he desired. One of those he was whose hearts, wild, but never going astray, are able only to breathe in the better and nobler elements of humanity.

Under a somewhat old-fashioned acquiescence with indifferent things and people he covered a heart that would have gladly defied death in vindication of any vital truth, often most loudly proclaiming what might most likely compromise himself; a passionate advocate of inquiry and freedom and progress in all ways—civil, religious, and scientific; as passionate a hater of all that would retard or fetter it; and sometimes inclined to defend a dogma *because* bold and new and likely to be assailed. For there was much of the noble and Cervantic humourist in him, beside a certain quaintness of taste, resulting from a simple nature, brought up in simple habits and much country seclusion. And if a boy in feeling, he was a child in expressing his feelings, especially of enjoyment in little and simple things, which those more pampered by the world mistook for insincere. And whatever his intolerance of *verse*, he was far more the poet's son than he believed, bowing his white head with more than botanic welcome over the flower which reminded him of childhood, and convinced him of the Creator's sympathetic provision for His creatures' sense of beauty; or in some of his long and strong walks, whether in solitary meditation or earnest conversation on the only subject he cared for, stopping to admire some little obscure parish church in which he could discern cathedral proportions, or to lament over some felled oak trees, by whose however needful fall he declared the guilty landowner " scandalously misused the globe." For like many magnanimous men he had a passion for great trees and buildings ; indeed, an aptitude for architecture which, if duly cultivated, might have become his real genius.

Not long before his death he left a short paper to be read by his children immediately after it, affirming up to the last period of responsible thought, that he was satisfied with the convictions he had so carefully come to ; bidding nobody mourn over one who had lived so long, and on the whole so happily ; and desiring to be buried as simply as he had lived, " in any vacant space on the south side of the churchyard." Thither, accordingly, he was carried, on Tuesday, September 22 ; and there, attended by many more than were invited, and scarce one but with some funeral crape about him, were it no bigger than that about the soldier's arm, was laid in death among the poor whose friend he had been ; while the descending September sun of one of the finest summers in living memory, broke out to fling a farewell beam into the closing grave of as generous a man as he is likely to rise upon again.

Printed in the United States
68626LVS00002BA/173